DEATHRIDGE, John. Wagner's Rienzi: a reappraisal based on a study of the sketches and drafts. Oxford, 1978 (c1977). 199p music (Oxford monographs on music) bibl index 78-303657. 29.00 ISBN 0-19-816131-X

Written as a doctoral dissertation at Oxford University, this study examines three facets of Wagner's third opera: its origin, certain aspects of its style, and the problem of its performance. Lacking the autograph score, last in the possession of Adolf Hitler, and the presumably lost autograph libretto, Deathridge, now co-editor of Wagner's *Sämtliche Werke* and of the *Wagner Werk-Verzeichnis,* relies on the extant prose, verse, and compositional sketches and drafts to reconstruct working methods that, he says, remained fundamentally the same from the genesis of *Rienzi* to the completion of *Parsifal.* After an introductory chapter, Deathridge traces the evolution of the libretto from its sources to Wagner's prose sketch and draft settings of them. The longest chapter deals, through the analysis of selected scenes, with the transformation of prose into verse and its setting to music. The problem of arriving at a suitable performance edition is examined by comparing the composition draft and subsequent published versions, most notably the vocal score by Gustav Klink, published in 1844. Three

Continued

DEATHRIDGE

appendixes list the manuscript sources, present transcriptions — not translations — of the prose sketch and draft, and give a detailed comparison of the composition draft and Klink's score. A bibliography and index complete this model of musico-literary scholarship. Extensive, beautifully reproduced musical examples and other illustrations contribute to a volume that is indispensable for advanced undergraduate and graduate research libraries.

OXFORD MONOGRAPHS ON MUSIC

Wagner's
Rienzi

John Deathridge is co-editor of the Richard Wagner Collected Edition currently in progress in Munich, and is director of music at the church of St. Wolfgang there.

Wagner's *Rienzi*

A reappraisal based on a study of the sketches and drafts

JOHN DEATHRIDGE

Clarendon Press · Oxford

1977

Oxford University Press, Walton Street, Oxford OX2 6DP

OXFORD LONDON GLASGOW NEW YORK
TORONTO MELBOURNE WELLINGTON CAPE TOWN
IBADAN NAIROBI DAR ES SALAAM LUSAKA ADDIS ABABA
KUALA LUMPUR SINGAPORE JAKARTA HONG KONG TOKYO
DELHI BOMBAY CALCUTTA MADRAS KARACHI

British Library Cataloguing in Publication Data
Deathridge, John
  Wagner's 'Rienzi': a reappraisal
  based on a study of the sketches and drafts.
  —(Oxford monographs on music)
  Bibl.—Index
  ISBN 0-19-816131-X
  1. Title. 2. Series
  782.1'092'4   ML410.W132
  Wagner, Richard. Rienzi

Text set in 14 on 15 pt Monotype Bembo, printed by photolithography,
and bound in Great Britain at The Pitman Press, Bath

To Anne

Preface

OF all Wagner's works, *Rienzi* has the most enigmatic reputation. Not only his opponents, but also many of his admirers have been at one in their condemnation of it—a thorn in the flesh to be dismissed with half-hearted epithets and fragile explanations. Certainly, its belligerent fanfares and sexless heroics seem, at first sight, a strange contrast with the sensuality of the later works; and the totalitarian implications of its libretto, which even the blindest cannot ignore, have been understandably cold-shouldered by the guardians of Wagner's post-war reputation. Yet enthusiasm has not been lacking. Gustav Mahler, for example, conducted his own arrangement of the work in Vienna (1901) when, in a moment of inspired eccentricity, he is said to have called it 'Wagner's most beautiful opera' and 'the greatest musical drama ever composed'. Richard Strauss, too, saw fit to conduct the work on several occasions, and Cosima Wagner, together with her fellow Bayreuthians (a term coined by H. S. Chamberlain), did not hesitate to transform it into an ideological shop-window at odds with its obviously cosmopolitan origins. But despite this powerful, if sometimes misguided advocacy, *Rienzi* has received little serious attention from scholars and critics. It has been banished from the portals of Bayreuth and, elsewhere, has long ceased to adorn the regular repertory. In a sense, it is Wagner's eleventh commandment: a rebellious, yet stridently conformist work in exile from the ten admired summits of his later achievements between *Holländer* and *Parsifal*.

This book is an attempt to clear away the débris of contention surrounding *Rienzi* by returning to Wagner's sketches and drafts. It is not a comprehensive analysis of the work, nor does it claim to do justice to the complicated history of its performance. Its aim is simply to clarify Wagner's original conception in the face of subsequent transformations imposed upon it, and to offer a concentrated study of his working methods in a critical and biographical context. Since *Rienzi* is a relatively unknown work, this approach must seem unduly narrow if the circumstances enveloping its history are not clarified at the outset. As the introduction to the study explains, a balanced appreciation of the work has been seriously hindered not only by the conflicting judgements of its critics, but also by the loss of the original score and the lack of a complete edition. Within this complex of misunderstanding and practical neglect, the sketches and drafts serve two purposes: first, the illumination of a particularly turbulent stage in Wagner's development—the almost chameleon-like transition from mediocrity to genius which most commentators, including Wagner himself, have been at a loss to explain; and second, the determination of the contents of the missing original score. Further, a study of the genesis of *Rienzi* provides a good opportunity for considering, at least briefly, its sources and social ambience. In view of its uncanny premonition of twentieth century fascism, Adolf Hitler's interest in the work, and the well known involvement of Wagner's heirs in the Third Reich, *Rienzi* casts unpleasant shadows which require at least some reflection on its origins and political background if easy moral outrage is to be avoided. Indeed, when seen through the intimacy of Wagner's working methods, the political content of the work—its public intention so to speak—seems more complex and contradictory than has hitherto been supposed. Although confined in its initial scope, then, the study hopes, by virtue of this limitation, to bring a number of larger issues into sharper focus. It is not intended as a final judgement, but as a starting-point for a more serious attitude towards *Rienzi*, and an indication of its wider implications in any appraisal of Wagner's social and artistic personality.

The present study was completed in 1973 and accepted by Oxford University for the degree of Doctor of Philosophy in 1974. It also served as an initial guideline for the first complete performance of *Rienzi* broadcast by the BBC on June 27 1976, and played a small, though not unimportant role in the preparation of a new edition of the work published by Schott (1974–77) as part of their Wagner Collected Edition. Fortunately, the appearance of the *Rienzi Dokumentenband* (1976) as volume xxiii of this Edition has enabled me to reduce the apparatus of the original study to more manageable proportions. Nevertheless, the complete prose draft and extracts from the verse draft relevant to the discussion had to be included if the reader were not to be entirely dependent on another publication. Even this overlap is not without value, however, since the transcriptions in both publications were made independently, and show, as can be expected from documents of such recalcitrant legibility, some variant readings and a different presentation of layout and orthography.

My thanks are due to Professor Martin Geck who first pointed out the editorial problems of *Rienzi* to me, and who kindly commissioned me to examine the Burrell composition draft and Klink vocal score for the Collected Edition of which he was then an editor (1970). The results of this investigation form the basis of the last part of the present discussion. My thanks are also due to Reinhard Strohm and Egon Voss, two of the present editors, for their advice and readiness in placing the resources of the Edition at my disposal. Further, I would like to thank Professor Robert Bailey for some thought-provoking ideas on terminology, and Professor Gerald Abraham for his expert scrutiny of the original text. Gordon Mapes, former librarian of the Curtis Institute Philadelphia, kindly provided me with a microfilm of the Burrell Collection, and promptly answered a number of questions concerning its incompleteness—in one instance providing me with copies of missing frames in the verse draft. I also received friendly help from Gertrud Strobel of the Wahnfried Archives Bayreuth, where I had the opportunity to inspect a large amount of material at my leisure. In the practical task of writing the study I was greatly assisted by Kathleen Eberlein, who prepared the original typescript, and by some conscientious proof-reading undertaken by Lucy Russell. A mutual interest in the fascinating subject of Rienzi, also led to some stimulating conversations with the artist Sven-Roland Hooge, the result of which can be seen on the jacket of this book.

Lastly, I would like to express my warmest gratitude to Frederick Sternfeld who first stimulated me to examine Wagner more closely, and who, with consideration and great patience, supervised this study from its inception to its conclusion.

Munich, 1976   JOHN DEATHRIDGE

Contents

List of Illustrations

Translations

In order not to disrupt the continuity of the English text, all shorter quotations from foreign sources have been translated. Longer quotations broken off from the main text have been left in the original, together with foreign titles of works, books, periodicals, and articles included in the main body of the English text. In all cases, references for translated quotations are to editions in the original language, even where a separate English translation of the source in question exists. With one exception (Paul Bekker, *Wagner: Das Leben im Werke*, Berlin, 1924), all translations have been made direct from the original sources.

Abbreviations

Ap.	Appendix
Sämt. Briefe	Richard Wagner, *Sämtliche Briefe*, eds. Gertrud Strobel and Werner Wolf, 15 vols. (projected), Leipzig, 1967– .
Sämt. Werke	Richard Wagner, *Sämtliche Werke*, ed. Carl Dahlhaus, 30 vols. (projected), Mainz, 1970–. Vols. iii (1–5) have been prepared by Reinhard Strohm and Egon Voss, vol. xxiii by Reinhard Strohm, and vol. xxx by Martin Geck and Egon Voss.
Schriften	Richard Wagner, *Gesammelte Schriften und Dichtungen*, 10 vols., Leipzig, 1871, and its extension in the 'große Ausgabe', 12 vols, Leipzig, 1911. (References in parentheses are to *Sämtliche Schriften und Dichtungen*, 'Volksausgabe', 16 vols, Leipzig, 1911.) Rererences to the 'Volksausgabe' are *not* in parentheses for vols. xiii–xvi, which appear only in this edition.
Vocal Score	Richard Wagner, *Rienzi, der letzte der Tribunen*, vocal score by Carl Gustav Klink, Dresden, 1844. (References in parentheses are to the vocal score by Otto Singer, Leipzig, 1914.) N.B. All other vocal score editions are shorter versions, and are only to be consulted with the greatest caution.

Examples

Unless specifically indicated otherwise, all music examples from the final version of *Rienzi* have been freely transcribed from the Klink and Singer vocal scores. In all transcriptions of the verse draft, additions are indicated by italics, deletions with a line through the text and underlinings of proper names by capital letters. Stage directions are in parentheses. Transcriptions of musical MSS. are as faithful to the original as possible, including Wagner's use of short-hand. Except for missing rests and punctuation marks, obvious mistakes are marked *sic*. In all cases, square brackets indicate editorial additions.

N.B. The recording of *Rienzi* issued by EMI Records in 1976 is not based on the version by Cosima Wagner and Julius Kniese as Curt von Westernhagen erroneously states in the accompanying booklet. The recording adheres to the first printed score (1844) which contains a considerably shortened version authorized by Wagner.

Ich entsinne mich noch, um mein dreißigstes Jahr herum, mich innerlich zweifelhaft befragt zu haben, ob ich denn wirklich das Zeug zu einer höchsten künstlerischen Individualität besäße: ich konnte in meinen Arbeiten immer noch Einfluß und Nachahmung verspüren und wagte nur beklommen auf meine fernere Entwicklung, als durchaus originell Schaffender, zu blicken.

Richard Wagner an Mathilde Wesendonk
Biebrich, 9 Juni 1862.

I still remember asking myself with deep uncertainty around the age of thirty whether I really had the makings of a supreme artistic individuality; I could still see the influences and imitation in my works, and only with a heavy heart did I dare contemplate my future development as a thoroughly original artist.

Richard Wagner to Mathilde Wesendonk
Biebrich, 9 June 1862.

I

Introduction

1. Wagner and the Bayreuthians

IN the enlarged edition of his biography of Richard Wagner, Carl Glasenapp wrote the following about *Rienzi*:

> Wer sich im Betreff des heroischen Jugendwerkes, gegen dessen Beurteilung als Erstlingswerk sich der junge Meister im Bewußtsein seiner bereits gewonnenen dramatischen und technisch-musikalischen Erfahrung mit solcher Bestimmtheit verwahrt hat, wer sich im Betreff dieses Werkes nicht einer bewußten Selbsttäuschung hingeben will, muß vor allem zugestehen, daß er es nicht *kennt* und nicht kennen *kann*, in Ermangelung der beiden einzig ermöglichenden Hilfsmittel für eine solche Kenntnis: einer richtigen Aufführung oder auch nur einer vollständigen Partitur.[1]

Glasenapp was attempting to make three points with this sentence, all of which have a bearing on the present study. First, perhaps in answer to Nietzsche's description of Wagner's youth as one of a 'many-sided dilettante with no prospects of any particular distinction',[2] a remark later developed by Thomas Mann[3] and T. W. Adorno,[4] he wanted to emphasize that at the age of twenty-nine, when *Rienzi* was first presented to the world in Dresden on 20 October 1842, Wagner was already an experienced composer fully in command of his musical technique. Second, conscious that the Wagnerites as well as the anti-Wagnerites of his generation were ill-disposed towards the work, he was insisting, like Eduard Reuss before him,[5] that a 'correct performance', which could lead to a knowledge of the work free of 'self-deception', had still not taken place in the theatres of his time. Third, he wanted to point out the lack of a published full score which reproduced Wagner's original manuscript in its entirety.

Unfortunately, Glasenapp's last observation is still true. This is particularly serious since the original manuscript score which, according to Otto

---

[1] *Das Leben Richard Wagners*, 5th edn., 6 vols., Leipzig, 1916–23, i. 306.

[2] 'Richard Wagner in Bayreuth', *Gesammelte Werke*, 23 vols., Munich, 1922, vii. 252.

[3] 'Leiden und Größe Richard Wagners', *Gesammelte Werke*, 12 vols., Frankfurt, 1960, ix. 375 f.

[4] 'Versuch über Wagner', *Gesammelte Schriften*, 20 vols., Frankfurt, 1971– , xiii. 26 ff.

[5] 'Rienzi', *Bayreuther Blätter*, xii (1889), 151, 160–2.

Strobel, consisted of 798 beautifully written pages bound in four volumes,[6] and which, until the end of the Second World War, was in the possession of Adolf Hitler, is now considered missing, together with the two complete copies which were made from it. In addition, the published full scores and the extant copies which Wagner ordered to be made from the original manuscript for use in Dresden and other theatres all contain, in one form or another, extensive cuts which Wagner introduced for the first and subsequent performances in Dresden during the 1840s. The missing autograph score, therefore, means that a complete edition of *Rienzi* as it was originally conceived is impossible.[7]

The only full score which claims to be a *restitutio in integrum* of the original is the conductor's score published by Fürstner in 1898/9—a score on which most performances of *Rienzi* have been based since the turn of the century. Despite the fact that the title-page of this edition misleadingly describes it as being 'based on the original score', it contains the most astonishing cuts and revisions which amount to a grotesque distortion of Wagner's original intentions. It stems from a version prepared by Cosima Wagner and Julius Kniese, one of her Bayreuth collaborators, and attempts in short to convert *Rienzi* from 'grand opera' into 'Musikdrama' by haphazard cutting of choruses, word repetitions, ornaments, and anything considered 'inessential' to the dramatic action.[8] The present study is an attempt to examine this and related topics arising from the examination of Wagner's sketches and drafts[9] for *Rienzi* which, besides showing us some aspects of his working methods with a direct bearing on the development of his so-called 'musico-dramatic style', raise some important questions about the exact nature of the original score and the motives which led Cosima Wagner and Kniese to treat *Rienzi* in the way they did— a subject which can be better understood by further consideration of Glasenapp's second point.

---

[6] 'König Ludwigs Wagner Manuscripte', *Bayreuther Festspielführer*, 1936, p. 108. See Ap. i. 159 (source 1).

[7] Due to a lack of authentic source material, even the most reliable edition is forced to omit almost a fifth of the work from its main text (1,710 out of a possible 8,327 bars). See *Sämt. Werke*, iii (1–5).

[8] See Martin Geck, 'Rienzi-Philologie', *Das Drama Richard Wagners als musikalisches Kunstwerk*, ed. C. Dahlhaus, Regensburg, 1970, pp. 186–96. The discussion is limited to the circumstances surrounding the making of the arrangement and includes a brief account of some of the alterations. The full extent of the changes made can be seen by comparing the Fürstner score (plate number 5000) with *Vocal Score* (Klink and Singer). See also Guido Adler, *Richard Wagner: Vorlesungen*, Leipzig, 1904, pp. 50–2.

[9] The terms 'sketch' and 'draft' are defined in Ap. i. 158–9.

After remarking that the publication of a complete full score probably would not protect *Rienzi* from further distortion in the theatres, Glasenapp goes on to explain what he means by a 'correct performance' of the work. More important than a complete score, he says, is a recognition of the fact that even *Rienzi* was conceived by its creator as a 'drama' and not as a 'grand opera'. This is the work's true significance, he maintains, quoting Reuss, and it will only attain its proper place in the history of art when all theatres make the effort to regard the music of the work as a means of clarifying its action (*Handlung*). During rehearsal, therefore, performers should not be content with simply learning the musical part of the work; the text is of equal, if not greater importance because it announces something really 'new'—an ideal towards which Wagner was unconsciously striving, i.e. the 'drama', but for which he had not yet found the right form. The lack of an immediate model, Glasenapp continues, led Wagner to clothe his ideal of the 'drama' in purely 'theatrical' forms typical of 'grand opera'. It is this difference between the 'dramatic' and the purely 'theatrical' elements in the work, he insists, again quoting Reuss, which has been generally overlooked and which has led to the most nonsensical comparisons of the work with that of the Meyerbeer school.[10]

According to Glasenapp, then, a 'correct performance' of *Rienzi* is one which emphasizes its action or 'drama' as the object of expression and its music as a means of clarifying this object—an interpretation perfectly in keeping with the basic tenet of Wagner's theoretical work 'Oper und Drama'[11] written 10 years after the completion of *Rienzi*, and one which C. Wagner and Kniese attempted to realize in their arrangement of the work although Wagner's later theory was intended as a radical rejection of precisely that 'operatic' form in which *Rienzi* was originally conceived. Perhaps aware that he might be guilty of a misplaced application of Wagner's later theories to one of his early works, Glasenapp goes on to verify his interpretation by quoting Wagner himself, but without giving the source or date of his quotation:

Daß diese Auffassung des 'Rienzi' die einzig richtige sei, wird durch die eigenen Worte Wagners bestätigt, der . . . gegen sein Jugendwerk viel gerechter war, als unsere großen Wagnerianischen und Un-Wagnerianischen Kunstrichter. 'Als ich . . . die Komposition meines "Rienzi" begann, band ich mich an Nichts, als an die *einzige Absicht, meinem Sujet zu entsprechen.* Ich stellte mir kein Vorbild,

---

[10] Glasenapp, op. cit. i. 306–7. Quotations from Reuss, op. cit., pp. 161, 157.
[11] Cf. *Schriften*, iii. 282 (231).

sondern überließ mich einzig dem Gefühl, [das mich so verzehrte, dem Gefühl,] daß ich nun so weit sei, von der Entwickelung meiner künstlerischen Kräfte etwas Bedeutendes zu verlangen und etwas nicht Unbedeutendes zu erwarten. Der Gedanke, mit Bewußtsein—wenn auch nur in einem einzigen Takte—[seicht oder] trivial zu sein, war mir entsetzlich.'[12]

Glasenapp is conveniently quoting from Wagner's 'Autobiographische Skizze' written for Heinrich Laube's *Zeitung für die elegante Welt* in 1843 a few months after *Rienzi's* highly successful first performance in Dresden. Wagner, naturally wanting to capitalize on his first great success, was therefore not inclined to place the work in anything but the most favourable light. Even so, the fact that he takes the trouble to describe the single driving force behind the composition of *Rienzi* as the feeling of at last being able 'to expect something not insignificant' from his artistic powers suggests, together with his ostensible aversion against consciously writing anything 'shallow or trivial', that his attitude towards the work was not entirely positive even at this early stage. Indeed, we find him in his later writings expressing a distinctly negative opinion about *Rienzi* which Glasenapp ignores completely. Although still emphasizing the 'real enthusiasm'[13] he had for the subject when composing the work, he makes no bones about the fact that *Rienzi* and the stage works before it were intended only as 'operas' and as such have little in common with his later works.[14] Not surprisingly then, we find him drawing a sharp dividing line between *Rienzi* and the rest of his works, beginning with *Der fliegende Holländer*—a division he first makes in his essay 'Eine Mittheilung an meine Freunde' (1851) written during his work on the initial conception of the *Ring*:

Noch mit dem 'Rienzi' hatte ich nur im Sinne, eine 'Oper' zu schreiben . . . Mit dem 'fliegenden Holländer' . . . schlug ich eine neue Bahn ein . . . Ich war von nun an in bezug auf alle meine dramatischen Arbeiten zunächst *Dichter*, und erst in der vollständigen Ausführung des Gedichtes ward ich wieder Musiker.[15]

Nine years later, in the essay 'Zukunftsmusik' (1860), written shortly after the completion of *Tristan und Isolde*, he makes the division more emphatic:

[12] Glasenapp, loc. cit. His quotation is from *Schriften*, i. 17 (13). Glasenapp's omissions are included in square brackets. The emphasis is his own and not Wagner's.

[13] *Schriften*, iv. 319 (258).

[14] An opinion which would have inconveniently contradicted Glasenapp's own view of Wagner's complete *oeuvre* as a large unified *Gesamtkunstwerk*, had he mentioned it. See Glasenapp, op. cit. i. 214.

[15] *Schriften*, iv. 385–6 (316).

Ich lege auf dieses Werk ['Rienzi'], welches seine Konzeption und formelle Ausführung den zur Nacheiferung auffordenden frühesten Eindrücken der heroischen
Oper Spontinis sowie des glänzenden, von Paris ausgehenden Genres der Großen
Oper Aubers, Meyerbeers und Halévys verdankte,—ich lege, sage ich, auf dieses
Werk . . . keinen besonderen Nachdruck, weil in ihm noch kein wesentliches Moment meiner später sich geltend machenden Kunstanschauung ersichtlich erhalten
ist.[16]

Finally, in the introduction to the first edition of his Collected Writings
(1871)—an introduction which amounts to an apology for including
Rienzi in the Wagner canon at all—he laments the 'neglect of diction and
verse' in the text of the work, ascribing it to a 'frivolous tendency' in his
development, and explains that he was not acting as a poet when writing
it, but simply as a composer wanting to fashion an efficient piece for the
operatic stage. He then continues:

Der 'Rienzi' möge somit als das *musikalische Theaterstück* angesehen werden, von
welchem meine weitere Ausbildung zum musikalischen Dramatiker . . . ihren
Fortgang nahm . . . So weit meine Kenntnis reicht, vermag ich im Leben keines
Künstlers eine so auffallende Umwandlung, in so kurzer Zeit vollbracht, zu
entdecken, als sie hier bei dem Verfasser jener beiden Opern ['Rienzi', 'Holländer']
sich zeigt, von denen die erste kaum beendigt war, als die zweite fast fertig schon
vorlag.[17]

In contrast to the impression given by Glasenapp, it is clear from these
quotations that the mature Wagner regarded *Rienzi* as an 'opera' and
nothing more. As for a 'correct performance' of the work, the only hint
he gave to this effect was in a footnote added as an afterthought to the
passage quoted above where, more positively, he expresses the hope that a
presentation of the complete text in his Collected Writings[18] will serve
as a means of correcting the judgement of those who only know the work
from the 'well-loved mutilation' of it currently being performed in the
theatres of that time. From this we may deduce that, like Glasenapp, he
wanted the Wagnerites to give *Rienzi* a fairer hearing, but, unlike Cosima
Wagner and Kniese, he wanted to make this possible by offering them a
complete or nearly complete version of the work as he originally conceived
it. Although he says in 'Eine Mittheilung an meine Freunde' that the form

---

[16] Ibid. vii. 160 (119).

[17] Ibid. i. 2–3 (2–3).

[18] Ibid. i. 41–122 (30–89). There are a number of sheets in the Wagner–Gedenkstätte Bayreuth
containing numerous alterations which Wagner made for this edition of the text. The revisions
relate mostly to the stage directions. The only substantial omission is the entry of the ambassadors
(Act II/finale) which is included in *Schriften*, xvi. 184. The other 'variants' in the latter volume are
not in Wagner's original verse draft.

of 'grand opera' in *Rienzi* was only so to speak the 'pair of spectacles'[19] through which he saw his material, he was not prepared to interpret the work as a 'drama', and even less inclined to regard it as one of his significant works.

The different attitudes of Wagner and his interpreters towards *Rienzi* are even more striking when we realize that the interpretations offered by Reuss and Glasenapp are only two of several which appeared during Cosima Wagner's reign in Bayreuth.[20] They are all in the same vein: an enthusiasm for *Rienzi* the 'drama' or 'tragedy'; criticism of current performances (except those using the C. Wagner/Kniese version); surprise that the work is not valued more highly by the 'Wagnerites'; and a marked inclination to discuss the text at the expense of the music.[21] Houston Stewart Chamberlain, for example, goes as far as saying that, as a creator of dramatic character, Wagner 'almost stands at the peak of his mastery' in *Rienzi*,[22] and even claims elsewhere that the work is the only one in Wagner's *oeuvre* which merits the title 'Musikdrama'.[23] Hugo Dinger is equally enthusiastic and claims to see in *Rienzi* the 'first work in which Wagner's great intellectual power breaks through with respect to the content of the work as well as its form'; already in *Rienzi*, he says, we can see Wagner's 'virtuoso command of technique', and he goes on to compare the dramatic disposition of the work with Shakespeare, Greek

---

[19] *Schriften*, iv. 319–20 (259), 386 (316).

[20] Hermann von der Pfordten, *Handlung und Dichtung der Bühnenwerke Richard Wagner's*, Berlin, 1893, pp. 25–38; Houston Stewart Chamberlain, *Richard Wagner*, Munich, 1901, pp. 330–9; W. Köhler, 'Wagners "Rienzi" in alter und neuer Gestalt', *Musikalisches Wochenblatt*, xxii (1901), 648–9; Wolfgang Golther, 'Rienzi—ein musikalisches Drama', *Die Musik*, i (1902), 1833–9; Robert Petsch, 'Das tragische Problem im "Rienzi",' *Zeitschrift für Philosophie und philosophische Kritik*, cxxviii (1906), 44–55; Max Koch, *Richard Wagner*, 3 vols., Berlin, 1907, i. 332–40; H. S. Chamberlain, *Das Drama Richard Wagners*, 3rd edn., Leipzig, 1908, pp. 12, 42–4; Hugo Dinger, 'Zu Richard Wagners Rienzi', *Richard Wagner Jahrbuch*, ed. Ludwig Frankenstein, 5 vols., Berlin, 1908, iii. 88-132 (Review by Golther, *Die Musik*, viii/4 (1908–9), 51); Arthur Seidl, *Neue Wagneriana*, 3 vols., Regensburg, 1914, i. 174–83.

[21] The only one to include music examples is Pfordten, op. cit., pp. 37–8. However, these are intended more as a guide than an analysis.

[22] Chamberlain, *Richard Wagner*, p. 336.

[23] Chamberlain based his claim on an essay by Wagner (1872) entitled 'Über die Benennung "Musikdrama"' in which the implications of the term are carefully scrutinized. At this period, Wagner's view was that the label 'Musikdrama' indicated a 'real drama set to music' and not, as he would have wished, a 'drama' in which musical laws act as a formative element. Chamberlain therefore regarded *Rienzi* as an independent 'drama' set to music, but one which stretched the 'capabilities of music' to their extreme limits and which hence showed a logical step in Wagner's 'intuitive striving' towards the 'perfect art-work of the searching word-tone poet', i.e. his ideal of the 'drama'. See Chamberlain, *Das Drama Richard Wagners*, pp. 42–3, and Wagner, *Schriften*, ix. 359–65 (302–8).

Tragedy, and Hegel's interpretation of tragedy as an expression of the 'dialectical' World-process.[24] The similarity of these interpretations, particularly the continual emphasis on 'drama', suggests that they have a common source, but one which is difficult to pin-point with certainty. Glasenapp was the first to publish an interpretation of *Rienzi* with an emphasis on its 'dramatic' aspects;[25] but this relatively early description of *Rienzi* as 'drama' was intended more to prove the work's alleged influence on a number of German plays on the same subject which appeared in the wake of Wagner's Dresden success. The first published interpretation of *Rienzi* describing the work as a 'drama' in the sense of Wagner's later works is the one written by Reuss on the occasion of a performance of *Rienzi* in Karlsruhe on 13 January 1889 under the direction of Felix Mottl—a performance which Reuss praises for observing the 'dramatic' side of the work and for completely dissociating it from the label 'grand opera' hitherto applied to it.[26] However, Cosima Wagner also took a great interest in this performance and supervised most of the rehearsals.[27] Although there is no concrete evidence to prove it, it is possible that her strong attraction to the work was the moving force behind Reuss's interpretation.

2. Further appraisals

For a 'not insignificant' work by a major nineteenth-century composer, *Rienzi* presents us with an unusually confused picture due in no small measure to the interpretations which have been imposed on it. Bearing in mind that, since the advent of the Cosima Wagner/Kniese edition, most listeners have become acquainted with the work on the basis of this version, Glasenapp's warning that no one can claim to 'know' *Rienzi* in the absence of a 'correct performance' or a 'complete full score' retains its validity— providing we assume, unlike Glasenapp, that a 'correct performance' is one which follows the composer's original intentions and not one based on a tendentious interpretation of the work as 'drama'.[28] Symptomatic

[24] Dinger, op. cit., pp. 94, 107, 109.

[25] 'Aus dem deutschen Dichterwälde', *Bayreuther Blätter*, iii (1880), 36–40.

[26] Reuss op. cit., pp. 160–1.

[27] Geck, op. cit., p. 187.

[28] Ironically enough, Glasenapp ingenuously extols the virtues of the Cosima Wagner/Kniese version in a footnote to the passage quoted at the beginning of this study. Without realizing that it is an even greater distortion of the original than the previous versions he rightly criticizes, he praises the edition for its 'emphasis on the drama' and claims that it is 'completely in accordance with the intentions of the Master'. See *Das Leben Richard Wagners*, 5th edn., i. 306–7.

of the situation is also the fact that even critics and scholars sympathetic to Wagner's cause have not been able to give us a clear idea of what the work's significance in Wagner's development actually is, least of all Wagner himself. Judgements on it have been either full of special pleading and enthusiastic respect, like those of Glasenapp and Chamberlain, or, like Wagner's, simply expressions of critical embarrassment. Paul Bekker, for example, claims that the clear-cut distinction which Wagner made between *Rienzi*, the 'opera', and his 'new path' in *Holländer* is already to be seen in *Rienzi* itself. According to his interpretation, which will be discussed in detail at a later stage, the first part of the work (Acts I-II) is 'Spontini's music under Wagner's showmanship', i.e. heroic grand opera *par excellence*; whereas the second part (Acts III-V)—and here he echoes Glasenapp and Chamberlain—is 'grand opera in intention only'—a 'drama' which 'abandons the sphere of historic incident for that of human passion'.[29] At the other end of the scale, Ernest Newman, who usually had a kind word to say about even Wagner's most insignificant creations, says of *Rienzi* that it 'will always be something of a puzzle to the student'; he calls it the 'least satisfactory' of all Wagner's works and proceeds to dismiss it with a string of adjectives which are extreme, to say the least.[30] Wagner's own attitude is perhaps the strangest and has certainly contributed most towards the critical schizophrenia to be found amongst his admirers. On the one hand he is prepared to include the entire text of the work in his Collected Writings with an additional footnote to the introduction pleading for a juster appreciation of it. On the other hand he attempts to interpret the 'striking transformation' which took place between *Rienzi* and *Holländer* as the beginning of his development as 'poet' and 'musical dramatist', and makes it quite clear that he wants us to regard the latter work as the beginning of the 'serious' Wagner and the former as a product of a 'frivolous tendency' which has little bearing on his significance as an artist—a generally accepted interpretation which is doubtless the main reason why *Rienzi* has never been performed at Bayreuth.

One explanation of Wagner's attitude is the fact that *Rienzi*, unlike his other early stage works *Die Feen* (1833/4) and *Das Liebesverbot* (1835),[31] was successfully performed in his lifetime, and remained one of his most

---

[29] *Wagner. Das Leben im Werke*, Berlin/Leipzig, 1924, pp. 103, 118.

[30] *Wagner as Man and Artist*, 2 edn., London, 1923, pp. 160-1.

[31] Wagner did not include the texts of these works in the first edition of his Collected Writings. They are to be found in *Schriften*, xi. 5-58 (5-58), 59-124 (59-124).

popular works until the close of the century. In fact, it is the only work in his whole output which met with unqualified success from the very beginning, even though most theatres were slow to take it up largely for practical reasons. In Dresden alone, it reached its 100th performance in 1873 and its 200th in 1908. In 1869, after a delay of over twenty-five years, it had its première in Paris, the city for which it was originally intended,[32] and ran to twenty-six performances. In 1871, the year in which Wagner wrote the introduction to his Collected Writings, it was performed for the first time in Augsburg, Karlsruhe, Vienna, and Munich, i.e. *after* the Munich premières of *Tristan*, *Meistersinger*, *Rheingold*, and *Walküre*. Besides further first performances abroad (New York 1878, London, 1879), it was regularly given by most major German theatres towards the end of his life, and could count as one of his most widely performed works, if only in versions which were always extravagantly cut.[33] Wagner was therefore in the difficult position of wanting to reject the work on the one hand for fear of 'confusing'[34] the public as to the real nature of his ideals, and of wanting to profit financially from its success on the other. His numerous references to *Rienzi* in the correspondence of his mature years almost always treat the work as an *affaire d'argent*[35]—a means of gaining a quick success which could prepare the way for his other works and further financial rewards. The fact that he mentions *Rienzi* at all in his later essays is because he knew it could still bring him the 'operatic' success he badly needed, but which he also despised.

However, the mixed attitudes of Wagner and his admirers towards *Rienzi* have deeper roots than this. It is significant that Glasenapp's point about Wagner's 'technical and musical experience' when writing *Rienzi* recurs with surprising frequency in practically all interpretations of the work so far discussed. Indeed, the fact that Wagner's admirers go out of their way to emphasize a point which we would normally take for granted in a composer of almost thirty is a sure sign that there is more to it than they are prepared to admit. The only discussion of *Rienzi* which touches on

[32] See Wagner's open letter to Judith Gautier on the occasion of this performance. *Schriften*, xvi. 114–6.

[33] Scores used for these performances were either hand-written copies with cuts, or copies of the first published full score (Dresden, 1845) consisting of a shortened version Wagner prepared for the Dresden stage in 1843. At the time of Wagner's death, the work had been performed in 38 theatres in 12 different countries. See Oscar Eichberg, 'Zum 50 jährigen Jubiläum des "Rienzi",' *Bayreuther Taschenbuch*, viii (1892), 74 f.

[34] *Richard Wagner an Freunde und Zeitgenossen*, ed. Erich Kloss, 2nd edn., Berlin, 1909, p. 193.

[35] See e.g. *Briefwechsel zwischen Wagner und Liszt*, 2nd edn., 2 vols., Leipzig, 1900, ii. 191, 193, 217.

this question with any insight comes, not unexpectedly, from Wagner's opponent Eduard Hanslick. Writing after its first performance in Vienna (1871), Hanslick delivered a scathing attack on the work which, without resorting to an interpretation of it as 'drama', attempts to place it in the context of Wagner's later style:

Ein so scharfer und feiner Kopf wie Wagner mußte trotz des Rienzi-Erfolges in Dresden bald einsehen, daß ihm auf *diesem* Felde keine weiteren Lorbeeren sprießen. Im Schaugepränge und Orchesterlärm noch weiter zu gehen, war unmöglich, in den alten Formen durch Reichtum und Schönheit musikalischer Ideen zu entzücken, erlaubten seine Mittel nicht—was blieb übrig, als einen neuen Weg zu suchen? . . . Wagner's eigenartiges, mehr poetisch-theatralisches als musikalisches Talent bedurfte der Zuführung ganz neuer oder neu combinierter Elemente in die Oper. Wagner schuf sich einen neuen Styl und neue Formen und hat daran wohlgetan. Nicht als ob er durch sein declamatorisches "Musikdrama" die bisherige "Oper" beseitigt hätte, diese wird allezeit daneben fortbestehen, solange es reich begabte musikalische Erfinder gibt. Aber gerade Wagner hätte in dieser Richtung nur mittelmäßiges geleistet . . . Für das Verständniß von Wagner's späterer auffallender Stylwendung ist dieser Rienzi unschätzbar.[36]

Assuming for the moment the validity of Hanslick's argument, the probable reason for the confused reception of *Rienzi* is that it poses a riddle which, either by special pleading or puzzled rejection, Wagner's admirers prefer to leave unsolved: how was it possible for a composer of such formidable influence to begin as a mediocrity? And how did his rapid and 'striking change of style' come about? The central part of this study is an attempt to give detailed consideration to these questions (and hence to test the validity of Hanslick's argument) by returning to Wagner's sketches and drafts for *Rienzi*. It is an attempt to study the question of the work's style not simply in terms of its external influences, but in terms of Wagner's efforts to fashion an original musical language from these influences. A feature of *Rienzi* which Hanslick does not consider—perhaps because he was basing his judgements on a shortened version of the work[37]—is that it contains not only the routine imitation typical of Wagner's earlier operas, but also, as Bekker points out, the first clear signs of his later

[36] *Die moderne Oper*, Berlin, 1875, pp. 277–8.

[37] The score on which the 1871 performances were based is now in the Nationalbibliothek Vienna. It is a hand-written copy of the first published score (1845) with additional cuts and alterations. These additional emendations amount to a shortening of finales and a further distortion of long-range dramatic effects. The extra cuts were probably not all introduced for the 1871 performances; the different handwritings in the score suggest that it was used by several conductors, including perhaps Gustav Mahler who revived *Rienzi* in Vienna (1901) with cuts of his own.

dramatic style. If Wagner's 'new path' was an astute move to compensate for his 'mediocre' musical talent, as Hanslick argues, the sketches and drafts for *Rienzi*, provided they show Wagner's working methods in sufficient detail, should therefore be able to offer some indication of how this transformation afforded a way out of his technical and musical limitations. Taking concentrated examples from each act, and thus reconstructing a chronological picture of Wagner's stylistic development during the composition of *Rienzi*, it is possible to glimpse something of the unbridled methods which disturbed Hanslick's critical decorum. Indeed, an analysis of the sketches and drafts suggests that Wagner's almost breathtaking *laissez-faire* in matters of musical technique—the 'dilettantism' his admirers and detractors ignore or misjudge[38]—was one quality which encouraged his break with operatic convention and the conservative aesthetic norms Hanslick later espoused. The sketches and drafts for *Rienzi* are, to paraphrase Hanslick, invaluable for an understanding of Wagner's striking change of style, for they show an uninhibited, sometimes reckless handling of traditional forms and an increasing reliance on extra-musical stimuli clearly foreshadowing the provocative originality of his mature works—an originality which Hanslick failed to understand.

The 'conscious self-deception'[39] which Glasenapp invokes for those who want to 'know' *Rienzi* is, except for the narrower issue of the 'complete score', an ironically good description of his own unwillingness to see the ambiguous position of the work in Wagner's stylistic development. But apart from this, his words would also be applicable, if he were writing today, to another questionable attitude of which he could only have had the slightest premonition, and which, in the light of subsequent events in Germany, has cast an unpleasant shadow on the work's character. Although Adolf Hitler's possession of the original *Rienzi* score may be regarded simply as an unfortunate fact,[40] especially in view of its subsequent loss and the complex editorial problems arising from this, his possession of the score was only part of an intense attraction towards the work which, as Hitler himself is alleged to have said, played a significant

---

[38] Adorno, for example, places a derogatory emphasis on Wagner's 'dilettante' traits without realizing their anti-bourgeois potential—a potential he would have secretly admired. See *Gesammelte Schriften*, xiii. 26–7.

[39] See p. 1 above.

[40] See p. 2 above.

role in the initial formation of his political ideals.[41] Not surprisingly, then, the stigma of Fascism and the terrible events of the Second World War has thrown its cloak around *Rienzi*, and, especially in the hands of Adorno, the 'self-praise and pomp'[42] it undeniably contains have become symbolic terms of abuse for Wagner's entire production. It is in order to modify this over-simplified and polemical attitude that this discussion includes a consideration of the sources and influences behind *Rienzi* seen in conjunction with an analysis of the prose draft which Wagner made as a preparation for the final libretto. Thus in the first part of this study, Wagner's working methods in *Rienzi* become, so to speak, a mirror-image of the work's origins in the nationalistic fervour and idealism which began to emerge in the fragmented and predominantly *petit-bourgeois* society of early nineteenth-century Germany—an idealism nourished by, but by no means identical with, liberal and so-called Utopian philosophies current in the intellectual circles of more advanced societies such as France and England. In this sense, Wagner's prose draft for *Rienzi* provides a useful springboard for placing any glib comparisons between its idealistic rhetoric and the brutal *Realpolitik* of Hitler and Mussolini in their proper perspective.

Wagner's working methods which are to be described in the following pages remained, externally at least, fundamentally the same for all his works up to and including *Parsifal*.[43] In fact his mechanical adherence throughout his life to the same procedure is perhaps proof of the inartistic, uncreative element in his works which Hanslick never tired of pointing out, and which was even noticed by one of Wagner's most intelligent

[41] Hitler's remarks on *Rienzi* are attributed to him in a book by one of his closest school-friends August Kubizek. The book is the main source for an unusually obscure period in Hitler's life (up to his apprentice years in Vienna) about which *Mein Kampf* is strangely reticent. Kubizek not only mentions *Rienzi*, he devotes an entire chapter to it and its effect on the young Hitler after a performance they both saw together in Linz (1906 or 1907). According to Kubizek, the work made a strong impact on Hitler, stronger in fact than any of the other Wagner works they saw. Most interesting of all, when Kubizek reminded Hitler of the experience during the Bayreuth Festival of 1939, the latter reacted enthusiastically, recalling details of the performance, and, as Kubizek reports, with the words: 'In jener Stunde begann es' ('es' referring to the growth of Nazism). See August Kubizek, *Adolf Hitler mein Jugendfreund*, Göttingen, 1953, pp. 133–42.

[42] Adorno, *Gesammelte Schriften*, xiii. 13. 'Eigenlob und Pomp—Züge der gesamten Wagnerschen Produktion und Existentialien des Faschismus . . .'

[43] This is not to say that the contents of Wagner's sketches did not change. Particularly in the sketches of the later works, there are changes of emphasis to accommodate the increasing importance of orchestration, although the external method of working in clear-cut stages from prose to verse, and then through various drafts of the music to the full score remains constant. See John Deathridge, 'The Nomenclature of Wagner's Sketches', *Proceedings of the Royal Musical Association*, ci (1974–5).

admirers, Thomas Mann.[44] But the sketches and drafts for *Rienzi* are not only valuable because they are the first relatively complete example of Wagner's working methods we possess, but also because they are the only authoritative source to which we can refer in determining the contents of the missing original score. Besides examining Wagner's procedure in *Rienzi* in order to gain a clearer view of his origins and stylistic development, therefore, the present study also hopes to prove that an authentic performing edition and, to use Glasenapp's phrase, a 'correct performance' of *Rienzi*—not necessarily complete, but with a full awareness of Wagner's original intentions—can only be undertaken with the sketches and drafts of the work in mind.

The scope of this study is therefore limited to three separate, but interrelated topics arising from an examination of the sketches and drafts for *Rienzi*: the origin of the work, the question of style, and the problem of performance. Using the sketches and drafts as a basis, we shall attempt a reappraisal of the work with these three aspects in mind which should help us towards a better understanding of Wagner's social and creative personality, and the unusual position of the work in the Wagner canon— as Glasenapp might have said, an understanding with less risk of a 'conscious self-deception' and a better claim to really 'know' the work in its original form.

[44] *Gesammelte Werke*, ix. 376. 'Es ist etwas zweifelhaftes um seine Beziehung zu den Künsten; so unsinnig es klingt, haftet ihr etwas Amusisches an.'

II

The Prose Draft and its Origin

1. Main features

IN describing Wagner's style as an 'artefact', Nietzsche[1] was attempting to define a rational anti-Romantic element in Wagner's works which provides an important key to an understanding of his origins and his working methods. The 'abstract' quality of his motivic technique noticed by Adorno,[2] the notorious theorizing of his prose works and the social criticism inherent in many of his libretti are all part of an objective, if not openly didactic side of his personality, which, despite the intense subjectivity of his music and the Romantic apparatus of his music dramas, clearly sets him apart from the norms of nineteenth-century art he is generally supposed to represent.[3] Although more recent generations have tended to challenge rather than endorse his ideals, the vacillations between highly rational and irrational elements which is a central feature of twentieth-century music clearly reflects a similar ambiguity in his works. The 'split' which Stravinsky noted between Wagner's 'genius' and 'the accessory parts of his mental *mise-en-scène*'[4] may be more accurately, though paradoxically, described as a form of emotional didacticism which is evident not only in the discrepancy between his theories and his music dramas, but also in the works themselves, and particularly in the way he set about composing them. His prose draft for *Rienzi*, although a relatively early example, provides an excellent starting-point for a study of his working methods from this point of

---

[1] *Gesammelte Werke*, xvii. 22.

[2] *Gesammelte Schriften*, xiii. 46–7.

[3] It is perhaps worth mentioning in this context that both an admirer of Romanticism, Thomas Mann, and one of its opponents, Bernard Shaw, were strongly attracted to Wagner's works. Notwithstanding Mann's interest in 'Wagner the psychologist'—one of the latter's most modern traits—he still saw him as the peak of German Romanticism. Shaw on the other hand, was more inclined to praise the rational side of Wagner's art—the 'far reaching ideas' of the social critique inherent in the *Ring* for example—while condemning his more Romantic tendencies (e.g. Alberich's 'curse') as 'stagey and old-fashioned'. See T. Mann, *Gesammelte Werke*, ix. 363 f., 373 f.; B. Shaw *The Perfect Wagnerite*, Leipzig, 1913, p. 73.

[4] 'Wagner's Prose', *Themes and Episodes*, New York, 1966, p. 138.

view—a study which is particularly appropriate when we consider that the constellation of political events in early nineteenth-century Germany which stimulated his choice of Rienzi as a dramatic subject was one, if not the main, formative influence on the socially critical, anti-Romantic attitudes we also find in his later works.

At first sight, there seems nothing unusual about the way in which Wagner began crystallizing his ideas for a dramatic composition. Clearly, the sensible thing to do when planning a large-scale musical work for the stage, especially one which involves elaborate re-working of previous material, is to write a scenario outlining the main points of the dramatic action in order to provide clear guide-lines for the creation of text and music, much as Verdi did for his librettist Piave before writing *Macbeth*.[5] In Wagner's case, however, the long and detailed prose draft with which he usually began the composition of a dramatic work is considerably more than a scenario in the ordinary sense of the term.[6] As a cursory glance at the prose draft for *Rienzi* shows, his first impulse was to provide not only a very exact idea of the action, even down to the gestures and emotions of individual characters, but also a considerable portion of the dialogue as well. Using this dialogue as a basis, he then went on to create the verse form of the final text, the first signs of which we can already see in the margin of the prose draft. There is even a single musical entry at this stage which, although it appears to be more like a stray jotting than a significant idea, bears a tenuous, but nevertheless distinct relation to the corresponding moment in the finished score.[7] The interval of a fourth is expanded to a diminished fifth and filled out with a quick

---

[5] See Carlo Gatti, *Verdi*, 2 vols., Milan, 1931, i. 176.

[6] See Ap. ii. 165–87. As this book was going to press, a short prose sketch (originally thought to be lost) was discovered by the author in the Burrell Collection in Philadelphia—unfortunately too late for inclusion in *Sämt. Werke*. The document now counts as the first extant sketch for *Rienzi*. A commentary is to be found in Ap. i. 159 (source 2a) and a transcription in Ap. ii. 165. It should be mentioned here that the terms 'prose sketch' (*Prosaskizze*) and 'prose draft' (*Prosaentwurf*)—first coined by Otto Strobel in 'Richard Wagner als Arbeitsgenie', *Allgemeine Musikzeitung*, lvi (1929), 525—distinguish between two types of document: a brief outline of the dramatic action in short, telegraphic sentences, and a more detailed working-out in prose with dialogue. There are extant prose sketches for the *Ring* and *Tristan*, but not for any of the earlier works with the exception of *Rienzi*. However, prose drafts exist for all the stage-works from *Rienzi* to *Parsifal*. For a comparison with *Rienzi*, see the prose drafts of *Tristan* and *Meistersinger* in *Schriften*, xi. 326ff., and *Parsifal* in *Sämt. Werke*, xxx. 68–87.

[7] Ap. ii. 181. Wagner rarely made musical entries in the prose draft. The only other example is in the prose draft for *Lohengrin* (Wahnfried) where a theme in E major from the bridal chamber scene is entered into the margin.

descending scale. The impression of a rapid downward movement followed by a rest is therefore retained in the final draft of the music as the
following comparison shows:

EXAMPLE 1

Prose draft   *Vocal Score*
Ap. i. 159 (source 2b, p. 6)   ii. 112 (437)

Although with this exception he left the invention of musical ideas to a
later stage, notably in the margin of the verse draft, the prose draft
shows the beginnings of a distinct chain reaction between prose, verse,
and music, which originates less with any poetic or musical 'inspiration'
than with the declamation of dialogue quite literally 'prosaic' in character,
and so closely intertwined with the stage directions that it often seems to
grow out of the stage action itself. Wagner's prose drafts are perhaps the
most revealing documents relevant to his working methods, for they have
a didactic, almost inartistic aura which was clearly not without influence
on the final music.

A striking feature of the prose draft for *Rienzi* is the relatively cursory
treatment of static or lyrical moments for which either little or no
dialogue is provided. At the end of scenes and acts particularly, Wagner
often writes the word 'Ensemble' to indicate a set piece during which
the movement of the action is suspended to give the singers a chance of
launching into a lyrical effusion of emotion and vocal display. Yet
although Wagner takes little trouble over these moments in the prose
draft, they take up a surprisingly large amount of space in the final score.
The two typically operatic movements which close the finale of Act II,
for example,—'O laßt der Gnade Himmelslicht' (Adagio) and 'Rienzi
dir sei Preis' (Allegro)—are represented by only four lines in the prose
draft,[8] but were later given such extensive musical treatment that they

[8] Ap. ii. 177 (lines 25–30).

form almost a third of the finale excluding the ballet music—a finale which in any case is over three times as long as any comparable examples of the period.[9] A similar instance is to be found at the end of the scene and trio in Act I.[10] As the prose draft shows, Wagner was concerned here with outlining a confrontation between Rienzi and Irene's lover Adriano, who, as a member of the nobility whose power Rienzi is intent on destroying, is nevertheless sympathetic towards Rienzi's ideals but highly critical of his methods of achieving them. During the course of the scene, Rienzi succeeds in convincing Adriano that the proposed revolution will not destroy the latter's status as a noble, but simply curb the anarchic activities of his family by making them answerable to the 'law'. Adriano succumbs to the argument, and his quixotic conversion is celebrated in an 'Ensemble' for which Wagner writes no dialogue at all, but which occupies well over a third of the whole scene in the final score.[11] As a study of the composition draft will show, Wagner had great trouble in finding the right form for this scene, largely on account of the conflicting motives behind it. On the one hand he wanted to present an aggressive, but nevertheless didactic argument between Rienzi and Adriano. On the other hand he wanted to show Adriano's feelings towards Irene which eventually influence his decision to side with Rienzi. The scene will be analysed in detail at a later stage;[12] but it is worth mentioning in this context that these two opposing motifs in the action led Wagner to arrive at an uneasy compromise between varied and powerful *recitativo accompagnato*, reflecting the exchange between Rienzi and Adriano, and a comparatively banal, four-square melody for the concluding 'Ensemble' in which Irene also participates. Indeed, Wagner's difficulties in reconciling the didactic and lyrical elements in the action can already be seen in the prose draft where, possibly when writing the ensuing verse draft or the prose draft itself, he crossed out Adriano's line 'Ha, du zeigst mir einen neuen Zustand der Welt . . .'[13] representing the latter's conversion to Rienzi's vision of a new society. Significantly, the line recurs in varied form during the following duet between Adriano and Irene where, possibly

[9] See *Vocal Score*, i. 203–351 (184–331). The length of the finale is 2,405 bars, i.e. longer than any single act in *Walküre* or *Parsifal*. The ballet music occupies 1,500 bars, and the last two movements 257 out of the 905 remaining bars.

[10] Ap. ii. 170 (line 6).

[11] 100 out of 175 bars. See *Vocal Score*, i. 81–93 (79–85); *Sämt. Werke*, iii (1). 158–74.

[12] See pp. 60–79 below.

[13] Ap. ii. 170 (lines 3–5).

sensing that it would disrupt the emotional atmosphere between the lovers, Wagner also saw fit to delete it.[14] Perhaps as compensation for the deletion of this didactic gesture, he briefly introduced a typically Romantic element at this point which is in none of his sources. At the end of the duet, Adriano calls upon 'night and death' and welcomes 'death and destruction' as he lies with Irene in an embrace during the breaking of day. The situation is strikingly reminiscent of *Tristan* and shows that the equation between sexual desire and resignation in death was part of Wagner's *Weltanschauung* long before he read Schopenhauer.[15]

Altogether, the word 'Ensemble' occurs seven times in the prose draft and almost always represents, when compared with the final score, an extended movement which usually occupies a third of the scene it adorns. The overriding impression given by the document, then, is that Wagner's initial interest was concentrated less on the lyrical or purely musical moments of his opera than on those sections involving the exposition of ideas and events. When recalling the genesis of *Rienzi* in later years, however, Wagner gives a somewhat different impression:

Aus dem Jammer des modernen Privatlebens, dem ich nirgends auch nur den geringsten Stoff für künstlerische Behandlung abgewinnen durfte, riß mich die Vorstellung eines großen historisch-politischen Ereignisses, in dessen Genuß ich eine erhebende Zerstreuung aus Sorgen und Zuständen finden mußte, die mir eben nichts anders, als nur absolut kunstfeindlich erschienen. Nach meiner künstlerischen Stimmung stand ich hierbei jedoch immer noch auf dem mehr oder weniger rein musikalischen, besser noch: opernhaften Standpunkte; dieser Rienzi, mit seinem großen Gedanken im Kopfe und im Herzen, unter einer Umgebung der Roheit und Gemeinheit, machte mir zwar alle Nerven vor sympathischer Liebesregung erzittern; dennoch entsprang mein Plan zu einem Kunstwerke erst aus dem Innewerden eines rein lyrischen Elementes in der Atmosphäre des Helden.[16]

The quotation is taken from the autobiographical essay 'Eine Mittheilung an meine Freunde' (1851) in which, as also in *Mein Leben*,[17] the initial plan for *Rienzi* is described as an attempt to write something so vast that only one of Europe's largest theatres, to which Wagner had no access at the time (1837), could think of producing it. The plan was meant as a means of escape from the crushing limitations of provincial theatrical life

---

[14] Ap. ii. 170 (lines 18–20).
[15] Ap. ii. 170 (lines 30–1, 40–1).
[16] *Schriften*, iv. 317–18 (257).
[17] Ibid. xiii. 211.

in which he found himself and—of great interest psychologically—from a serious marital crisis with his first wife Minna which almost led to divorce.[18] The vast dimensions of the final work which, as it turned out, not even Europe's largest theatres could accommodate in its complete form, were therefore the result of an Utopian element in its original conception—the typically Romantic longing to escape an 'artistically hostile' present we also find in E.T.A. Hoffmann for example. In the above quotation, Wagner attempts to qualify this fact by emphasizing his 'operatic' attitude towards the subject—implying, of course, that the 'great thoughts' in Rienzi's head were not commensurate with his 'purely musical' standpoint when he wrote the work. Later in the same essay, however, Wagner defines a similar antithesis, but places the emphasis the other way round:

Die "große Oper", mit all ihrer szenischen und musikalischen Pracht, ihrer effekt-reichen, musikalisch-massenhaften Leidenschaftlichkeit, stand vor mir; und sie nicht etwa bloß nachzuahmen, sondern, mit ruckhaltsloser Verschwendung, nach allen ihren bisherigen Erscheinungen sie zu überbieten, das wollte mein künstlerischer Ehrgeiz.—Dennoch würde ich gegen mich selbst ungerecht sein, wenn ich in diesem Ehrgeize alles inbegriffen sehen wollte, was mich bei der Konzeption und Ausführung meines "Rienzi" bestimmte. Der Stoff begeisterte mich wirklich, und nichts fügte ich meinem Entwurfe ein, was nicht eine unmittelbare Beziehung zu dem Boden dieser Begeisterung hatte. Es handelte sich mir zu allernächst um meinen Rienzi, und erst wenn ich mich hier befriedigt fühlte, ging ich auf die große Oper los.[19]

When the above quotations are compared, it is obvious that Wagner himself was undecided about how he should evaluate *Rienzi*. In the second quotation, he modifies the earlier impression of an 'operatic' impulse behind the work by suggesting that it was after all the figure of Rienzi and the dramatic substance of his material which took precedence over traditional forms.[20] Judging on the evidence of the prose draft, there is no reason to doubt the accuracy of this. Although he is exaggerating when he reduces the influence of 'grand opera' to the level of an afterthought, the draft does indeed show a concentration on dramatic development and, as we have indicated, a brief handling of the ensembles —in many ways the most traditional elements in the work. The word

[18] Ibid. xiii. 192, 197.
[19] Ibid. iv. 319 (258–9).
[20] A statement naturally influenced by his theoretical position in the essay 'Oper und Drama (1851) completed in the same year as 'Eine Mittheilung . . .'

'Arie', for example, occurs only once,[21] and it is noticeable even at this stage that the work was conceived less in terms of individual numbers giving the singers an opportunity to display their vocal virtuosity, than in terms of composite scenes in which traditional operatic forms are welded together to create a series of large-scale dramatic units[22]—a technique closely related to the works of Gluck and particularly to the 'heroic' operas of Spontini.

But if the prose draft offers proof of Wagner's attempt to make the forms of traditional opera subservient to the dramatic content of his subject, it is the final work which shows that his openly admitted ambition not only to imitate, but also to outbid, all previous grand operas with 'unreserved extravagance' was a major factor in its conception. Indeed, the fleeting musical entry in the prose draft is perhaps a sign that the musical 'brilliance' of grand opera, which Wagner wanted to imitate, and which came to dominate the dramatic elements of the work in its final form, was already in his mind at this stage. It is also likely that his enthusiasm for *Rienzi* was not only due to the Utopian idealism inherent in the subject, but also to the fact that he was lucky enough to find a 'historical–political event' which gave him a unique opportunity to imitate the effective features of so many successful grand operas of the time, even though the technique he used to realize his material belonged, in its initial stages at least, to the older tradition of Gluck and Spontini. The revolutionary leader Masaniello in Auber's *La Muette de Portici* (1828), Eléazer's prayer at the beginning of Act II in Halévy's *La Juive* (1835), the power of the Catholic Church represented by Cardinal Brogni's curse in Act III of the same work, the conspiracy of the nobles in Act IV of Meyerbeer's *Les Huguenots* (1836), are just a few effective moments which Wagner faithfully imitated in his prose draft (1837) in the form of Rienzi himself, the hero of 'freedom' who delivers the people of Rome from the oppression of the nobility, his 'prayer' at the beginning of Act V,[23] his excommunication by the Catholic Church at the end of Act IV,[24] and the conspiracy of the nobles to assassinate him in the finale of Act II.[25]

Despite these resemblances, however, *Rienzi* differs in two important respects from its predecessors: first, it is not simply a 'historical–political

---

[21] Ap. ii. 178 (line 31).

[22] e.g. the 'Introduktion, Duett u. Terzett' commencing Act IV. See Ap. ii. 181 (line 19).

[23] Ap. ii. 184 (lines 27–39).

[24] Ap. ii. 183 (lines 27 ff.).

[25] Ap. ii. 173 (lines 31 ff.).

event' in operatic clothing designed to satisfy the musical (and political) prejudices of its audience, but a didactic and somewhat pessimistic attempt to envisage the consequences of a 'new state of the world'[26]—the aftermath of a bloodless revolution which, in contrast to other 'revolutionary' operas of the period, takes place at the beginning of the work; second, the dramatic effects, and particularly the music of *Rienzi* in its complete form, differ from their models not in the sense that they are strikingly original, but because their sheer size and weight far exceed even the most extravagant works of Wagner's contemporaries. Hanslick was right for the most part in reproaching Wagner for not investing the traditional operatic forms of the work with original musical ideas;[27] but a fact he does not mention is that the tendency of Auber, Halévy, and Meyerbeer to 'spoil' their audiences with formal and melodic repetitions is taken to a point in *Rienzi* where it can be said to assume an extramusical character already to be felt in the prose draft—a Utopian gesture which, corresponding to the 'great thoughts' in Rienzi's 'head and heart',[28] was at odds with the conventional opera-going habits of nineteenth-century middle-class society.[29] In this sense, the traditional 'lyrical' elements or 'ensembles' which are only roughly outlined in the prose draft, but which contribute greatly toward the excessive length of the final work, are just as much part of the 'revolutionary' rhetoric inherent in the original conception of the opera as those sections in the draft provided with more detailed dialogue.

2. Sources and influences

(a) Mary Mitford and Bulwer-Lytton.

A fact often forgotten today is that Wagner's dramatization of *Rienzi* was only one of a number in a century which saw frequent revivals of the

[26] Ap. ii. 170 (lines 3–4).

[27] *Die Moderne Oper*, p. 276.

[28] See p. 18 above.

[29] Although *Rienzi* was substantially cut for its première, it still managed to encroach on the daily routine of its audience. One sympathetic critic, for example, remarked: 'Ohnstreitig würde man den Hauptfehler der neuen Oper, daß sie erst eine halbe Stunde vor Mitternacht endete, derselben für eine besondere Tugend angerechnet, wenn eine so lange Dauer nicht in manche Lebensgewohnheiten zu grausam eingriffe. Der Eine will um diese Zeit schon eine Stunde geschlafen haben, ein Anderer bei seinem Souper bereits bis zum Zahnstocher vorgerückt seyn, und ein Dritter des Comforts traulicher Häuslichkeit auf irgend eine Weise froh werden.' See H. Kirchmeyer, *Das zeitgenössische Wagner-Bild* 1842–5, Regensburg, 1967, p. 53. For details on the length of *Rienzi*, see Ap. iii. 189–90.

subject in literary and scholarly circles. The best known adaptation for the
theatre before Wagner's was Mary Mitford's five-act tragedy *Rienzi*—
first performed with great success in London at the Drury Lane Theatre on
4 October 1828, and later transferred to America where it was received
with equal enthusiasm. Before Mitford's play—to which we shall
return—there were two French dramatizations by Laignelot (1791) and
Drouineau (1826), both of whom, together with Mitford, drew their
inspiration from the eighteenth-century accounts of Rienzi's life by the
Abbé de Sade[30] and Edward Gibbon[31]. Contemporary with Wagner's
operatic version, and particularly after its Dresden success (1842), there
have been at least fifteen Rienzi dramas, mostly by third-rate Italian and
German authors long since forgotten.[32] In addition, the nineteenth century saw the publication of a number of important studies on Rienzi,
e.g. including the first critical edition by Zefirino Rè of an anonymous
biography by one of Rienzi's contemporaries[33] (the primary source for
our knowledge of the historical Rienzi) and the first transcription of
Rienzi's letters by Felix Papencordt.[34]

But the most successful and widely-circulated work on Rienzi in any
form during the nineteenth century was the novel by Bulwer-Lytton,
Rienzi—the Last of the Roman Tribunes,[35] which was stimulated by Mitford's play and draws largely on the *Vita* as well as a number of more
minor sources. The novel was Wagner's main source. Not uncritically, it
portrays a political figure and close friend of Petrarch active in fourteenth-
century Rome who, with a cunning mixture of pragmatism and mysti-
cism, attempted to deliver the city from anarchy and corruption by creating an allegedly egalitarian state in which rulers and ruled alike were equal

---

[30] *Mémoires pour la vie Petrarque*, 3 vols., Amsterdam, 1764–7, ii. 48–50, 320–416, iii. 221 ff.

[31] *The History and Decline of the Roman Empire*, 12 vols., London, 1790, xii. 339–62. This is still
the best short account of Rienzi and should be consulted for a quick resumé of his life.

[32] Including versions by Riekhoff (1837), Giocometti (1838), Engels (1840/1), Mosen (1840),
Kirner (1845), Gaillard (1848), Esselen (1848), Grosse (1854), Kühn (1872), Hamann (1873), Pirazzi
(1873), Vergilii (1877), Cossa (1882), v. Delius (1903), and Namneek (1938). Wagner was only
acquainted with the versions by Mosen and Gaillard. For his comments, see *Schriften*, xiv. 24;
Sämt. Briefe, ii. 398.

[33] *La Vita di Cola di Rienzo*, ed. Zefirino Rè Cesenate, Fiorli, 1828. Unfortunately, the edition
does not include the original MS. in its entirety. The most complete published text is to be found in
vol. III of Muratori's collection *Antiquitates italicae* . . . (Medialoni, 1740). All references are to the Rè
edition, however, since this is more readily available. (Hereafter *Vita*.)

[34] *Cola di Rienzo und seine Zeit*, Hamburg, 1841.

[35] London, 1848. The first edition appeared in 1835. All references are to the 1848 edition,
however, because it includes a substantial preface by Bulwer pointing out the relevance of his
subject to the revolutions which shook Europe in that year. (Hereafter *Bulwer*.)

before the law. Although Bulwer lays substantial claim to historical accuracy in his novel,[36] his idealized portrayal of Rienzi,[37] which was intended as a refutation of the less flattering account by Gibbon, stands in sharp contrast to the distinctly negative impression given by the original sources available to him and on which Gibbon also based his judgements.[38] Rienzi's modern biographer Konrad Burdach, while remaining aloof from any real estimation of the former's political goals, has published evidence which, unwittingly perhaps, confirms the tendentiousness of Bulwer's interpretation. Burdach's painstaking transcription of Rienzi's letters, and his equally meticulous account of the age in which he lived, show unmistakably that Rienzi was less an enlightened visionary who wanted to reform a corrupt state with his idea of a *Reformatio boni status urbis*,[39] than an ambitious politician who, despite some truly progressive ideas, was forced to maintain an uneasy equilibrium between the interests of the propertied classes and those of the masses[40] by using techniques of 'mass persuasion'—allegoric paintings on houses, street demonstrations, magic ceremonies, and the like—to create a dictatorship strikingly similar in its methods to the modern totalitarian state.

Wagner, of course, was more interested in making an 'efficient piece for the operatic stage'[41] out of Bulwer's novel than questioning the latter's interpretation of historical facts. In later years, during a conversation with Bulwer's son in Vienna, Wagner described his opera as a 'direct outcome'[42] of the novel and, judging by his numerous references to the work, he seems to have had no direct knowledge of any other source except a translation of the book by Bärmann[43]—one of no fewer

[36] Ibid., pp. ix–x, 441–7.

[37] The correct spelling is 'Rienzo' since the name was a popular corruption of 'Lorenzo'. To avoid confusion, the more familiar spelling 'Rienzi' used by both Bulwer and Wagner has been adopted throughout.

[38] This has been convincingly demonstrated by A. Warncke, *Miss Mitfords und Bulwers englische Rienzibearbeitung*, Rostock, 1904, pp. 8, 22, 54 f.

[39] Burdach, *Briefwechsel des Cola di Rienzo*, 5 vols., Berlin, 1913–29, i. 499.

[40] See Max Horkheimer, 'Egoismus und Freiheitsbewegung' (1936), *Traditionelle und kritische Theorie*, Frankfurt, 1970, pp. 109–10.

[41] See p. 5 above.

[42] Lytton, *The Life of Edward Bulwer by his Grandson*, 2 vols., London, 1913, i. 441. Lytton gives no date for the meeting; according to *Mein Leben*, however, it was probably in 1863. See *Schriften*, xv. 347.

[43] Bulwer, *Rienzi, der letzte der Tribunen*, tr. G. N. Bärmann, 4 vols., Zwickau, 1836. (This translation will be referred to in parentheses after each reference to the English 1848 edition.)

than five different German translations to have appeared since the book was first published.[44] There is evidence to suggest, however, that Wagner also knew Mitford's play, the existence of which was either drawn to his attention by Bulwer's laudatory account of it in the original preface to the novel, or by an entirely different source which predates his reading of Bärmann's translation. In his 'Autobiographische Skizze' (1843), for example, he states that the novel brought him back to a 'favourite idea'[45] he had already been considering; and in a letter from Paris (20 September 1840) to his former schoolfriend and companion Theodor Apel, Wagner clearly indicates that the idea for *Rienzi* originated at a time when he was still seeing a good deal of his friend, i.e. before he first read the novel in Blasewitz in the summer of 1837 when their ways had already parted:

Es ist über 4 Jahre, daß wir uns nicht sahen . . . Und siehst Du, wie ich *in Dir*, ganz Eins mit Dir gelebt habe;—mein eben fertig gewordenes Werk heißt: *Rienzi*, der letzte der Tribunen! Wer hatte die erste Idee davon?—Ich glaube auch, wir haben die Arbeit zusammengemacht! Wenigstens ist sie meine beste. Laß Dir sagen . . . unser *Rienzi* ist eine Oper in fünf Akten geworden.[46]

From this quotation it may be supposed that the idea for *Rienzi* originated with Apel who was himself keenly interested in the theatre and wrote a play, *Columbus*, for which Wagner composed an overture (1835). In a letter to Apel dated 27 October 1834, i.e. a year before Bulwer's novel was first published, Wagner expresses an ambition to travel with Apel to Italy and then to Paris where he would compose a 'French opera'.[47] It is possible, then, that the idea of using Rienzi as a subject for a 'grand opera' was suggested by Apel at this time; and of the three Rienzi dramatizations before Wagner's own, it may well have been the success of Mitford's play which drew Apel's attention to the dramatic possibilities of the subject. Certainly, there are broad resemblances between the play and Wagner's opera which make it probable that either he or Apel managed to procure a copy of it—perhaps through the publisher Friedrich Brockhaus, with whose family Wagner had close connections. Besides the fact that both Mitford and Wagner compress Rienzi's two periods

---

[44] Other translations are: O. v. Czarnowski (1836), Gustav Pfizer (1839), Theodor Roth (1845), R. Wichtbold (1920).

[45] 'Eine bereits gehegte Lieblingsidee', *Schriften*, i. 16 (12).

[46] *Sämt. Briefe*, i. 406, 409.

[47] Ibid. i. 168.

of power as tribune and senator[48] into one, thus simplifying the intricate causes of his rise and fall described by Bulwer, both works are in five acts and centre on a love relationship between a relative of Rienzi's and a member of the nobility (Claudia/Angelo in Mitford, Irene/Adriano in Wagner) which only plays a subordinate role in the novel. In addition, there are other similarities between the two works—notably Angelo/Adriano's intervention to save his father from the sentence of death placed upon him by Rienzi (Mitford IV/i,[49] Wagner II/finale[50])—which are not to be found in Bulwer or any other source. Though possibly due to a coincidence of dramatic instincts, they suggest that Wagner, despite his rudimentary English (the play was not translated), knew Mitford's adaption in some detail.[51]

(b) Heinrich Laube and the Saint-Simonians.

Another important, though indirect influence on Wagner's conception of *Rienzi* was the writer Heinrich Laube (1806–84), who, besides helping Wagner with the practical realization of the work,[52] was also the moving force behind its political *Tendenz*. To try and unravel a coherent aesthetic or political viewpoint from Laube's writings after the French and Polish revolutions of 1830/1 is, it must be admitted, an almost impossible task. His enthusiastic articles for the *Zeitung für die elegante Welt* on subjects ranging from Schröder-Devrient[53] and Spontini's *Olympia*[54] to Bulwer-Lytton,[55] all probably known to Wagner since he was also a contributor

[48] For a useful survey of Rienzi's career, see Rè's 'Sommario Cronologico' in *Vita*, pp. 330–8.

[49] *Rienzi*, London, 1828, pp. 38–45.

[50] Ap. ii. 176 (lines 11 ff.).

[51] A further indication that either Wagner or Apel had access to printed editions of successful English plays of the period is the publication of a 'nautical drama' by Edward Fitzball called *The Flying Dutchman* (1826) by the same publisher who printed Mitford's *Rienzi* (John Cumberland). Wagner himself reports in 'Eine Mittheilung . . .' that he first became acquainted with the subject of the Dutchman when planning the first stages of *Rienzi* (*Schriften*, iv. 319 (258)). Although he implies that it was Heine's account of the story which drew his attention to it, it is possible, especially in view of his hazy recollection, that he was first attracted to it by glancing through a copy of Fitzball's 'drama'. The play bears little resemblance to Wagner's *Holländer*, but it has some vivid theatrical effects (e.g. the sudden appearance of the 'Phantom Ship' at the end of Act II) which clearly point to the operatic possibilities of the subject.

[52] Laube helped to acquire the services of Schröder-Devrient for *Rienzi* and was the mediator between Wagner and Liszt for their first meeting. Liszt later became one of the opera's most influential advocates. See *Sämt. Briefe*, i. 455, 461.

[53] *Zeitung für die elegante Welt*, xxxiii (1833), 17–19, 21–4.

[54] Ibid. xxxiv (1834), 579–81.

[55] Ibid. xxxiv (1834), 525–7.

to the periodical, are coloured by an emotionalism of almost studied superficiality and a political philosophy derived mainly from the German Youth Movement (*Burschenschaften*) and the French Utopian Socialists. If any consistency is to be found in his early writings, including the first part of his prose-poem *Das junge Europa* to which Wagner refers in his autobiography,[56] it is the tendency to give political or historical concepts an aesthetic value which robs the former of any rational validity and effectively transforms them into an irrational quantity. Laube's extensive article on Bulwer-Lytton, written a year before the novel *Rienzi* appeared, is interesting from this point of view because, unlike his articles on Schröder-Devrient and Spontini, it takes up a critical stance towards its subject which reflects this mixture of rational and emotional attitudes. While praising Bulwer for his 'liberal' political views (Bulwer was a Whig and Member of Parliament at the time), Laube reproaches him for a lack of original and creative 'Poesie' and attributes the success of his novels to their strong didactic flavour and its appeal to the same 'philistine' element in the general reading public.[57] The significance of Laube's critique is that, although he points to Bulwer's most serious deficiency (his argument agrees with present-day assessments of Bulwer's works), he is still prepared to acknowledge him as an important artist, on a par with Victor Hugo and Heinrich Heine. On the one hand he condemns Bulwer's didacticism for its lack of fantasy. On the other hand he praises the erudition of Bulwer's novels and suggests that this 'modern' feature is a positive asset, if only because it catches the spirit of the times and the attention of the public. Laube's argument, which only becomes clear when seen in the context of his other articles, is based on a twofold view of the artist: first, as an ideological instrument of progressive opinion capable of 'educating' society;[58] second, as a vehicle of 'sublime' emotion transcending history and affairs of state.[59] For Laube, these two viewpoints do not contradict one another, since the artist is in a position not simply to demonstrate objective knowledge, but also to inject it with a subjective force impossible in any other form of communication; he therefore becomes a powerful instrument of propaganda with an ability

[56] *Schriften*, xiii. 110, 113.

[57] *Zt.f.d.e.W.*, xxxiv (1834), 526.

[58] Ibid. xxxiii (1833), 123 ff.—Laube comments here on the didactic role of the actor and theatre in society.

[59] Ibid. 18, 22. Laube describes Schröder-Devrient as an embodiment of a new age concerned with 'strong emotions' as opposed to the 'affairs of state' represented by her rival Henriette Sontag.

to convince and persuade his audience without the necessity of rational argument—a faculty which ordinary statesmen and historians do not have. According to Laube, therefore, an author must not only study history in order to write a good historical novel, he must also be able to 'feel' history and to exploit its Romantic possibilities to the full.[60] This, he implies, is precisely what Bulwer does not do—an argument which may well have influenced Wagner in his response to Bulwer when he later came to read *Rienzi*.

Laube's and Wagner's political opinions of the post-revolution years 1831–7 have often been described as 'liberal', but in fact they go much further than this, especially in their glorification of the irrational as a political (and artistic) principle. As Laube states in his autobiography, it was the doctrine of the Saint-Simonians—a religious political sect active in Paris (*circa* 1829–31)—which was the main formative influence on his early writings.[61] The totalitarian basis of this doctrine has been analysed by Georg Iggers, and it is interesting to note that many aspects of the Simonian philosophy he brings to light, particularly the view of the artist as a propagator of political ideas,[62] often resemble similar views in the early writings of Laube and Wagner. It must be said straight away that Laube did not realize the implications of the authoritarian society proposed by the Simonians. He firmly believed that the Simonian conception of 'freedom' in an 'integrated' class society was a significant and truly 'socialist' solution to the unsettled political situation of the time.[63] Nevertheless, the shadows of totalitarianism are implicit in the doctrine and it would be foolish to ignore their presence, both in Laube's early writings and Wagner's *Rienzi*, which, although not directly influenced by Saint-Simonism, reflects a political mood very similar in content.

---

[60] See Laube's review of König's novel *Die hohe Braut*, *Zt.f.d.e.W.*, xxxiii (1833), 531. Wagner also converted this novel into a prose draft before proceeding to *Rienzi*. See *Schriften*, iv. 317 (256), 337 (273).

[61] *Gesammelte Schriften*, 50 vols, Leipzig, 1908/9, xli. 300. 'Ich glaube auch, daß die Aufmerksamkeit, welche meine Redaktion der "Zeitung für die elegante Welt" erweckte, von dieser Gedankenwelt (i.e. the Saint-Simonians) herrührte. Denn sie pulsierte in jedem meiner Artikel.'

[62] Georg G. Iggers, *The Cult of Authority. The Political Philosophy of the Saint-Simonians*, The Hague, 1958, pp. 19, 158, 173.

[63] Laube, op. cit., xli. 284. 'Die Nachrichten über den in Paris aufstehenden St. Simonismus erweckten mir wieder jenen Gedanken an Freiheit. Sie sprachen von einer ganz neuen Organisation des Begriffes von Freiheit, sie verbreiteten ihn auf alle Theile der Gesellschaft ... Es war der Beginn des Socialismus in ausgedehntestem Sinn.'

One of the central ideas of the Simonian doctrine is that of an 'organic' society in which freedom is defined not in the Hegelian sense as the use of reason to determine social activity, but as the unconditional, and hence totally irrational surrender of the individual to the good of the community as a whole. The 'organic' society, according to the Simonians, is a form of religious order in which the goal of activity is clearly defined through a rational ordering of institutions by a select élite, and which, as opposed to the anarchy of 'critical' or pluralistic societies, is based on the unanimous consent of the governed who have no part in the formulation of policy. The mediator between the governing élite and the governed is the 'genius leader' who, by virtue of his 'natural' superiority and ability to inspire the masses, acts as the principal agent in creating an organized people or *foule ordonné* (equivalent to Rienzi's *Volksgemeinschaft*) from the disorganized mob, or *foule chaos* typical of critical epochs[64]—including of course the rise of French bourgeois society against which this doctrine was directed. As Iggers remarks, the classification of anti-capitalist movements as left and right first ceased to make sense with the Simonians.[65] The conservative demand for order and hierarchical organization with the socialist demand for equality of opportunity, and this combined with a mystical belief in the supremacy of the totality over the individual, accurately summarizes the contradictions of the Simonians' 'benevolent totalitarianism'[66] which also emerges in Laube's early writings and Wagner's *Rienzi*, and which, less certainly, may also have been known to Bulwer.[67] Wagner himself described the 'whole ideal' of his *Rienzi* as the transition from the 'confused anarchic conditions in Rome under the nobles' to the 'enthusiastic confidence' in the Good Estate, or *buono stato* which Rienzi brings into being[68]—a description which not only reflects the Simonian notion of critical and organic societies, but also defines a cultural criterion which Wagner retained with surprising consistency to the end of his life.

3. Organization

Besides defining his conception of an organized anti-bourgeois society

---

[64] Iggers, op. cit., p. 94.

[65] Ibid., pp. 2–3.

[66] Ibid., p. 64.

[67] In the preface to the 1848 edition of his *Rienzi*, Bulwer extols the virtues of a 'mild despotism' and a constitution which 'asks but of its subjects to submit to be well governed—without agitating the question "how and by what means that government is carried on" '. See *Bulwer*, p. xiv.

[68] *Wagner Briefe. Die Sammlung Burrell*, ed. John N. Burk, Frankfurt, 1953, p. 148.

based on subjective principles,[69] Wagner's passion for order as a means to an irrational end is very much in evidence in his sketches, the almost pedantic neatness of which stand in sharp contrast to the *émotions fortes* of his music. It is true that, apart from questions of calligraphy, the extent to which this need for order affected the substance of a work is not easy to determine. But the simple fact that Wagner always began with a prose sketch or draft and worked systematically from this point through definite stages to the final score suggests that, if any conscious organization is to be found at all, it is already present at this initial stage, i.e. in the conception of a work as a scenic entity aside from the poetical and musical elements added later. The elaborate symmetries which Alfred Lorenz[70] thought he saw in the mature music dramas, for example, are, if one observes closely, most convincing when related to clearly organized scenic (and sometimes verbal) parallels which can often be traced to the prose draft of the work in question. *Rienzi* is no exception to this and is in fact the first of Wagner's works in which this type of scenic organization can be seen.

When the prose draft for *Rienzi* is stripped of its emotional dialogue, a rational ordering of scenes and events emerges which surpasses all of Wagner's models, including the libretto for Spontini's *Ferdinand Cortez*,[71] and even Scribe's libretti for *La Muette* and *La Juive*—greatly influential in their clear organization of plot and judicious handling of entrances and exits. It is immediately obvious, for example, that each act runs a similar course between an introduction, through one or two individual numbers, to a large-scale choral finale. There is, of course, nothing particularly remarkable about this; but what is unusual is that these set pieces are arranged in a clear symmetry corresponding exactly with Rienzi's rise to power (Acts I–II), his change of fortune (III) and downfall (IV–V). As shown by the table below, the only aria in the work is placed at its centre; it is flanked in Acts II/IV by a duet and trio on both

---

[69] Particularly noticeable in his later revolutionary writings: see, e.g., *Schriften*, iii. 51 ff. (42 ff.), xii. 218 ff. (220 ff.).

[70] *Das Geheimnis der Form bei Richard Wagner*, 4 vols., Berlin, 1924–33.

[71] The libretto is by Esménard and Jouy, and the work was first performed on 28 November 1809. Wagner saw a performance of it in the company of Laube in Berlin during 1836. He describes his impressions as follows: '. . . das außerordentlich präzise, feurige und reich organisierte Ensemble des Ganzen . . . (war mir) . . . durchaus neu. Ich gewann eine neue Ansicht von der eigentümlichen Würde großer theatralischer Vorstellungen, welche in allen ihren Teilen durch scharfe Rhythmik zu einem eigentümlichen, unvergleichlichen Kunstgenre sich steigern konnte. Dieser sehr deutliche Eindruck lebte drastisch in mir fort, und hat mich bei der Konzeption meines "Rienzi" . . . geleitet.' *Schriften*, xiii. 168.

sides which are further matched by a striking parallel in the action: the nobles' plot to assassinate Rienzi in opposition to Adriano (II),[72] and the citizens' conspiracy against Rienzi, this time with Adriano's support (IV).[73] It is also clear that Wagner deliberately arranged the entries and exits of his characters to focus maximum attention on Rienzi. At the beginning of each finale, Rienzi enters in the middle of a crowded stage: in Acts I–IV with great pomp amidst mass processions, and in Act V in the face of a mob intent on destroying him. With the exception of Act IV, Rienzi also appears at or near the beginning of each introduction, exits later in the act, and thereby causes a change in the action which enables him to make an effective re-entry in the finale. This in turn allows Wagner to set Rienzi in relief by using a strikingly symmetrical constellation of characters: Adriano/Irene (I), Adriano/Nobles (II), Adriano (III), Citizens/Adriano (IV), and Irene/Adriano (V). This scheme may be represented as follows:

Rienzi's Rise		*Peripeteia*	*Rienzi's Fall*	
Act I	II	III	IV	V
Intro.	*Intro.*	*Intro.*	*Intro.*	*Intro.*
R. enters.	R. enters.	R. enters		R. on stage.
	R. exits.	R. exits.		
Sc. a. Trio.	*Duet.*		*Duet.*	*Duet.*
R. exits.	Nobles		Citizens	R. exits.
	plot		plot	
	the		the	
	assassination	*Aria.*	downfall	
	of R.		of R.	
	Adriano		Adriano	
	resists		supports	
	the		the	
	plan.		plan.	
Duet.	*Trio.*		*Trio.*	*Sc. Duet.*
Adriano/Irene		Adriano		Irene/Adriano
Finale.	*Finale.*	*Finale.*	*Finale.*	*Finale.*
R. re-enters.	R. re-enters.	R. re-enters.	R. re-enters.	R. re-enters.
Pentecost	Festivities,	Battle San	Excommuni-	Fall at the
Revolution,		Lorenzo,	cation,	hands of people,
19/20 May	1/2 August	21 November	3 December	8 October
1347.	1347.	1347.	1347.	1354.
Bulwer, p. 135ff.	277ff.	244ff.	261–3,	432 ff.
(ii. 70ff.)	(iii. 76ff.)	(iii. 116ff.)	(iii. 152–6)	(iv. 273ff.)

[72] Ap. ii. 173 (lines 31 ff.).
[73] Ap. ii 182 (lines 10 ff.).

Obviously, the table raises an important question: did Wagner consciously construct this symmetry? Or was it merely intuitive? Since there are no extant sketches earlier than the prose draft showing any advance structural organization, this is impossible to answer for certain. However, there is one method we can use as a sounding-board and that is to determine whether any aspect of this structure is dramatically superfluous, but formally necessary in terms of the symmetry alone. If this is so, it would imply that Wagner, who was usually very economical in shaping the action of a work, had the symmetry in mind when writing the draft and for some reason placed it above the interests of dramatic coherence and precision. For the most part, the elements of the symmetry dovetail smoothly with the action; but there is one moment where this does not occur and that is the scene and duet between Irene and Adriano in Act V.[74] Viewed in a dramatic context, this piece is redundant since the situation it presents—Irene's rejection of Adriano in favour of her brother's ideals—is a repetition of a similar event at the end of Act IV.[75] It would have been more effective, for example, to have continued the preceding Rienzi/Irene duet in Act V[76] directly into the finale, thus creating an unbroken line of tension up to the final catastrophe. In view of Wagner's scenic economy in the rest of the work, it is surprising that he failed to do this. But when the 'scene and duet' is compared with its opposite number within the symmetry—the Adriano/Irene duet in Act I —a clear connection emerges between them: Adriano's metaphysical references to 'death and destruction',[77] for example, and the fact that both pieces are flanked by Rienzi's departure in directly antithetical situations: his triumphant appearance before the people (Act I/finale),[78] and his degrading reception by the mob (Act V/finale).[79] It is possible, therefore, that Wagner was less interested in making the 'scene and duet' in Act V serve a strictly dramatic purpose, than in using it to create a clear formal parallel with Act I—a kind of large-scale rhetorical emphasis in the action which, although superfluous, consciously rounds off the symmetry of the whole.

[74] Ap. ii. 186 (lines 1 ff.).
[75] Ap. ii. 184 (lines 8 ff.).
[76] Ap. ii. 184 (lines 40 ff.).
[77] Ap. ii. 170 (line 40); 186 (lines 13, 15).
[78] Ap. ii. 171 (lines 13 ff.).
[79] Ap. ii. 186 (lines 38 ff.).

The above table suggests, too, that Wagner was equally ingenious in his adaptation of Bulwer's novel, particularly in his selection of the historical facts forming the basis of its narrative. Although he did not study any historical sources,[80] it was this didactic element in the book which seems to have attracted him. In his prose draft, the episodic form of the novel (an unsubtle imitation of the technique used in Shakespeare's historical plays) is transformed into a linear sequence of situations which culminates at the end of each act in a massive choral scene based on a key event in Rienzi's political career. By a stroke of good fortune, the five 'brilliant'[81] finales Wagner had in mind for his opera were ideally suited to the public, often extravagant nature of these events as reported by the *Vita*. This fabric of historical fact, however, is by no means limited to the scenic presentation of *Rienzi*; it also extends to the music itself. On a more detailed level, there are two historical motifs in the prose draft (also traceable via Bulwer to the *Vita*) which Wagner transformed into two distinctive musical symbols in the final work: (i) the trumpet sound marking the beginning of Rienzi's Pentecost Revolution[82]—heard as a 'long-sustained tone'[83] at the beginning of the overture:

EXAMPLE 2

and at appropriate moments during the opera, e.g. before Rienzi's words 'Doch höret ihr der Trompete Ruf' in Act I:[84]

---

[80] In a letter to Tichatschek (the first tenor to sing Rienzi), Wagner writes: 'Es ist historisch, daß Rienzi zur Zeit als er sein großes Unternehmen ausführte ein junger Mann von ungefähr 28 Jahren war.' (*Sämt. Briefe*, i. 507. The date of the letter is probably September 1841.) As neither the *Vita* nor *Bulwer* give any indication of Rienzi's age, the only source where Wagner could have found this piece of information is Papencordt (op. cit., p. 60) who was the first to determine this fact. However, Papencordt places Rienzi's birth in the middle of 1313, which makes him almost 34 at the time of the Pentecost revolution (May 1347). Although Wagner may have read or heard of Papencordt's book in 1841 when it was first published, it seems more likely that he was either inventing or modifying Rienzi's age in order to make it agree with his own.

[81] *Schriften*, iv. 320 (259).

[82] 'Allora Cola di Rienzo mando 'l bando a suono di tromba . . .'; *Vita*, p. 43. 'Suddenly, there was heard the sound of a single trumpet! It swelled—it gathered on the ear.' *Bulwer*, p. 137 (ii. 74).

[83] '. . . als die [*sic*] von Ferne den langgehaltenen Ton einer Trompete hören'. Ap. ii. 170 (lines 43–4).

[84] *Vocal Score*, i. 63 (61); *Sämt. Werke*, iii (1). 121–2.

EXAMPLE 3

(ii) Rienzi's desire to avenge his brother's death at the hands of the nobles which, as the *Vita* implies, became the driving force behind his political career.[85] Both Bulwer and Wagner use this psychological element as a recurring motif in their respective versions: Bulwer quotes its source in the *Vita* at the beginning of his novel, and Wagner turns it into a 'reminiscence' motif of the kind he used later in the *Ring*, i.e. an amalgam of music and text so close that a repetition of the motif, even without text, inevitably recalls the extra-musical idea originally associated with it. The text underlying the motif is already to be found in the prose draft.[86] It first occurs in Act I when Rienzi indicates to Adriano that the duty to avenge 'a relative's blood' has become a self-pitying moral obligation, and one of the incentives behind his revolution against the nobility:[87]

EXAMPLE 4

[85] 'pensa lunga mano vendicare 'l sangue di suo frate; pensa lunga mano dirizzare la cittate di Roma male guidata.' *Vita*, p. 17.

[86] Ap. ii 169 (lines 42–3).

[87] Cf. *Vocal Score*, i. 80 (77–8); *Sämt. Werke*, iii (1) 155. There is some confusion about the text at this point. In all published scores except the Fürstner edition (pl. no. 5000), the Singer vocal score and *Sämt. Werke*, the words have been altered to 'Weh dem, der mir verwandtes Blut vergossen hat'—a not inconsiderable change of emphasis which transforms the motif from a self-pitying to an openly aggressive call for vengeance. The version in the prose draft is derived from Bärmann's translation ('Gesegnet bist Du, der Du kein Dir verwandtes Blut zu rächen hast', iii. iv. 249) and is used in all further drafts—suggesting that it is also in the full score. The first vocal score by Klink (Dresden, 1844) already contains the altered version—a certain indication that it was introduced during the first performances of the work, probably on account of its comparative simplicity. In his Collected Writings, Wagner reverts to the original version. See *Schriften*, i. 53 (42).

Later in the work, Wagner introduces the motif again with great effect in Act III,[88] and particularly in Act IV where it underscores Adriano's meeting with the citizens. Although without text in Act IV, it is clearly associated with Adriano's intention to avenge his father's death[89] by conspiring against Rienzi and provoking his downfall. Originally at the root of Rienzi's will to power, therefore, the idea of vengeance associated with the motif is turned against him in its new context; it becomes a major factor in his eventual ruin and hence a key element in the symmetry of the action. The following example is taken from the introduction to Act IV:[90]

EXAMPLE 5

Apart from drawing on the didactic content of the novel, however, Wagner was also prepared to fly in the face of historical fact, to 'feel'[91] history and to activate it with Romantic elements of a non-historical character.[92] Unlike Bulwer, he decided to compress Rienzi's two careers as tribune and senator into one and to give greater weight to the love interest between Adriano and Irene.[93] This piece of dramatic licence which, as already indicated,[94] he may have borrowed from Mitford's

---

[88] Ap. ii. 180 (line 37).

[89] At the hands of the Rienzi's soldiers during the off-stage battle in the finale of Act III: Ap. ii. 179–80, especially 180 (lines 26–8).

[90] Cf. *Vocal Score*, ii. 167–8 (494); *Sämt. Werke*, iii (4). 23. The origin of the text is to be found in the prose draft: Ap. ii. 182 (line 11).

[91] See p. 27 above.

[92] In the 1848 preface to his novel, Bulwer states that the book's 'interest is rather drawn from a faithful narration of historical facts, than from the inventions of fancy' (*Bulwer*, p. xi). Nevertheless, Wagner, although principally attracted to the factual side of the book, also drew to a lesser extent on the 'inventions of fancy'; the abduction of Irene from Rienzi's house (Act I/introduction), the dialogue between Rienzi and Adriano (Act I/sc. and trio), and the 'war hymn' *Santo Spirito* (Act III/introduction, finale) which, in the final text, is taken directly from Bärmann's translation. See respectively, *Bulwer*, pp. 45 ff. (i. 63 ff.), 68 ff. (i. 114 ff.), 246–7 (iii. 119).

[93] An aspect of the novel not to be found in the *Vita* or any other historical source. It is based directly on the Claudia/Angelo relationship in Mitford's play.

[94] See pp. 24–5 above.

play, concentrates Rienzi's rise and fall into a single phase and gives his
ascetic political ambitions (contrary to Bulwer, Wagner's Rienzi is not
married) an emotional penumbra well suited to the obligatory mixture
of historical fact and human passion typical of grand opera. In order to
reinforce the emotional weight of the action, Wagner condensed the
two key figures of Angelo and Adrian in the novel into the single role of
Adriano. In Bulwer, Angelo is a protégé of Rienzi who, when learning
of his father's death on Rienzi's orders, turns aginst his benefactor and
precipitates his downfall.[95] Bulwer's Adrian, on the other hand, is a
judicious observer of events who, though critical of Rienzi, never loses
respect for him and even attempts to save his life when his downfall is
imminent.[96] In uniting the figures of Angelo and Adrian, therefore,
Wagner created a character both critically sympathic towards Rienzi in
the first half of the opera, and one of his bitterest opponents in the second.
Within this framework, Adriano's vacillations between his love for Irene
and loyalty to his father Steffano Colonna become the centre-point of
the action and the principal motivation behind his confrontation with
Rienzi.

Hanslick complains in his critique of *Rienzi* that, unlike Bulwer's
novel, the opera leaves its audience completely in the dark about the
political causes of Rienzi's rise to power and subsequent decline.[97] The
remark was doubtless provoked by the fact that Wagner, in focusing
on the confrontation between Rienzi and Adriano, deliberately created
an emotional rather than a political catalyst for Rienzi's actions, and,
given the conventions of grand opera, it is difficult to see what else he
could have done. However, there is another side to this which suggests
that, far from simply adapting the novel to suit the traditions of grand
opera, Wagner actually used these traditions to emphasize 'the sinister,
demonic foundation of Rienzi's character',[98] and even to gain an
occasional insight into its real political nature. He realized, perhaps only
intuitively, that the basis of Rienzi's power was not 'political' in the
ordinary sense of the word, but something far broader and less easy to
define. With the 'scenic magnificence' and 'musical mass pathos'[99] of
grand opera in mind, he cleverly selected a subject in which, as two

[95] *Bulwer*, p. 421 ff. (iv. 249 ff.).
[96] Ibid., p. 432 ff. (iv. 274 ff.).
[97] *Die moderne Oper*, p. 279.
[98] *Schriften*, xiv. 36.
[99] See p. 19 above.

modern studies have pointed out,[100] the term 'political' extends its
meaning to include public display and 'mass pathos' used in the form of
premeditated propaganda as a means of inculcating non-rational concepts
such as blood, community and people (*Volk*)—a technique which the
historical Rienzi exploited to win support of the masses and simultaneously to hide his real political interests, i.e. an identification with the
ruling classes. By intensifying the calculated emotions and effects of grand
opera in an attempt to 'outbid'[101] all previous works in the genre,
Wagner reproduces this facet of Rienzi's 'political' methods with great
accuracy and occasionally with a real awareness of its significance. It is
interesting, for example, that Wagner gives to the citizens' representative,
Baroncelli, a critical consciousness quite different from Bulwer's description of him as 'not an eloquent nor gifted man'.[102] In the introduction to Act IV, Baroncelli insinuates that Rienzi's actions are guided
more by the interests of the ruling classes than those of the people,[103] and
that his love of 'pomp and festivities' only serves to smother the 'just
complaints'[104] of the people—an insight into the hypocrisy of Rienzi's
political affiliations and the duplicity of his propaganda which is not
to be found in Bulwer. Indeed, it seems as if Wagner could already sense
this sinister side of Rienzi's 'benevolent totalitarianism'[105] long before it
became a reality in the modern age. There is no question, of course, that
he identified with the demagogic personality of Rienzi in a way well
demonstrated by the Utopian rhetoric and underlying formalism of the
prose draft just discussed. But it must not be forgotten that there is also
a critical element in the work which places his attitude towards its
subject in a different perspective. In this sense, Wagner has forestalled
those of his critics who see *Rienzi* as a reflection of its creator's inherently
'Fascist' personality,[106] for it is clear even in the prose draft that the
essence of this critique is already a part of the work itself.

---

[100] See Franz Neumann, *Behemoth*, New York, 1963, pp. 465–7; Horkheimer, *Traditionelle und
kritische Theorie*, pp. 107–16.

[101] See p. 19 above.

[102] *Bulwer*, p. 267 (iii. 164).

[103] Ap. ii. 182 (lines 3 ff.).

[104] Ap. ii. 182 (lines 22–4).

[105] See p. 28 above.

[106] See e.g. Adorno, *Gesammelte Schriften*, xiii. 12–13.

III

The Composition of Verse and Music—the Question of Style

1. Biographical survey

WITH the exception of Stravinsky, Wagner would still be right in saying that there has never been such a 'striking transformation'[1] in the works of any artist within so short a time as that between *Rienzi* and *Holländer*. The sudden shift from the noisy public events of the former to the more intimate world of German Romantic opera in the latter is one which Wagner does not explain, except by oblique reference to a series of essays he wrote in Paris depicting, too self-pityingly perhaps, the struggles of a 'German musician in Paris'.[2] The reaction against the sophisticated emptiness of Parisian musical life which emerges in these essays doubtless contributed towards, and probably affirmed, Wagner's change of artistic direction; but a fact which he nowhere mentions is that the 'striking transformation' he speaks of in reference to *Holländer* is present at a stage in the composition of *Rienzi* when his attitude towards Paris was still a positive one. In order to focus upon this 'striking transformation', therefore, we shall begin by outlining some biographical facts connected with the composition of *Rienzi*—a period in which Wagner's personality underwent perhaps its most intensive development.

After making an initial plan of *Rienzi* in Blasewitz (1837) at a low point in his fortunes,[3] Wagner undertook a long journey to Riga (at that time part of Russia) where he had obtained a conductor's post, possibly making further notes for the opera during an eight-day stop in Travemünde on the way.[4] During his routine work in Riga, where he rehearsed and conducted some fifteen operas, including Bellini's *Romeo*, Cherubini's *Wasserträger* and, with great admiration, Méhul's *Joseph*,[5]

---

[1] See p. 5 above.
[2] *Schriften*, i. 3 (3), 113 ff. (90 ff.).
[3] Ibid. xiii. 192.
[4] See Ap. i. 159 (source 2a).
[5] Wagner singles out this work as the high point of his Riga activities several times in his Collected Writings. Cf. *Schriften*, i. 17 (13), vii. 134 (97), xiii. 201.

he completed the verse draft of Rienzi by 24 July/6 August 1838[6] and the composition draft of the first two acts, and the full score of the first act by 9 April 1839. After a period of separation from his first wife, Minna—a not unimportant factor in the conception of *Rienzi*[7]—Wagner was reunited with her in Riga and, after a number of difficulties with ambitious rivals who sought to oust him from his job, he decided, with an uninhibited recklessness also noticeable in his music at this time, to throw everything to the winds and to take Minna with him on a hazardous journey to Paris in the hope of having *Rienzi* performed there with the help of recommendations from Scribe and Meyerbeer. After a series of narrow escapes from the police and near shipwrecks (the journey was undertaken without passports to avoid creditors), the couple arrived in Boulogne (via London) on 20 August 1839, where Wagner completed the full score of the second act by 12 September. Armed with recommendations from Meyerbeer, whom Wagner had visited in Boulogne,[8] they proceeded to Paris to begin the long, and, as it turned out, futile struggle for recognition.

Wagner arrived with his wife in Paris during September 1839. Having completed the first two acts, he now put *Rienzi* to one side and began to compose a number of short songs (including an additional bass aria with chorus for Bellini's *Norma*[9]) in order to catch the interest of prominent singers who would possibly perform them in one of their concerts. However, apart from the economic difficulties he could foresee, it was the simple fact that he was now among the leading musical figures of Europe whose standards were well above those of a provincial *Kapellmeister* from Germany which prompted a period of self-examination and, inevitably, disappointment. Although he later attributed his lack of success to a money-mad Paris bourgeoisie, it must be remembered that all he had to convince others of his 'genius' were two and a half operas and a number of instrumental works, all highly imitative and below the level of even average composers like Boieldieu and Lortzing.

The realization that his musical equipment was not equal to his ambition

---

[6] More correctly 24 July/5 August or 25 July/6 August since the Russian calendar was at that time twelve days behind European time. The double dating appears at the end of the verse draft. See Ap. i. 160 (source 3).

[7] See p. 19 above.

[8] Cf. *Schriften*, xiii, 228–9.

[9] Published in vol. xv of the incompleted Wagner edition edited by Michael Balling (Breitkopf, 1912–23).

came to Wagner, as he openly admits in *Mein Leben*,[10] during a rehearsal of Beethoven's Ninth Symphony in November or December 1839 by the Paris Conservatoire Orchestra, then one of Europe's leading orchestras. The experience of at last hearing a coherent performance of this work, having once rejected it as a lost cause on account of abortive provincial performances he had heard earlier in Leipzig, proved to be a turning point. He immediately turned his attention from opera to the world of instrumental music in an attempt to create something comparable. The result was an orchestral work, based on the first part of Goethe's *Faust*, which was completed on 12 January 1840.[11] According to *Mein Leben*, the work was intended as the first movement of a *Faust* symphony which never came to fruition, despite the fact that Wagner already had the theme of the second movement 'Gretchen' in his head.[12] It is clear from a later letter to Liszt (9 November 1852)[13] that the plan of providing the 'lonely' Faust with a feminine counterpart was then dropped in favour of *Der fliegende Holländer*, thus transforming Gretchen into Senta and Faust into a descendant of the Wandering Jew. Accordingly, a plan was sketched out for *Holländer* and sent to Scribe for approval on 6 May 1840.[14] Part of the music was even composed at this early stage, as is clear from a letter to Meyerbeer (26 July 1840) where Wagner reports that a 'few numbers' are ready for audition.[15]

As a counterpoint to this burst of activity in new creative directions, Wagner started work again on *Rienzi*, completing the composition draft of Acts III–V between 15 February and 19 September 1840, the overture by 23 October, and the finished score by 19 November.[16] The full score of *Holländer* was completed exactly a year later on 19 November 1841[17] and set the seal on his decision to leave Paris for Germany where *Rienzi* had already been accepted for performance by the Dresden Court Theatre. Besides his musical activities, however, he had already started to publish

---

[10] *Schriften*, xiii. 237.

[11] Revised 15 years later and published as 'Eine Faust-Ouvertüre'. The second version is to be found in vol. xviii of the Balling edition.

[12] *Schriften*, xiii. 237–8. Wagner wrote down the 'Gretchen' theme on the back of a sketch for the 'Spinnerlied' in *Holländer* now in the Wahnfried Archives, Bayreuth (AI d2).

[13] *Briefwechsel zwischen Wagner und Liszt*, 2nd edn., 2 vols, Leipzig, 1900, i. 102.

[14] *Sämt. Briefe*, i. 390.

[15] Ibid. i. 401. According to *Mein Leben*, these 'numbers' were Senta's Ballad, the song of the Norwegian sailors and the 'Spuk-Gesang' of the Flying Dutchman's crew. See *Schriften*, xiii. 273.

[16] Wagner gives the date in *Mein Leben*. See *Schriften*, xiii. 254.

[17] Cf. Otto Strobel, *Richard Wagner, Leben und Schaffen—Eine Zeittafel*, Bayreuth, 1952, p. 23.

a series of essays during the latter stages of work on *Rienzi*, some of which, notably 'Eine Pilgerfahrt zu Beethoven',[18] contain a clear premonition of his 'new path' towards the synthesis of music and drama, and the first signs of an ever-increasing bitterness towards France aggravated by his failure in Paris, but containing an immanent critique of commercial interests and their effect on musical performance which is still valid today.

From this short chronology it is clear that Wagner must have been working for a time on the music of *Rienzi* and *Holländer* simultaneously.[19] Also, two significant experiences in Paris—the Conservatoire rehearsal of the Ninth Symphony and a performance of Berlioz's *Romeo and Juliet* (winter 1839-40) which, according to *Mein Leben*, opened a 'new world' of orchestral virtuosity completely new to him[20]—occurred in the five-month break between the completion of the second act of *Rienzi* and the beginning of work on the third. Not unexpectedly, therefore, there are signs of stylistic change in the second half of the work which clearly point to *Holländer* and beyond.

The only commentator to stress this fact is Paul Bekker, who claims that the interval separating Acts II and III of *Rienzi* 'deeply affected its organic form' and 'profoundly changed the composer's attitude towards his subject'.[21] Bekker's critique, which is based on the assumption that the two halves of the work build an 'inner antithesis' (*innere Gegensätz-lichkeit*),[22] delineates, in effect, two genres within the same work: a 'grand opera' and a 'drama' (*dramatisches Geschehen*)[23]—an overemphatic division certainly, but one which contains an element of truth. Many of the differences which Bekker emphasizes between the two halves of the work—e.g. the use of the reminiscence motif 'Weh dem, der ein ver-wandtes Blut . . .' and the increasing emphasis on individual characters

---

[18] First published as part of a series in the 'Gazette musicale' on the day *Rienzi* was completed i.e. 19 November 1840.

[19] The artist Friedrich Pecht, who often visited Wagner in 1840, says that the latter was then working alternately on both operas. Although Pecht had left Paris by July 1841 when, according to *Mein Leben*, the composition of *Holländer* was begun, he claims to have heard both works 'almost complete' during his visit. Pecht is probably mistaken about *Holländer*; but his remarks suggest that Wagner was more involved with the music while also working on *Rienzi* than the account in *Mein Leben* implies. See *Schriften*, xiii. 272-3; Glasenapp, *Das Leben Richard Wagners*, i. 382. See also Ap. i. 164 (source 17).

[20] *Schriften*, xiii. 259.

[21] Bekker, *Wagner. Das Leben im Werke*, p. 118.

[22] Ibid. p. 103.

[23] Ibid. p. 118.

in the second half—are already implicit in the prose draft.[24] As we have seen, the conception of *Rienzi* owes more, technically speaking, to the tradition of Gluck and Spontini than to the grand opera of Auber and Meyerbeer.[25] The prose draft of *Rienzi* is fundamentally a return to the ideal of unity between operatic form and dramatic expression proposed by the experiments of Grétry, Lesueur, Méhul, Catel, and Berton, without whom Spontini would be unthinkable and whose historical significance was perfectly clear to Wagner.[26] If the description 'drama' is understood to mean an accord between form and dramatic content, then, it is applicable to *Rienzi* from the beginning, even including the mass disposition of the work which, unlike the operas of the Auber/Meyerbeer school, is, as we have seen,[27] thematically related to the political character of its subject. The most challenging task facing Wagner, however, was the discovery of a musical style to match his dramatic conception. He was faced with two difficulties: first, his musical immaturity, and second, the fact that the 'heroic' genre of Spontini and the Paris Conservatoire professors was too limited a vehicle for the development in musical language which had taken place in the meantime. The stylistic developments which Bekker rightly mentions—the less schematic use of orchestral recitative accompaniment and the more declamatory handling of vocal lines, for example—are not only present in the second half of the work, but also implicit in the first. Wagner's Paris 'experience' did not amount to a sudden *volte-face*, as Bekker implies, but to a gradual awareness of his limitations and those of the 'heroic' opera, and a more self-critical search, already begun in the first half of *Rienzi*, for a musical language better suited to his unique combination of literary and musical talents. In the light of his later achievements, the sporadic attempts to focus an original language documented by the sketches and drafts of *Rienzi* are a milestone in the history of opera, involving a reorientation of traditional operatic style, a greater emphasis on its gestural power, and the first signs of a flexible synthesis of word and tone to be found in the mature works. With the biographical facts in mind, we shall attempt to define the beginning of this 'striking transformation' of style, not, as Bekker does, with a nebulous account of Wagner's Paris 'experiences', but with the concrete evidence of the

[24] See e.g. Ap. ii. 180 (lines 37).
[25] See p. 20 above.
[26] Cf. *Schriften*, iii. 144 (122).
[27] See pp. 35–6 above.

revisions in the verse draft of *Rienzi*, and the relation of these revisions to the composition of the music.

2. Verse draft: the interaction of words and music

Not the least significant feature of *Rienzi* is the fact that it was one of the first successful operas in the history of the genre to have a libretto written by the composer. The lack of good librettists in Germany—the *Sich-nicht-finden-Können* of poet and composer as Ernst Bücken puts it[28]—was, together with the lack of a consistent and centralized operatic tradition as in France and Italy, the greatest impediment to the development of German opera in the early nineteenth century. Not only did this deficiency lead to the ruin of good music, as in Weber's *Euryanthe*, it also prevented composers from experimenting with operatic form, and hence from creating a unified dramatic style on a par with the great tradition of German instrumental music. Wagner, who, fortunately for German opera, considered his literary gifts as good, if not better than his musical talent, was conscious of this from the first.[29] Despite attractive offers from literary friends, including Heinrich Laube,[30] he was always insistent on remaining his own librettist, and thereby assured an essential condition, namely, the possibility of a supple interaction of verse and music not necessarily bound by traditional norms.

Wagner's first two complete operas, *Feen* and *Liebesverbot*, for which he also wrote the text, show little variation from conventional forms. The verse draft for *Rienzi*, however, shows the first fruits of Wagner's (for the period) unique procedure. It not only contains numerous alterations to the text introduced during the composition of the music, but also, in common with the verse drafts of the mature works,[31] numerous places where musical fragments have been inserted into the margin, generally next to the words which clearly inspired them. The text itself is based, sometimes word for word, on the dialogue already in the prose draft; the chain reaction between prose, verse, and music just noticeable in the

---

[28] *Der heroische Stil in der Oper*, Leipzig, 1924, p. 127.

[29] As shown by the opening paragraph of his first published essay 'Die deutsche Oper', *Zeitung für die elegante Welt*, xxxiv (1834), 441–2. Republished in *Schriften*, xii. 1 (1).

[30] Cf. *Schriften*, xiii. 97.

[31] Cf. Otto Strobel, *Skizzen und Entwürfe zur Ring-Dichtung*, München, 1930, pp. 112, 255–6. Strobel discusses the rhythmic outlines of Siegfried's 'Aus dem Wald fort in die Welt zieh'n' and Siegmund's 'Winterstürme wichen dem Wonnemond' written into the verse drafts of *Jung Siegfried* (the first version of *Siegfried*) and *Walküre*.

earlier draft is therefore developed to a point in the verse draft where it is possible to examine its effect on the genesis of the work more closely.

The appearance of musical outlines in Wagner's verse drafts—a total of eight in the case of *Rienzi*[32]—was interpreted by the German scholar Otto Strobel as follows:

> . . . ebenso enthalten fast alle Dichtungsurschriften schon Notationen musikalischer Themen: alles in allem also höchst anschauliche Beweise für das für Wagners Kunstschaffen charakteristische *gleichzeitige Entstehung von Dichtung und Musik* . . .[33]

Strobel, whose examination of Wagner's working methods was highly coloured by an uncritical acceptance of the latter's official image of himself as a musical 'poet', is certainly going too far in his conclusions. Whether or not one can speak of a 'simultaneous conception of poem and music' on the evidence of the musical fragments in the verse draft needs careful consideration before any conclusions can be drawn. In one case where text and music appear in immediate conjunction in the verse draft of *Rienzi*—'Rienzi, dir sei Preis' from the finale of Act II—the rhythmic character of the melody closely fits the iambic pattern of the words, as the following transcription shows:

EXAMPLE 6

Verse draft
Ap. i. 160 (source 3, p. 8)

[Ri - en - zi, dir sei Preis dein Na-me hoch ge-ehrt]

so lang als Ro-ma steht an's En-de al-ler Welt dein

[sic]

Na - - - - - - me nie ver-geht du ho-her Frie-dens-[held]

ADRIANO. IRENE
(Rienzi zu Füßen fallend)

Rienzi, dir sei Preis
Dein Name hoch geehrt;
Dich schmücke Lorbeerreis
Gesegnet sei dein Heerd [sic].
So lang' als Roma steht
An's Ende aller Welt,
Dein Name nie vergeht,
Du hoher Friedensheld!

[Text repeated by CHORUS]

The syncopation in the second bar, for example, matches the accentuation of the words exactly—even the word '*hoch*geehrt' has suggested the high

---

[32] Cf. *Sämt. Werke*, xxiii. 153–206.

[33] 'Richard Wagner als Arbeitsgenie', *Allgemeine Musikzeitung*, lvi (1929), 545. (Emphasis in the original.)

point of the melody in the fourth bar. But despite this close matching of text and music, it cannot be said for certain that both were conceived simultaneously. Certainly Wagner must have written in the melody before proceeding to sketch the music of the whole movement, since he would hardly have taken the trouble to draw musical staves into the margin of the verse draft if he had had proper manuscript paper to hand. However, a sketch fragment in the Bibliothèque Nationale Paris (MS. 2226)[34] suggests that the melody for 'Rienzi, dir sei Preis' first occurred to Wagner after he had completed the verse draft and had already begun to set it to music. The fragment contains various musical outlines for the trio and finale of Act I, and includes, in a slightly different and possibly instrumental form, the melody of 'Rienzi, dir sei Preis' without text immediately beneath the opening orchestral theme of the trio ensemble 'Noch schlägt in seiner Brust'[35]—a striking juxtaposition of themes, incidentally, clearly foreshadowing Wagner's penchant for fanfare-like motivic relations in his later works:

EXAMPLE 7

Composition sketch (fragment)
Ap. i. 163 (source 11, recto)

It is possible, then, that the C major melody was originally an instrumental invention intended for Act I. Having no immediate use for it, and realizing its suitability for the words of the final chorus in Act II, Wagner could well have jotted it down at the appropriate place in the verse draft for future reference. In any event, the existence of the Paris fragment is a strong indication that the words and music of 'Rienzi, dir sei Preis' were not conceived 'simultaneously', as Strobel might have claimed.

Another musical entry in the verse draft, however, shows the relation between poetic and musical form in a clearer and more complex light. As shown by Example 8 below, the entry occurs next to the words of Adri-

[34] Ap. i. 163 (source 11).
[35] Cf. *Vocal Score*, i. 81 (79); *Sämt. Werke*, iii (1). 158.

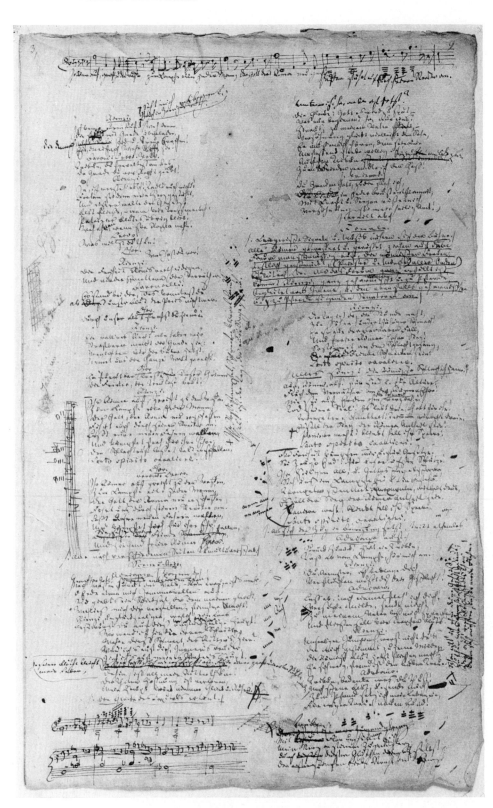

I. The Verse Draft, page 9, Act III

ano's scene and aria in Act III. In common with further transcriptions of the verse draft in this study, Wagner's additions are printed in *italics* and his deletions with a line through the text:

EXAMPLE 8

Verse draft
Ap. i. 160 (source 3, p. 9 – see Plate I)

Scene u. Arie

ADRIANO (kommt)

Gerechter Gott! so ist's entschieden schon,
Nach Waffen schreit das Volk, — kein Traum ist's mehr.
O Erde nimm mich Jammervollen auf!
Wo giebt's ein Schicksal, das dem meinen gleicht,
Wer ließ mich dir verfallen, finstre Macht!
Rienzi, unglückseel'ger, welch' ein Loos
Beschwurst du auf dieß unglückseel'ge Haupt!
    Wo wend' ich hin die irren Schritte,
    Wohin dieß Schwert, des Ritter's Zier?
    Wend' ich's auf dich, Irenen's Bruder,
    Zieh' ich's auf meines Vater's Haupt.

(*Er läßt sich wie erschöpft am Fuße einer zertrümmerten Säule nieder*)

In seiner Blüthe bleicht mein Leben,
Dahin ist all mein Ritterthum!
Der Thaten Hoffnung ist verloren
Mein Haupt krönt nimmer Glück u. Ruhm! ✛

(Die Glocke des Capitol's ertönt)

✛ ~~Verdüstert ist mein Jugendglanz~~
mit $\frac{\text{trübem}}{\text{bleichem}}$ Flor umhüllet, sich
Mein Stern in schönem Jugendglanz
Durch ~~düstre~~ düstre Gluthen dringet selbst
Der ~~ersten~~ schönsten Liebe Strahl ins Herz.

Wo war ich, ha, wo bin ich jetzt!
Die Glocke! Gott es wird zu spät, —
Was nun beginnen? Ha, nur eins!
Hinaus, zu meinem Vater fliehn, —
Versöhnung glückt vielleicht dem Sohn,
Er muß mich hören, denn sein Knie
Umfassend sterbe willig ich!
Auch der Tribun ————— *wird milde sein,*
Zum Frieden wandle ich den Haß!
    (knieend)
Du Gnaden Gott, zu dir fleh' ich,
Die Liebe in jeder Brust entflammt;
Mit Kraft u. Seegen [*sic*] rüste mich,
Versöhnung sei mein heilig Amt!
    (Er eilt ab)

The two parts of the musical fragment, both of which are connected with the central 'Andante' movement of the scene, are written on one and two staves respectively at the bottom of the first column on page 9 of the verse draft. From the first part of the fragment, it is clear that Wagner wanted a typical Italianate melody of periodic structure similar, for example, to that found in Romeo's cavatina 'Ascolta: Se Romeo t'uccise un figlio' from Act I of Bellini's *I Montecchi ed I Capuleti*.[36] The form consists of a basic melodic shape of two bars with a continuation of another two bars—a two-phrase structure which is then repeated in varied form with different words:

EXAMPLE 9

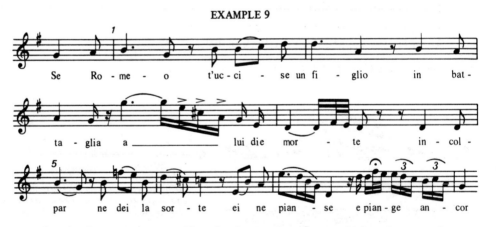

---

[36] The role of Romeo as portrayed by Schröder-Devrient was one which made a strong impression on Wagner. The memory of her performances in the part was doubtless one reason he wrote the part of Adriano for female voice. Cf. *Schriften*, vii. 134 (97), ix. 169 (140).

The example is a type of melodic structure which frequently occurs in Italian opera of the period and becomes increasingly predominant in the second half of *Rienzi*.[37] The first part of the fragment in the verse draft is a clear attempt by Wagner to imitate it. The fragment is a four-bar melody of the type just described. Although it is not repeated in the verse draft, the variation an octave higher in the second bar suggests that a varied repeat of some sort was intended, as we can see from the final form of the melody in the composition draft:

EXAMPLE 10

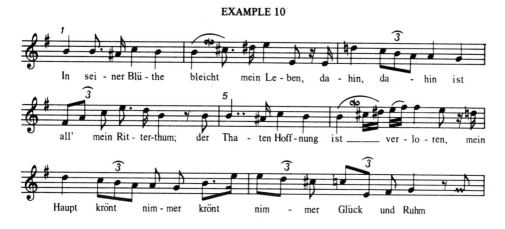

With the exception of the first syllable and the slightly clumsy setting of 'ist verloren . . .' in the sixth bar of this example, the rhythm of the melody matches the metrical accents of the verse. However, it would be unwise to assert that the melody was conceived simultaneously with the text; the number of word repetitions needed to make the text fit the music suggest that the melody was created only in apposition to the verse.

The second part of the musical fragment in the verse draft probably occurred to Wagner as a possibility for a continuation into the middle section of a ternary cavatina form with the intention of returning to his first idea in the last section. Another possibility may have been a development of the first part of the fragment to provide a transition to the next part of the scene. In any event, Wagner realized after writing down his musical ideas that he was going to need more words for the expansive Italianate form he envisaged for the movement. As shown in Example 8 above, he was forced, through lack of space, to write the extra words at

[37] e.g. 'Jungfrauen weinet' (Act III/finale), 'Mein Herr und Vater, O blick herab' (Act V/prayer). See *Vocal Score*, ii. 93–4 (418–19), ii. 210–14 (535–9); *Sämt. Werke*, iii (3). 227, (4). 85–96.

the side of the musical fragment, indicating the connection with a distinctive sign. The fragment is proof, therefore, that the relation between words and music was a two-way process, for it is clear that Wagner wrote down the additional words at the side of the column *after* the musical ideas had occurred to him.

When writing the first draft of the text, Wagner probably had an idea of the form the scene was going to take. The indentation of the text with the line 'Wo wend' ich hin . . .' happens to correspond in the final version with a return to the opening music of the scene;[38] but it is more likely that he originally intended this line as the beginning of the 'Andante' movement, later including it as part of the opening section which turned out to be longer than expected. This would explain the necessary additions to the text of the 'Andante' and the insertion of the direction 'Er läßt sich wie erschöpft . . .' which coincides with a formal break in the final version between the first two major sections of the scene. The nature of the direction clearly indicates a transition to a movement of different mood. Also, the direction 'knieend' preceding the last four lines of the scene ('Du Gnadengott . . .') corresponds to a formal transition in the music of the final version.[39]

Indentation is rare in the verse draft of *Rienzi* and it may well be that the correspondence with the final score at 'Wo wend' ich hin . . .' is coincidental.[40] As far as the stage gestures are concerned, they cannot be said to indicate anything more than broad formal divisions. But the verse draft for the scene does show how Wagner's role as his own librettist helped him to experiment with the form of the scene—one of the most powerful in the work.

It is true that the outline of the text determined the structure of the music in only a general sense; but we can see in the draft how Wagner's musical instinct influenced the form of the text as well. Although the insertion of the musical fragment was probably stimulated by the words, the lines added later clearly demonstrate that, in contrast, the extensive musical form implied by the fragment took precedence over the original form of the text. On a more detailed level also, it can be seen how the original

---

[38] Cf. *Vocal Score*, ii. 31 (363); *Sämt. Werke*, iii (3). 64.

[39] Cf. *Vocal Score*, ii. 37–8 (369); *Sämt. Werke*, iii (3). 83.

[40] In Wagner's later works, indentation of the text is frequent. The *Parsifal* text, for example, published in *Schriften*, x. 417 ff. (324 ff.) and separate copies exactly in the form of the original verse draft, contains numerous indentations of single lines and groups of lines which in no way correspond with the finished score.

structure of the text was sometimes adapted to the melodic form. The regular metre of the two lines beginning 'Mit trübem Flor . . .', for example, was transformed into a striking irregular structure when fitted to the second part of the fragment in the composition draft (including the substitution of 'in schönem' by 'im ersten'):

EXAMPLE 11

(a) *Verse draft*
    Mit trübem Flor umhüllet sich
    Mein Stern in schönem Jugendglanz

(b) *Finished score*
    Mit trübem Flor umhüll't
    Mein Stern sich im ersten Jugendglanz

(b) =

As the above examples demonstrate, the verse draft shows how Wagner's artistic intuition was already leading him towards the flexible synthesis of text and musical form which lies at the heart of his mature dramatic style. In this respect, it is interesting to compare Wagner's procedure in *Rienzi* described above with Cosima Wagner's account in her diaries of the conception of the 'Abendmahl' motif in *Parsifal*:

1877, 10 August.

. . . 'Nehmt hin mein Blut!'—Richard sagt mir er habe es aufgeschrieben . . . Nun habe er den Text dazu umzumodeln gehabt; . . . bei dem Meistersinger-Preislied habe er auch die Melodie zuerst gehabt, und er habe den Text darauf umgeformt. Gestern sagt er schon, man müsse sich hüten einer Melodie zu Liebe den Text verlängern zu müssen—heute nun ist die Hauptstelle 'Nehmt hin mein Blut um unserer Liebe willen; nehmet hin mein—[correct is 'meinen']—Leib und gedenkt mein ewiglich' gänzlich da . . .[41]

[41] 'Aussprüche des Meisters aus den Tagebüchern der Meisterin', *Bayreuther Blätter*, lix (1936), 61. If C. Wagner's account is accurate, Wagner changed the words again in the final version: 'und gedenkt mein ewiglich' becomes 'auf daß ihr mein' gedenkt'. The altered version was enclosed in a letter to Judith Gauthier dated 9 November 1877. Wagner wrote out the words and music of the complete melody with the direction 'Des voix d'alto (d'en haut du temple du St. Gral)' at the top. Facsimile in *Die Briefe Richard Wagners an Judith Gautier*, ed. Willi Schuh, Leipzig, p. 152.

From this account it is clear that Wagner allowed his musical instinct to influence the form of the text for the 'Abendmahl' motif, while at the same time expressing some caution about maintaining equilibrium between the two. Wagner's tendency to let musical form take precedence over text form (present in both his early and late creative periods) stands in sharp contrast to the theory and practice of the period after the flight from Dresden (1849). In both his theoretical works, 'Das Kunstwerk der Zukunft' (1850) and 'Oper und Drama' (1851), Wagner proposes a fusion of music and text in which music plays an equal and sometimes subordinate role to the poem.[42] The increasing dominance of musical over text form which can be seen in the works from *Tristan* to *Parsifal*[43] is, in a sense, a return to the position of Wagner's early creative period. However, the comparison of Wagner's practice in *Rienzi* with that of a late work such as *Parsifal* illuminates an essential difference as well as a similarity between the two. In contrast to his mature works, Wagner often let the structure of the *Rienzi* text stand in sharp contradiction to the melodic form:[44] the flexibility of musical and poetic structure was not yet sufficiently developed to create the subtle synthesis of word and tone one finds in the later works. However, the fragments which Wagner inserted into the verse draft of *Rienzi* show that even at this early stage there was a tendency towards interdependence of musical and poetic form. The proximity of music and text in the draft shows not, in Strobel's words, a 'simultaneous conception of poem and music', but rather an interaction of closely related poetic and musical conceptions.

3. Verse and composition drafts: Act I/introduction, trio

On a purely statistical basis, the number of omissions and additions introduced into the verse draft reveal a striking difference between the two halves of the work. Excluding modifications for the Dresden censor,[45] and disregarding additions which are substitutions for deleted passages, there

[42] . . . aber gerade die Musik (besitzt) die Fähigkeit . . ., ohne gänzlich zu schweigen, dem gedankenvollen Elemente der Sprache sich so unmerklich anzuschmiegen, daß sie diese fast allein gewähren läßt, während sie dennoch sie unterstützt.' *Schriften*, iii. 189 (160). See also ibid., iv. 136–47 (108–17).

[43] Cf. Jack Stein, *Richard Wagner and the Synthesis of the Arts*, Detroit, 1960, p. 149 ff.

[44] Ibid., pp. 18, 24. Stein quotes and analyses striking examples from Act I ('Doch höret ihr der Trompete Ruf') and from Act V ('Mein Herr und Vater . . .').

[45] The modifications were sketched into the draft after *Rienzi* was completed. Wagner later made a fair copy of the modified version and sent it to Lüttichau, the Intendant of the Dresden Opera. See Ap. i. 161 (source 7).

is a net total of 42 omitted and 11 additional lines in Acts I-II against 7 omitted and 57 additional lines in Acts III-V. The difference is more striking when we consider that the largest addition to the text in its first half—the herald's announcement of a pantomime to be enacted before Rienzi's guests in the finale of Act II[46]—arose less from an immediate musical need than from a new and ingenious idea which, since it is not to be found in the prose draft, occurred to Wagner either immediately before or during the composition of the libretto itself. Superficially, the idea of combining the obligatory ballet of grand opera with a pantomime is taken from Halévy's *La Juive* where, in the finale of Act III, the Major-domus announces a mimed play 'l'ouverture d'amour de la tour enchantée . . .' for the benefit of the Emperor's guests. In *Rienzi*, however, Wagner shows independence from these conventional flourishes: first, by including his ballet in the second act of his 'grand opera' instead of the third, as was customary; second, by choosing a subject for the pantomime—the rape of Lucretia by Tarquinius—with a clear relation to its dramatic context. Instead of a mere ornament, the pantomime becomes an allegorical mirror for the 'rape' of Rome by the nobles, their overthrow by Rienzi, and, in the context of the action, a highly relevant backdrop against which the nobles attempt to assassinate Rienzi.[47]

Leaving the herald's announcement aside, then, we have a clear antithesis in the verse draft: a tendency to shorten the text in Acts I-II, and a frequent inclination to expand it in Acts III-V. Since Wagner made most of these alterations when composing the music—a fact established by a comparison with the composition sketches and drafts—this contrast between the two halves of the verse draft would imply a similar contrast, or a different emphasis at least, in the musical style of the work. Let us examine the question more closely with reference to those alterations in the text, which, when compared with the sketches and drafts of the music, illuminate Wagner's reasons for making them.

The first change in the text, although not large, occurs at a dramatically sensitive moment, namely, Rienzi's first entrance 'Zur Ruhe . . .' and is therefore crucial in terms of dramatic effect. Wagner's first attempt to set the complete text at this point is contained in a draft fragment now in the Wahnfried Archives Bayreuth.[48] The draft is a perfect example of

[46] Cf. *Sämt. Werke*, xxiii. 175.
[47] Cf. *Vocal Score*, i. 223–46 (205–30); *Sämt. Werke*, iii (5). Appendix 9.
[48] Ap. i. 162 (source 9e).

Wagner's punctilious habits when composing. The opening movement of the opera—one of the few with a direct stylistic affinity to French opéra comique and the music of Meyerbeer—is already written out in its finished form. The only major deviation occurs at Rienzi's entrance, at which point the draft peters out. Yet Wagner took the trouble to write out the entire draft a second time (as part of the composition draft in the Burrell Collection[49]) complete with the same date at its head, and, having carefully deleted two superfluous lines in the verse draft, with a revised version of Rienzi's opening recitative.

The first part of the scene up to and including Rienzi's entrance demonstrates the stylistic diversity of the entire work in a nutshell. The opening, showing the seduction of Irene by the nobles, is a routine imitation of the contemporary opéra comique style based on a theme already to be found in the margin of the verse draft—a figure similar, for example, to the opening phrase of Boieldieu's overture to *La Dame Blanche* (1825):[50]

EXAMPLE 12

La Dame Blanche, overture

Verse draft
Ap. i. 160 (source 3, p. 1)

Hanslick considered the opening of the scene to be the best thing in the opera,[51] and, indeed, it is stylistically the most consistent moment in the work. This is reflected by both the Wahnfried and Burrell drafts which,

[49] Ap. i. 161 (source 8).

[50] The sustained chord with changing dynamics at the beginning of the Boieldieu overture is a well-tried device often used by opera composers to quickly catch the attention of their audience. The sustained trumpet-tone at the beginning of the *Rienzi* overture—the signal for revolution described by the *Vita* and Bulwer—is an application of the same device in a reduced and more pregnant form, once again showing Wagner's use of operatic convention to precise dramatic advantage.

[51] *Die moderne Oper*, p. 280.

except for minor changes, both contain the music up to Rienzi's appearance in its final form. With the entrance of Rienzi, however, Wagner wanted a radical change from the light-hearted atmosphere of the opening: a dignified speech from Rienzi and an emotional gesture from Irene, who, at the sight of her brother, throws herself into his arms. As shown by Example 13b, these abrupt transitions are matched by a rapid sequence of disparate musical styles, which, at the first attempt in the Wahnfried draft, was clearly unsatisfactory. After a modulation to the flattened supertonic of D major, Wagner introduces Rienzi with an unaccompanied

EXAMPLE 13a

Verse draft
Ap. i. 160 (source 3, p. 1)

RIENZI

Zur Ruhe hier!

(zum Volk)

und ihr, habt ihr
Vergessen, was ihr mir geschworen!
(Das Volk nachdem es den CARDINAL befreit, hat sogleich bei Rienzi's Erscheinen vom Streite abgelaßen)

RIENZI

(zu den Nobili)
Ist dieß die Achtung vor der Kirche
Die euch zum Schutze anvertraut?
~~Schont ihr selbst nicht den heil'gen Vater~~
~~Da den Legaten ihr beschimpft!~~
(Die Nobili sind unwillkürlich durch Erstaunen
über Rienzi's Auftreten u. seiner augenscheinlichen
Gewalt über das Volk sprachlos gefesselt. —
Irene ist auf Rienzi zugeeilt u. verbirgt schamvoll
ihr Gesicht an seiner Brust)

RIENZI

(erblickt die Leiter am offenen Fenster u. scheint sogleich
zu verstehen, was vorgefallen ist. Er wirft einen
tödlichen Blick auf die Nobili)

EXAMPLE 13b

Wahnfried composition draft (fragment)
Ap. i. 162 (source 9e, p. 3)

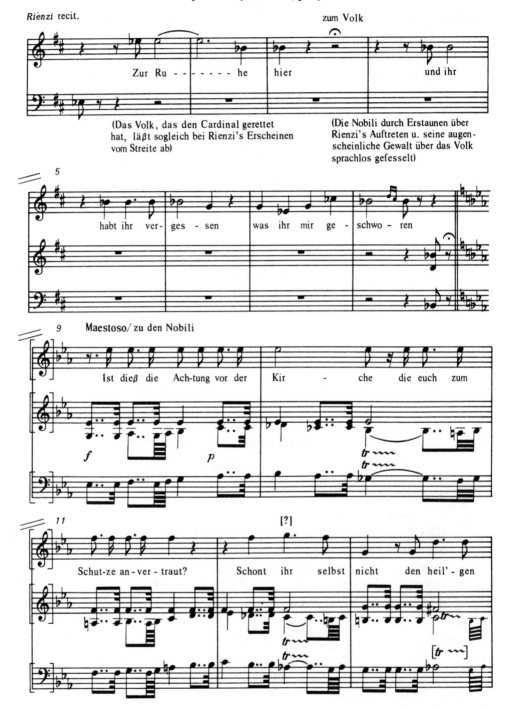

recitative,[52] after which he reverts to a march-like, 'heroic' passage consisting of a raw sequence (possibly intended for brass) moving up in regular steps from E flat to G major (bars 9–16). Rienzi declaims an admonition to the nobles above this chordal sequence with a vocal line of no particular distinction. This rigid passage is then 'softened', so to speak, with a syncopated figure (probably intended for strings) which alternates between G and F sharp, eventually rising through a modulation to E flat major, only to collapse over a diminished seventh chord in bar 18. Thus, within the space of the last five bars of the draft, Wagner attempts to transfer from an aggressive to a highly subjective style (delineating Irene's gestures and Rienzi's 'deadly glance' at the nobles) by changes in rhythm, key, and (presumably) orchestration which produce a less clear-cut definition of texture.

Wagner's second attempt at the passage (Example 14) is a vast improvement on the first. His solution is a simple one: instead of joining

[52] The recitative in its final form, which differs from both the original drafts, consists of a traditional formula disguised by more elongated treatment, but still clearly recognizable as a conventional flourish also to be found, for example, in the first acts of Mozart's *Don Giovanni*, (Leporello before no. 4) and Bellini's *I Montecchi* (recitative before no. 3). Cf. *Vocal Score*, i. 28 (25–6) and Hans Nathan, *Das Rezitativ der Frühopern Richard Wagners*, Dissertation, Berlin, 1934, pp. 66–7.

his changes of mood in a continuous passage, he makes a clear-cut separation between them. Indeed, the changes are so radical (excluding the
opening recitative) that the second version amounts to a recomposition
of the same text, which, presumably after completing the first draft,
Wagner effectively sharpened by deleting two lines in the verse draft.[53]
Rienzi's words 'Ist die dieß Achtung . . .' are now set to a vocal line of
greater agility (bars 8–11) and are punctuated by sharp chords which are,
in effect, a diminution of the original chordal sequence in the first draft.
These chords are followed by a musical figure of short duration built
on an E flat chord with accented appoggiaturas on the ninth, sixth, and
fourth degrees of the scale—a figure which, especially in its final version
shown in conjunction with the Burrell draft in Example 14 (bars 12–13),

EXAMPLE 14

Burrell composition draft
Ap. i. 161 (source 8, p. 9)

[53] See the verse draft extract in Example 13a. Wagner also omitted the word 'hier' from the
line 'Zur Ruhe hier!' in the second draft and also changed the phrase 'die euch zum Schutze' to 'die
eurem Schutze'.

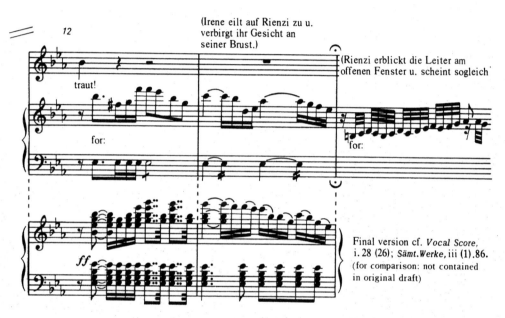

Final version cf. *Vocal Score,*
i. 28 (26); *Sämt.Werke,* iii (1).86.
(for comparison: not contained
in original draft)

is clearly an imitation of Weber's orchestral style. This brief orchestral
gesture, intended as an underlining of Irene's movement towards Rienzi,
is suddenly broken off in favour of an upward moving figure of great
rapidity which turns on itself in a chromatic downward rush, ending on a
trill in the bass (bars 14–15).

The individual elements of the whole passage are not particularly original. Their combination, however, represents something more unusual —a direct association between stage and musical gestures, not in the sense of the generalized content of the orchestral insertions used in traditional *rectitativo accompagnato*, but as specific carriers of defined moods and situations. Wagner's first drafting of the passage in Example 13b is particularly illuminating in this context because it shows an unsuccessful attempt to create logical cohesion between the stylistic elements involved. The final result in Example 14 is a resolution into separate units, held together not so much by any musical logic, but rather by the contingency of the stage gestures.

As separate entities, the stylistic elements involved have a powerful associative character due largely to their greater definition of form in the second version of the passage. Although they cannot be described as 'themes' or 'motifs', Wagner uses them later in the same act to underline moments clearly associated with their first appearance. The characteristic turn at the end of Rienzi's unaccompanied recitative on the word 'geschworen', for example, recurs when Rienzi later reminds the people again of their sworn allegiance to the Church:[54]

EXAMPLE 15

Ge - den - ket eu - res   Schwu - res!

The Weber-like flourish at bars 12–13 of Example 14 also recurs in varied form at the beginning of the trio in Act I where it underscores a similar emotional gesture between Rienzi and Irene:[55]

EXAMPLE 16

(Rienzi umarmt Irene mit heftiger Aufregung.)

[54] Cf. *Vocal Score*, i. 41 (37); *Sämt. Werke*, iii (1). 98.
[55] Cf. *Vocal Score*, i. 70 (68); *Sämt. Werke*, iii (1). 135–6.

Finally, the downward rushing chromatic scale in Example 14 (bars 14–15) which is associated with Rienzi's 'glance' towards the nobles, emerges again twice, almost note for note and, in the final score, with the same orchestration (bassoons and 'cellos). It first reappears when Rienzi refers to the nobles as 'bandits' in the introduction to Act I:[56]

EXAMPLE 17a

and again during the exchange between Rienzi and Adriano in the trio of Act I when Rienzi is reminded of his brother's murder at the hands of the nobles:[57]

EXAMPLE 17b

[56] Cf. *Vocal Score*, i. 31 (28); *Sämt. Werke*, iii (1). 89–90.
[57] Cf. *Vocal Score* i. 78 (75–6); *Sämt. Werke*, iii (1). 150.

In the last two examples, the identity of the music is further strengthened by two preceding chords, which give weight to the musical gesture, and by the interval of a diminished seventh (A flat/B natural) in the vocal line —an interval which occurs in both examples and with similar accentuation on identical notes of the scale.

The exactness with which Wagner reproduces these musical gestures is an indication of his efforts to correlate music and action, even with musical elements which are only transitory in character. As Example 13b above shows, however, this precise correspondence is achieved at the expense of musical flexibility; there is a distinct tendency towards a splintering of musical style, and, in the second draft of the same passage (Example 14), a 'fixing' of musical elements as specific signals rather than stages in a purely musical argument which articulates the action—a process which clearly arose from a need for dramatic accuracy on the one hand, but also from a technical deficiency on the other.

Wagner's inability to articulate a complex dramatic sequence in strictly musical terms, and his way of overcoming this limitation, is well demonstrated by his drafts for the trio between Rienzi, Adriano, and Irene in Act I. As the two large deletions in the verse draft suggest (Examples 18a and 19a below), he had considerable difficulty with this scene. The complex psychological situation already noted in our discussion of the prose draft[58]—Rienzi's attempt to influence Adriano and the latter's emotional relation to Irene—is well presented in dramatic terms, but proved too great a task for the musically immature Wagner. During the process of composition, the scene becomes less subtle instead of more so, and at least one important nuance is lost altogether: Rienzi's 'sharp observation' of Adriano and Irene—a direction already in the prose draft[59] implying his

---

[58] See p. 17 above.
[59] Ap. ii. 169 (line 17).

canny awareness of possibly exploiting the lovers' relationship to further a liaison with the nobility, much as Baroncelli accuses him of doing in Act IV.[60]

Wagner's struggle to find the right form for the scene is clearly shown by the Burrell composition draft. During the course of the trio, the draft shows two major deletions, both of which are connected with the omissions in the verse draft. In view of the fact that the composition draft was intended as a final copy of the work prior to the making of the full score, the alterations it contains at this point are unusual in the sense that they come relatively late in the process of composition. Indeed, it is not improbable that Wagner made outline sketches before this stage which are no longer extant. As it is, the Burrell composition draft shows two consecutive versions of the opening of the trio, the first of which has been heavily deleted. The second deletion occurs during the course of the second, and complete version of the trio which otherwise corresponds to the finished work. The two drafts of the opening have been transcribed side by side in Example 18b and the continuation of the second draft showing the second deletion in Example 19b below.

During the first part of the 'Allegro non tanto' in Example 18b[61] the two drafts are almost identical, again a demonstration of Wagner's painstaking diligence in taking the trouble to copy out the music a second time, even though only small alterations were involved. The opening theme, intended to underscore the didactic discussion between Adriano and Rienzi, is an undistinguished, march-like theme of regular periodic structure (4+4) with a continuation which is an inept attempt to create some harmonic variety, and at the same time a quick return to the tonic (bars 1–8). The theme is repeated, this time with its predictable contour matching the question and answer form of the text. As if wanting to imitate a schoolboy harmony book, Wagner leads his melody for the second time round into the dominant, where it remains for some time hovering around a tonic pedal in the new key (bars 16–24).[62]

---

[60] Ap. ii. 182 (lines 3–8).

[61] The transcription begins at bar 12 of the trio since the opening shows no significant change between the two drafts.

[62] From bar 16 the texts of the drafts are different, although the music remains largely the same. For the first draft Wagner made a cut in the text, but included the cut text again in the second draft. He bracketed the relevant portion of the text in the verse draft. The bracket is represented by a single black line at the side of the text in Example 18a.

EXAMPLE 18a

Verse draft
Ap. i. 160 (source 3, p. 2)

RIENZI

Adriano — du — wie, ein Colonna
Beschützt ein Mädchen vor Entehrung?

ADRIANO

Mein Blut, mein Leben für die Unschuld
Rienzi — wie kennst du mich nicht
Wer hielt mich je für einen Räuber?

RIENZI

Du weilst, Adriano, ziehest nicht
Hinaus zum Kampfe für Colonna?

ADRIANO

Weh mir, daß ich dein Wort verstehe
Erkenne, was du in dir birgst,
Daß ich es ahne, wer du bist, —
Und doch dein Feind nicht werden kann!

RIENZI

Ich kannte stets nur edel dich,
Du bist kein Gräuel dem Gerechten; —
Adriano, darf ich Freund dich nennen?

ADRIANO

Rienzi, ha, was hast du vor?
Gewaltig seh' ich dich, — sag' an,
Wozu brauchst du die Gewalt?

RIENZI

Nun denn, Rom groß u. frei ~~zu machen~~
Aus seinem Schlaf weck' ich es auf,
Und jeden, den im Staub du siehst,
Mach ich zum freien Bürger Rom's.

ADRIANO

Wodurch? Durch Blut — ich ahne es!

RIENZI

Ha, muß es sein, so fließe Blut!

ADRIANO

Unseeliger! Wie, und weißt du auch,
Daß du die Edlen Feinde nennst?
Und ihrer Rache du verfällst?
Willst du vertrauen diesem Volk,
Plebejern, Sclaven von Natur?

RIENZI

Erst wenn ich aus dem Staub sie hob
Zu freien Bürgern sie gemacht

ADRIANO

Entsetzlicher, — durch unser Blut!
Rienzi, wir haben nichts gemein!

(Er will sich zum Abgange, [sic] — sein Blick fällt auf
Irene, — er naht sich ihr zärtlich.)

EXAMPLE 18b

Burrell composition draft
Ap. i. 161 (source 8, pp. 20-2)

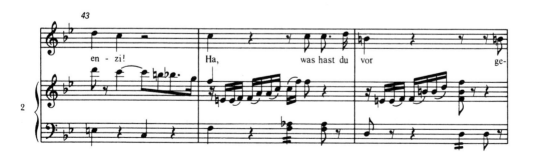

Staub sie hob zu frei - en Bürgern sie ge - macht! Ent - setz - lich - er!

wal - tig seh' ich dich. Sag' an! Wo - zu ge-brauchst du die Ge-

durch un - ser Blut Ri - en - zi wir ha - ben nichts ge-

walt. Nun denn Rom mach' ich groß u. frei; aus sei - nem Schlaf weck' ich es

end of deletion

conclusion of first draft

Second draft continues as in Example 19b below

It would be wrong to reproach Wagner for this mediocre beginning since, especially in view of the text, he almost certainly intended the music to have a mundane quality, a deliberately low-key mood, to prepare for the high emotion to come—a common enough device which also permeates his mature style. But he had to take the consequences of his commonplace inspiration. Because of its uniform character, the opening theme was not a fruitful one for development; at the moment in the first draft, for instance, where Wagner attempts to lead in to Adriano's more impassioned questions 'Wozu brauchst du die Gewalt?' and 'Wodurch? durch Blut . . .' (bars 26–32), the rhythmical triadic opening of the theme soon dissolves into a series of chords, increasingly sporadic, and momentarily giving the impression of *recitativo secco* in the middle of what presumably was intended to be a continuous texture. In addition, Wagner's concern for matching the expression of the text in the second question encouraged him to make a daring modulation (G major chord followed by E flat minor, first draft, bars 31–2) which, in the stark diatonic context of the preceding music, seems out of place.

The continuation of the first draft is a further attempt by Wagner to develop the music in accordance with the expression of the text by a quick alternation of different stylistic elements. Adriano's words 'Unseeliger! Wie' [*sic*], for example, are introduced with a semiquaver figure which is repeated and slightly, though clumsily, developed (bars 36–42). It is further accompanied by a figure in the bass which alternates with the semiquaver passages in the treble, but which, after a single transposed repetition, is not heard again. As in the previous instances, the attempt at musical development ends in a series of chords which have a fleeting *secco*-like character, leading this time to Adriano's words 'Entsetzlicher, durch unser Blut' accompanied by sustained chords (bars 43–52)—yet another swift stylistic change (*recitativo accompagnato*) which propels the music forward. The semiquaver figure used previously as a moment of musical development is now given the role of an intermediary gesture which, although it concludes the first draft, was probably intended as a transition to the next part of the scene.

In the first draft, Wagner's efforts to adapt his music to the detailed changes of mood in the text were clearly unsuccessful, as the strange disjunct effect of the modulation at Rienzi's words 'Nun denn, Rom groß u. frei . . .' prove (bars 28–31). In the second draft he resorts to less startling methods. At the point where the two drafts begin to differ, he introduces a sequence which eventually leads to a conventional cadence in F major (second draft, bars 29–30). He then begins to develop the main theme to the words 'Ich kannte stets nur edel dich', but on a simple basis: the rhythmic shape of the theme remains rigid, and, similar to the developmental texture of his mature style, the theme itself remains fundamentally unaltered while simultaneously passing through a number of modulations, which, in this case, return tamely to the dominant key (second draft, bars 32–44). But as in the first draft, this brief attempt at development gives way to a less continuous style, with the difference that Wagner does not try to integrate the semiquaver figure into the musical continuity, but leaves it as an interpolation between the declamatory phrases of the voice part (e.g. Adriano's words 'Ha! Was hast du vor . . .' bars 44–5).[63] The musical texture again disintegrates into a mixture of recitative-like moments and brief arioso passages (e.g. bars 50–5) which culminate, at greater length than in the first draft, in an isolated version of the semiquaver figure, this time associated with a specific stage-gesture (bars 62–3). Once more, then, Wagner finds a solution in the second draft not so much by developing a musical idea or ideas, but by introducing new stylistic elements which, as we can see in comparison with the first draft, tend to become dismembered as isolated gestures with only a loose connection to the musical context.

The continuation of the second draft in Example 19b contains another instance of this. In order to counteract the didactic discussion between Rienzi and Adriano, Wagner wanted to delineate the emotional tension between Adriano and Irene, with Rienzi as observer, by introducing an 'Andante' movement in D flat major. Probably taking the canonic quartet in *Fidelio* as his model, he wanted to represent the different emotional viewpoints of his protagonists with the same musical idea, the treatment of which, though not so much a canon in this instance, may nevertheless be described as three-part canonic imitation. The subtle dialectic of Beethoven's quartet, however, was beyond Wagner's reach. Although the diatonic melody he intended as the basis of the movement is potentially a good one for canonic treatment, his technique fails him when called upon to develop it. After an introduction leading down from a high F (presumably intended for strings), Adriano sings the melody alone, followed by Irene, who, after the opening phrase, sings a varied

---

[63] The semiquaver figure at this point is considered as a derivation of the figure in the first draft at bar 36.

EXAMPLE 19a

Verse draft
Ap. i. 160 (source 3, pp. 2-3)

ADRIANO

Und kann ich geh'n? Kann ich
Bezwingen dieses Herz? —
Deiner Augen milde Strahlen
Senke segnend in dieß Herz,
Löse meines Geistes Qualen
Richte milde meinen Schmerz

IRENE

Seines Auges dunkle Strahlen
Glühen mächtig durch dieß Herz;
Könnt' ich löschen seine Qualen
Trüg' ich freudig jeden Schmerz.

RIENZI (sie beobachtend)

Seiner Augen warme Strahlen
Drangen mächtig in ihr Herz;
Seines Zweifel's wilde Qualen
Füllen ihre Brust mit Schmerz.

EXAMPLE 19b

Burrell composition draft
Ap. i. 161 (source 8, pp. 22-3)

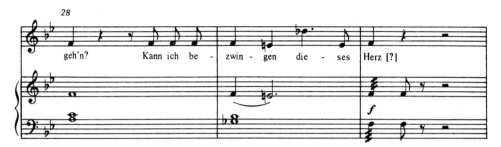

extension (bars 8–20). Rienzi enters last with a form of the melody altered according to the new harmonic context (bar 17). Having introduced all three voices, however, Wagner had trouble in maintaining the interest of the vocal lines. The voice-leading eventually becomes contrapuntally stagnant and leads to an exceptionally gauche modulation to the dominant key (bars 23–4). At this point the movement breaks off in the draft; it is deleted with heavy criss-cross pen-strokes since Wagner, justifiably, was clearly dissatisfied with it.[64] But instead of trying to improve on the idea, he omitted the 'Andante' movement altogether (carefully deleting the corresponding text in the verse draft) and substituted a continuation of the semiquaver figure which, before the 'Andante' trio was to begin, underlined Adriano's gesture of affection towards Irene (Example 18b, p. 71, bars 62–3). All that remains of the ensemble, then, is a new recitative-like setting of Adriano's introductory words 'und kann ich geh'n? . . .' and a preceding musical gesture for strings which rises to a high F to express Adriano's intense emotion towards Irene and at the same time the conflicting desire to leave Rienzi, and which then descends to a held G flat to indicate, by a sudden relaxation of tension, his decision to remain (Example 18b bars 62–3 and Example 19b bars 25–6).

The remainder of the scene (not transcribed in Example 19b since the draft is identical with the finished score) repeats the same cycle of events which Wagner focused in the first half of the draft: a broad, four-square development of the main theme leading to a free alternation of disparate stylistic elements. After Adriano's decision to remain (the half-way point of the scene), Rienzi intensifies his explanation of his political ideals.

[64] Since the next page of the composition draft begins with a B flat major key signature without any cancellation of the previous key of D flat, it is likely that Wagner extended his draft for the 'Andante' on to another page which he then tore out in order to continue the scene on a fresh sheet. The break between pages 22 and 23 of the composition draft is reproduced exactly at bars 24–5 of Example 19b.

Adriano responds with a passionate criticism of what he sees as Rienzi's potential violence. Once again the music passes from a didactic and prosaic style (a routine development of the main theme in E flat major[65]) to an emotive series of declamations between Rienzi and Adriano which mark the high point of their argument.[66] Seen in the context of Wagner's revisions for the first part of the scene, the development of the second part is an intensification of the same tendency towards musical gesture as the most effective carrier of dramatic movement. It is no coincidence that the most original and powerful moments in the music are those which allow the voice part to declaim freely between orchestral insertions serving more as melodramatic punctuation marks than stages in a real musical argument.[67] Indeed, proof that Wagner's talent is at its most original when not relying on a purely musical solution, but rather on the force of uninhibited gesture, is the concluding ensemble of the scene 'Noch schlägt in seiner Brust . . .'[68] After the excitement of the confrontation between Rienzi and Adriano, Wagner reverted to a conventional 'set piece' in which, because of its dramatic motionlessness, he was compelled to fall back on a purely musical idea. The result is a banal imitation of Spontini's 'heroic' style, which, as if to compensate for its lack of originality, is inflated with harmonic doubling, overloaded orchestration, and strenuous vocal parts. This tendency to exaggerate—difficult to demonstrate in a single quotation—is shown, for example, by a comparison of the main theme of the concluding ensemble with its less emphatic model from the duet between Licinius and Julia in the second act of Spontini's *La Vestale*:

EXAMPLE 20

[65] Cf. *Vocal Score*, i. 76–7 (73–4); *Sämt. Werke*, iii (1). 146–8.

[66] Cf. *Vocal Score*, i. 77–81 (75–8); *Sämt. Werke*, iii (1). 149–57.

[67] E.g. the syncopated figure which continually interrupts Rienzi's words 'Wer war es, der einst meinen armen Bruder . . .' Cf. *Vocal Score*, i. 78–9 (76); *Sämt. Werke*, iii (1). 151–2.

[68] Cf. *Vocal Score*, i. 81–93 (79–85); *Sämt. Werke*, iii (1). 158–74.

Rienzi, Act I

Noch schlägt in die-ser Brust ein frei-es Rö-mer-herz

This blatant, if not altogether tasteless imitation is a disconcerting decline from the excitement of the previous passage, but nevertheless typical of a nonchalant, almost reckless attitude towards the composition of the music which pervades the entire work. Wagner's penchant for the easy way out, his lack of patience in working at his musical ideas is well demonstrated by the drafts for the trio (e.g. the deletion of the canon-like 'Andante' without any attempt to improve its quality) and also by the exaggerated dimensions and dynamics of the final ensemble which takes on an exterior forcefulness out of all proportion to its inner substance.

4. Composition sketch (fragment): Act II/finale

Before proceeding to a consideration of the sketches and drafts for the second half of *Rienzi*, it is appropriate at this juncture to consider another MS. illuminating Wagner's procedure in the first half of the work. The document in question is now in the British Library (Egerton 2746 folio 3).[69] It is a composition sketch (fragment)[70] and is one of the few examples among the extant sketches and drafts of *Rienzi* to show Wagner's initial sketching of the music before proceeding to the more definitive and detailed version in the main composition draft. The document is a single folio sheet with musical sketches written on both sides. Except for seven disparate jottings on the verso, the greater part of the sketch consists of a continuous outline of the final chorus in Act II 'Rienzi, dir sei Preis' (systems 1–9 recto) with two fairly extensive alterations (systems 10–12

[69] Ap. i. 163 (source 12). The sketch remains as a fragment, but there is a number (306) written at the top of the page which indicates that it was part of a larger collection of sketches. The number is not in Wagner's hand, however, and was probably written in by a dealer or buyer in possession of a bundle of Wagner MSS. who quickly and not very expertly numbered them for sale. It is clear from the numbered sheets in the sequence so far located that the numbering does not relate to individual compositions or even to the correct sequence of sheets within any single work. For a complete list of the sketches in the series so far collected, see Egon Voss, 'Wagners fragmentarisches Orchesterwerk in e-moll . . .', *Die Musik-Forschung*, xxiii (1970), 51–2.

[70] The term is defined in Ap. i. 158.

recto, 1–2 verso) the first of which was modified at a later stage. The music is written on two staves without text and with clear indications of treble and bass parts which are occasionally filled out by the addition of a middle voice. It is almost certainly Wagner's first attempt at the composition of the passage and, judging by the dating of the subsequent composition draft for Act II (6 February–9 April 1839),[71] was probably written in Riga during the early part of 1839. It is transcribed in Example 21 below with the alternative versions parallel to the appropriate passages of the initial outline.

The first half of the movement is a symmetrical ternary form built from two melodic fragments which, as we have seen, are already to be found in the verse draft.[72] For the sake of convenience, the fragments have been marked 'x' and 'y' in the transcription of the sketch to clarify the structure of the initial outline as shown by the following diagram:

$$
\text{C major} \qquad A = 16 \left\{ \begin{array}{l} 8 = x\ (4\ \text{bars}) + x'\ (4\ \text{bars}) \\ + \\ 8 = x\ (4\ \text{bars}) + x'\ (4\ \text{bars}) \end{array} \right\} \quad \text{bars}\ \ 1\text{--}16
$$

$$
(\text{A flat major}) \quad B = \left[\begin{array}{l} 24 \left\{ \begin{array}{l} 8 = y \\ + \\ 8 \\ + \\ 8 \end{array} \right] = \text{continuation} \\[2em] 24 \left\{ \begin{array}{ll} 6 \\ + & = y\ \text{development} \\ 12 & + \\ + & \text{extension} \\ 6 \end{array} \right. \end{array} \right\} \quad \text{bars}\ 17\text{--}64
$$

$$
\text{C major} \qquad A = 16 \left\{ \begin{array}{l} 8 = x\ (4\ \text{bars}) + x'\ (4\ \text{bars}) \\ + \\ 8 = x\ (4\ \text{bars}) + x'\ (4\ \text{bars}) \end{array} \right\} \quad \text{bars}\ 65\text{--}80
$$

As the diagram indicates, the middle section B can be divided into two parts. The first is an exposition and continuation of melodic fragment 'y'

---

[71] See Ap. i. 161 (source 8).

[72] See Example 6, p. 43 above.

II. British Library Egerton MS. 2746, f. 3 (recto)

(which itself can be regarded as a continuation of 'x') leading towards the key of the flattened sub-mediant (A flat major). The second part is a sequential development and extension of 'y' leading back towards C major. Section A is then repeated in the same form as at the beginning of the movement. However, Wagner was unsatisfied with the somewhat clumsy sequential development in the second part of B and the mono-tonous four-square structure of its extension at bars 47–58 of the initial outline (2+2/2+2/2+2). He therefore rewrote the entire second half of B on systems 10–11 of the MS. indicating the alteration with two heavy pen-strokes at the beginning of the stave. In the alternative version at bars 40–47, for example, the sequential development of 'y' has been sharpened not so much by alteration of the harmony or harmonic rhythm (although this has sometimes been simplified), but by a reworking of its harmonic direction and the pointing of the rhythm in the bass line.[73] Instead of the sequence A flat–B flat–C–D, and the bass-line rhythm 𝅘𝅥𝅭 𝅘𝅥𝅮𝅘𝅥𝅮𝅘𝅥𝅘𝅥𝅘𝅥, Wagner has written A flat–E flat–F–G, and the rhythm 𝅘𝅥𝅮𝅘𝅥 𝅘𝅥𝅮𝅘𝅥𝅘𝅥𝅘𝅥𝅘𝅥—which is how the passage stands in the detailed composi-tion draft and in the finished score.[74] Also, the regular structure of the continuation in the initial outline at bars 47–63 has been transformed into a more irregular form (3+2+2+8) in the alternative version. Up to this point in the second version (at bar 61), the music corresponds exactly to the composition draft and the finished score. But the sketch also shows that Wagner intended this second version to be longer. From bar 62, the alternative outline continues with another seventeen bars, ten of which are deleted. The extension further indicates Wagner's inclination towards repetition and symmetry of form: it contains a repetition of melodic idea 'y' in its original form and repeated once through the deleted bars 69–78. Thus, the formation of a ternary form within the larger ternary structure ('y': development of 'y': 'y') was intended at this stage, but abandoned in the final work.

The second half of the movement ('più presto') falls clearly into two sections. The first is built from a new melodic fragment which, again for

[73] It is interesting to note that Wagner had similar difficulties in the slow movement 'O laßt der Gnade Himmelslicht' immediately preceding 'Rienzi, dir sei Preis' in the final work. An outline of the movement was sketched in a MS. now in the Public Library New York; see Ap. i. 162 (source 10). It shows that Wagner had to similarly rework and extend the sequence beginning with the words 'Bis in den Tod trifft dich sein Haß'. Cf. Vocal Score, i. 310 (294); Sämt. Werke, iii (2). 287.

[74] Cf. Vocal Score, i. 331–3 (313–14); Sämt. Werke, iii (2). 306–7.

EXAMPLE 21

Composition sketch (fragment)
Ap. i. 163 (source 12 — see Plate II)

the sake of convenience, has been marked 'z' at the repeated bars 80–8 in Example 21. The section begins with twelve bars containing motif 'z' aligned with an arpeggio figure based rhythmically on motif 'x' (bars 80–1, 88–91). At bars 92–5, motif 'z' is then expanded into a four-square phrase partially harmonized in parallel tenths and borrowed, incidentally, from one of Wagner's earliest compositions.[75] The phrase is repeated twice (second repeat varied) to form a twelve-bar unit which is itself repeated, thus creating a strong *Steigerungseffekt*, which, after an additional four bars (116–19), drives into the final section of the movement. Wagner's technique of incessant repetition to create tension and massive effect is nowhere more tangible than at this point. The tempo is now moving

[75] From a 'Szene und Arie' (1832) recently discovered by Gerald Abraham in the Burrell Collection. See 'A lost Wagner aria', *Musical Times*, cx (1969), 927–9. The fact that the phrase seems to grow from motif 'z' in the *Rienzi* sketch is an indication of the clever way Wagner has woven it into its new context. The phrase also appears twice in *Die Feen*: in the finale of Act I (in C major) and in Ada's 'Szene u. Arie' in Act II (last section D major).

almost twice as fast as in the first half of the movement,[76] and Wagner proceeds to reinforce this effect by reintroducing motif 'x', twice played, almost twice as fast and varied at bar 123 by the addition of motif 'z' in contracted form.

In the initial outline, the final thrust of this mounting line of tension is the addition of fifteen bars which consist of nothing more than constant reiterations of the V–I cadence in C major (bars 127–42). The second version of this conclusion, which Wagner wrote on the reverse side of the Egerton MS. (systems 1–2), shows that he was clearly dissatisfied with this primitive effect. The fact that the two versions have only one musical feature in common—the isolated chords at bars 140–2 of the first version and bars 142–4 of the second—shows that Wagner completely recast the music at the second attempt. At first, this may seem to contradict a general characteristic of Wagner's working methods, i.e. that they seldom show any reworking and refinement of initial ideas (in contrast to the stringent self-criticism of Beethoven's sketches, for example), but rather concentrate on a restructuring of material already formed in order to enhance its outer effect (as opposed to its inner form). This tendency is clear in the first reworking at bars 40–78 of Example 21, which, as we have seen, involves more extensive alteration in the sequence of material rather than the fundamental shape of the material itself. By contrast, it might be argued that the later revision at bars 128–50 shows the original outline in a thoroughly revised and sharpened form—a process which occurs frequently in Beethoven's sketches. However, when the passage is viewed in context, it can be seen that the two outlines are not two versions of the same material, but rather two different continuations of the preceding music. In the first version, Wagner continues by repeating a varied and contracted form of motif 'z' (bars 127–34). In the second version, he continues by developing the melodic and particularly the rhythmic characteristics of motif 'x' (bars 128–36). The second version does not therefore show the process of thematic revision which is typical of Beethoven's sketches, but the working-out of a new idea for continuing the preceding music.

This new 'end effect' or *Schlußwirkung*, as it may be aptly described, is both longer and more distinctive in outline than its predecessor. The monotonous regularity of the first version is replaced by a passage more irregular in construction, but nevertheless built upon the principle of

[76] The relevant metronomic indications given by Wagner in the final work are $\,\downharpoonright = 88$ ('Allegro vivace') and $\,\downharpoonright = 160$ ('più Presto').

incessant repetition which pervades the whole movement. Indeed, the two new features of the second version—its greater length and definition—can be said to be characteristic of both Wagner's revisions in the Egerton MS. The sketch shows clearly how Wagner inclined towards even greater extension of form during the composition of the movement. It also reveals a tendency to disguise banal regularities, (e.g. the more irregular revision at bars 47–62), not so much in melodic construction, but rather in the formal repetition which permeates the entire fabric of the music. An analysis of the sketch shows that the march-like uniformity of Wagner's melodic inspiration in *Rienzi* and the exaggerated demands he places on his performers, both of which contribute to the Utopian, extra-musical ambition behind the opera as a whole,[77] are transformed in 'Rienzi, dir sei Preis' into a formal gesture—a total mass-effect which outweighs the trivial nature of the musical material behind it. We have seen how he literally piles up effect, sometimes with material grafted into the movement from another work,[78] and in such a way that the shape of the music itself becomes only a secondary consideration. The two extensive alternative versions, for example, serve as replacements for passages which are not simply without distinction, but positively unmusical in character (e.g. the illogical sequences and hammering chords in the first version at bars 40–7 and 127–34 respectively). In these instances, Wagner seems to have been more concerned with gauging a line of tension in the initial outline, which, pointedly expressed, he turned into music in the second. On the basis of these examples alone, it is true to speak of an estrangement between effect and musical content which is perhaps greater than anything to be found in other operas of the period, including the more agile and varied textures of the final movement in Act III of Auber's *La Muette*, for example, or the concluding 'Stretta' of Act II in Meyerbeer's *Les Huguenots*, both of which are also in C major and make extensive use of repetition to create a feeling of exhilaration. Indeed, Adorno's mischievous comment that Wagner's operas are 'huge cardboard boxes' with music first 'measured through' according to the conductor's beat, and then 'filled out' in retrospect,[79] finds a certain confirmation in an analysis of the Egerton sketch.

[77] See pp. 19, 21 above.
[78] See p. 88 (note 75) above.
[79] *Gesammelte Schriften*, xiii. 30. 'Die Riesenkartons seiner Opern werden durch die Schlagvorstellung aufgeteilt. Die ganze Musik scheint erst durchtaktiert, dann ausgefüllt . . .'

The total effect of 'Rienzi, dir sei Preis' is difficult to judge in real terms since it has never appeared complete in any performing score.[80] Nevertheless, it is possible, even without the tangible evidence of a complete performance, to sense the discrepancy between the overpowering totality of the movement, and the trivial banality of its details. It is significant that Wagner, when asked by the chorus-master of the Dresden Court Theatre, Wilhelm Fischer, for extensive cuts in *Rienzi*, expressed great reluctance to shorten 'Rienzi, dir sei Preis', even though he simultaneously acknowledged the unusual dimensions of the movement[81]— a sign that Wagner himself was conscious of his dependence on outward formal exaggeration as compensation for a lack of effective musical ideas.

5. Verse draft, composition sketches and drafts: Act III/finale

The tendency in the Egerton sketch towards greater extension and exaggeration of outer form increases significantly in the second half of *Rienzi*. Although it is not true to say that Acts III–V create, in Bekker's words, an 'antithesis'[82] to the style of the first half of the opera, they do show less defined formal divisions and, as the increased additions to the second half of the verse draft suggest,[83] a more active interaction of text and music. The juxtaposition of 'normal' musical development and a free declamatory style which Wagner focused in the trio of Act I presents two contrasting vehicles of dramatic expression which often become intertwined in the second half of the work; the rhetorical gestures of Wagner's recitatives spill over, as it were, into the more stable fabric of his 'set pieces'. This incursion of gestural elements into the crevices of the 'operatic' ground-plan in the second half of *Rienzi*—a process involving an extension in time-scale and hence a corresponding increase in the quantity of text— is demonstrated by Wagner's working methods in two examples from the finale of Act III: Adriano's attempt to stop Rienzi from entering into battle with the nobles ('Zurück! Halt ein Tribun . . .')[84] and the passage in B minor after Rienzi's return from battle—a movement which can be

---

[80] Including the most authentic edition in *Sämt. Werke*. Since the MS. full score has been lost, the only complete version of the movement is in the composition draft. The Klink and Singer vocal scores contain slightly shortened versions. In all editions the movement is extensively cut. The cuts in 'Rienzi, dir sei Preis' are discussed on pp. 149–53 below.

[81] *Sämt. Briefe*, i. 559.

[82] *Wagner: Das Leben im Werke*, p. 103.

[83] See pp. 50–1 above.

[84] Cf. *Vocal Score*, ii. 50 ff. (382 ff.); *Sämt. Werke*, iii (3). 134 ff.

described as a 'lament' for the victims of Rienzi's Pyrrhic victory over the nobles (Baroncelli: 'Ach, blutig ist die Strafe erkauft . . .').[85] Wagner's first attempts at the composition of these passages are in the Wahnfried Archives Bayreuth.[86] In order to highlight his musical improvements in relation to the corresponding changes he made in the text, the appropriate extracts from the verse draft are transcribed in Examples 22a and 23a below, and his first attempts at the music, together with subsequent musical drafts of the same passages in Examples 22b and 23b.[87]

If Wagner had written the finale of Act III earlier in his career, he might have chosen to set the confrontation between Rienzi and Adriano (Example 22b) as a *recitativo accompagnato* with wide-ranging vocal lines interspersed with energetic orchestral insertions—much as he had done in the equally dramatic dialogue of the trio in Act I.[88] Instead of this, however, he decided to extend the scope of the passage by combining a broadened declamatory vocal line with a continuous instrumental accompaniment kept in motion by the repetition of definite motivic cells, or, more accurately, in this instance, rhythmic textures. There are three textures marked into Example 22b which occur throughout in various forms: a sustained chord followed by an upward moving scale ('a' bars 1–2), a syncopated rhythmic figure ('b' bar 9), and a similar figure in both treble and bass with the two voices moving chromatically towards one another ('c' bar 15).

If the vocal line were contracted and the textures isolated as insertions between the phrases of the vocal part, we would have, in effect, a conventional *recitativo accompagnato* built from this material. By elongating the vocal line, however, and by repeating varied forms of the accompanying textures simultaneously with the voice part, Wagner allows the orchestra to come into its own, not simply as a commentator, but as generator of the extra rhetorical energy he wanted to give the singers. Instead of allowing free reign to the orchestra, as he could have done in the flexible style of a normal recitative, he is compelled to introduce some

---

[85] Cf. *Vocal Score*, ii. 90 ff. (415 ff.); *Sämt. Werke*, iii (3). 217 ff.

[86] Ap. i. 162 (source 9c, pp. 1–3, 7).

[87] In the case of 'Ach, blutig ist die Strafe . . .' a second fragmentary sketch written on one stave, identical in essentials with the finished score, appears on side 8 of the relevant Wahnfried MS. Because of the compression on to one stave, it has been rejected, for the purposes of comparison in Example 23b, in favour of the appropriate portion of the main composition draft which is clearer and more detailed.

[88] See p. 78 above.

form of musical argument in order to maintain continuity. At the same time, this continuity was to serve as the vehicle for the heightened pathos and rhetorical gesture he wanted at this point. It was this merger of continuous musical texture and free-ranging gestural emphasis which posed technical difficulties for Wagner in focusing a stylistic balance between the two.

It is clear from the beginning of the first draft that the outer turbulence which Wagner wanted to present is based on a mechanical alternation of two-bar phrases, and on motifs or textures repeated in sequence rather

EXAMPLE 22a

Verse draft
Ap. i. 160 (source 3, p. 9 – see Plate I)

(Als sich der Zug in Bewegung setzt, tritt athemlos
    ADRIANO auf)

Zurück! Zurück! Halt' ein Tribun,
Laß ab vom Kampfe, hör' mich an!

RIENZI

Du Aermster, ich beklage dich,
Verfluchen mußt du dein Geschlecht!

ADRIANO

Laß ab, noch einmal fleh' ich dich!
Versuche Milde, sende mich!
Schon eilt' ich ohne dein Geheiß,
Zu thun, was hohe Pflicht gebeut;
Doch ach! verschlossen jedes Thor,
Drum sieh mich hier, u. hör mein Flehn!
Zu meinem Vater laß mich sprechen
Und fließen soll kein Tropfen Blut's!

RIENZI

Unseel'ger Jüngling, warst nicht du's,
Der mich gestimmt zu jener Milde,
Die Römisch Blut jetzt fließen macht?
Ha schweig, fremd ist den Buben Treue!

EXAMPLE 22b

Wahnfried composition drafts (fragments)
Ap. i. 162 (source 9c, pp. 1-3)

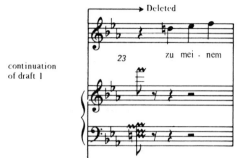

continuation
of draft 1

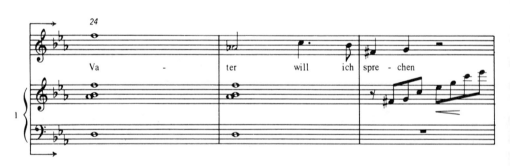

than developed in any real sense.[89] In order to maintain the dynamic forward motion essential to the dramatic effect of the whole passage, therefore, Wagner resorts to a constant change of texture and tonal direction as a means of counteracting the static quality of his phrase construction. In the first draft, the importance of these elements (particularly that of tonal direction) was not clear to him. For this reason he introduced a substantial deletion (bars 22–8) and then went on to the second page of the Wahnfried MS. to write a second draft which begins at the point where the deletion was introduced into the first draft.[90]

Although the first draft of the passage looks as though it could work, on paper at least, when it is played over on the piano, i.e. when its physical effect becomes a reality, the return to B flat minor at the end of the deletion (bar 29) seems lame and weak, largely because it is an over-hasty return to the tonal field of the opening bars. Instead of thwarting the expectations of the listener, Wagner composes the obvious cadence, with the result that the flux of the music almost comes to a standstill. In addition, the voice part lies too low and is too short-breathed to make a convincing impression. In order to correct these deficiencies, Wagner, who realized that he needed a greater time-span to create the right effect, returned to the verse draft to provide himself with more text.

The additional text which Wagner wrote into the margin of the verse draft,[91] presumably before proceeding to the second draft of the music, adds nothing new to the action. It is, in effect, a rhetorical gesture in every way comparable to its musical realization. Instead of proceeding towards a B flat minor cadence as in the first draft, Wagner uses the extra text to create an extended drive over a rising chromatic bass-line towards a cadence in E flat major (second draft, bars 23–33).[92] He does this by repeating a short quaver figure in triplets (in essence a variation of 'a') alternating with an extension of 'a' without triplets (e.g. bar 27)—a

---

[89] The first 20 bars of Example 22b, for instance, consist only of two-bar phrases and simple, or sequential repetitions of rhythmic textures.

[90] The transcription of the first draft in Example 22b has been split up in bar 23 to accommodate the extra length of the second draft.

[91] The extra text is printed in *italics* in Example 22a. The transcription shows, incidentally, that Wagner did not always keep strictly to the verse draft when composing the music. In the first draft, for example, 'Zu meinem Vater laß mich sprechen' becomes 'Zu meinem Vater will ich sprechen' (bars 23–6). Also, the ending of the extra text '. . . mein Fleh'n' becomes simply 'mich' in the second draft (bar 33).

[92] Since Wagner obviously intended the second draft as a continuous alternative to his initial attempt, it has been numbered on continuously from the first draft.

rhythmic contrast which helps to drive the music forward. Above this repetitive texture, the vocal line constantly rises and reaches a climax on a high A flat at the cadence point (bar 32), only to surge on with a double repetition of 'c', and with a bass-line which rises twice to a perfect cadence in E flat (bars 36–7, 40–1). It is clear that the music does not develop in any real sense, but, as in the first draft, relies on repetition of regular, often two or four-bar phrases. But Wagner also uses his insistence on a single tonality (E flat) to carry the music forward: at the third perfect cadence, he frustrates the listener's expectation of an E flat major chord after the dominant B flat by suddenly reverting to E flat minor (bar 41). The deception is further strengthened by the voice part which rises to a climax on a high A flat, thus reinforcing the connection with the earlier cadence, and highlighting the subsequent surprise.[93]

The extra text, then, is the basis of a double cycle of events which, paradoxically, exploits tonal repetition for the purpose of creating the impression of variation and development—a simple technique applied frequently in the later works.[94] The next passage, too, shows a similar tendency. Once again, Wagner leads up to a deceptive cadential climax in D minor with a modification of 'b' or 'c' (second draft, bars 43–4), a diminution of 'a' repeated three times (bars 45–8), and a further six bars which are a version of 'c' (bars 49–53). Although the music clearly moves towards the tonal field of D, the expectation of a perfect cadence in D minor is thwarted by the intrusion of a diminished seventh chord in place of the new tonic (bar 54). But the most interesting feature of the manoeuvre is that it only occurred to Wagner in the second draft. The same moment in the first draft is a static V–I cadence in D minor similar in effect to the tonal stagnation of the deleted bars before the introduction of the new text. It is possible, then, that Wagner's setting of the additional lines in the second draft prompted the expansion of a similar rhetorical principle

---

[93] Cf. bars 32 and 40 in the second draft. In the latter case, the high A flat is altered in the finished score to an extended G with a pause, followed by an F and an E flat to complete the cadence. The similar emphasis of the two cadences remains nevertheless the same, and is even more effective in the final version. See *Vocal Score*, ii. 53 (384); *Sämt. Werke*, iii (3). 142.

[94] The passage before the opening of the 'Great Door' in *Walküre* Act I/ii is a good example. The music is built around a double cycle divided between Sieglinde (to the words '. . . umfing' den Helden mein Arm') and Siegmund (to . . . 'fühl' ich dein schlagendes Herz'). The ends of both cycles are marked by closes which promise to be V–I cadences in G major, but which turn out to be, in the first instance, a surprise substitution of a G minor chord for G major, and, in the second, an interrupted cadence leading to a prolonged diminished seventh chord marking the opening of the door. See the Breitkopf vocal score (1910), pp. 52–6.

to the music he had already composed in the first. In common with a process typical enough of his mature style, the second draft shows a conscious and adroit interjection of interrupted cadences to activate an immobile passage relying less on real musical argument for its articulation[95] than on the repetitive force of essentially static elements and declamatory gestures in the vocal line. Indeed, the only musical events of any consequence are the cadential surprises just described. For the rest, Wagner is content to repeat motifs and textures, practically unchanged, but on different tonal levels according to the degree of tension he wants at a particular moment. Nevertheless, the gain in physical intensity is undeniable and an usually precise premonition of the frenetic pathos characteristic of his later music.

Our second example from the Wahnfried MS. is a composition sketch (fragment) of a later moment in the finale of Act III. The sketch is written fleetingly on two staves and corresponds, as Example 23b shows, to the first version of the text in the verse draft in Example 23a. A comparison of this first attempt with the final version in the Burrell composition draft reveals a complete reorganization and mutation of initial ideas amounting to two different settings of the same dramatic situation—a process found only rarely in extant examples of Wagner's working methods. Before proceeding to an analysis of the two versions, however, it is necessary to outline the fabric of the action which the passage in question is meant to delineate.

Despite Adriano's offer to seek a reconciliation between the nobles and the citizens of Rome led by Rienzi—a plea which forms the basis of the Adriano/Rienzi exchange discussed above—Rienzi ignores all compromises and enters into a fierce battle which takes place off-stage.[96] Rienzi wins the battle and he returns triumphant, but with a sadly depleted army. Towards the end of the Act III finale, the mood on stage is one of joy muted by the growing realization, as the scene proceeds, of the crippling loss of human life involved. The dead bodies of the nobles are dragged on stage. Seeing Steffano Colonna among them, Adriano cries out

---

[95] The logical progression in the music is so tenuous that it enabled Wagner to sew in the extra bars of the second draft without significant alteration to the surrounding music. Rienzi's phrase 'Unseel'ger Jüngling', for example, remains fundamentally the same in both drafts, even though the preceding two bars are transposed up a fourth in the second version. Cf. Example 22b bars 29–30, 41–2, first and second drafts respectively.

[96] Cf. *Vocal Score*, ii. 58 ff. (388 ff.); *Sämt. Werke*, iii (3). 156 ff.

EXAMPLE 23a

Verse draft
Ap. i. 160 (source 3, p. 10)

BARONCELLI

Ach blutig ist die Straf' erkauft, —
Auch uns trifft furchtbarer Verlust.
Wie viele unter diesen Frau'n
Seh'n nie den Mann, den Bruder mehr!

ADRIANO (richtet sich todtenbleich von der Leiche empor, — mit Bedeutung:)

Weh' dem, der ein verwandtes Blut
Zu rächen hat! — Blut'ger Tribun,
Blick' hieher, sieh dieß ist dein Werk!
Fluch über dich u. deine Freiheit!

RIENZI

Er raset, hört ihn nicht!
Ein ew'ger Tod sei jener Loos
Die euer Muth zu Staub zertrat!
Ihr Jungfrauen weint, ihr Weiber klagt
Gerecht u. groß ist euer Schmerz.
Doch Römerinnen rüstet auf
Wen wir verloren, fiel für Rom!

Ewiger Tod sei jener Loos
Die euer Muth zu Staub zertrat!
Das Blut, das Roma heut' entfloß,
Komm' über sie u. ihren Verrath!
Jungfrauen weinet, ihr Weiber klaget!
Wehrt nicht der Thränen heiligem Strom, —
Doch euren Herzen tröstend dann saget:
Die wir verloren, fielen für Rom!

BARONCELLI. CECCO, CHOR

Furchtbar entschied das Schlachtenloos,
Das Feind u. Freund darnieder trat!
Das Blut, das Roma heut' entfloß,
Bring' ew'gen Fluch dem schwarzen Verrath!
Jungfrauen weinet, ihr Weiber klaget, . . .

ADRIANO

Furchtbar erfüllt ist das Loos,
Entschieden ist des Schicksal's Spruch!
Sie ist vollbracht, die grause That!
Das Blut, das dieser Wund' entfloß,
Laut klagt es an des Sohnes Verrath!
Nicht weih' ich dir des Kindes frome Klagen,
Nicht milder Thränen heiligen Strom;
Doch soll die Nachwelt von dir einst sagen:
Furchtbare Rache ward ihm vom Sohn!

IRENE

Furchtbar erfüllt ist das Loos,
Was ich gefürchtet, nun ist's That.
Das Blut, das Roma heut' entfloß,
Keimt wild empor als Schmerzens Saat!
Nicht darf ich weinen, nicht darf ich klagen,
Lindernde Thräne wehr' ich den Strom;
Stolz meinem Herzen darf ich nur sagen:
Was du verlierest, opferst du Rom!

ADRIANO

Fluchwürdiger, der du von dir
Mich stießest, da den Frieden ich
Mit meinem Leben dir verbürgte,
Geschieden sind wir fortan,
Nur Rache haben wir gemein, —
Die deine stilltest du, doch zittre
Vor meiner, du ~~verfielest~~
      bist ihr verfallen!

RIENZI

Unsinniger! Verzeiht ihm Römer!

EXAMPLE 23b

Wahnfried composition sketch (fragment)
Ap. i. 154 (source 9c, p. 7)

Burrell composition draft
Ap. i. 153 (source 8, pp. 116-23)

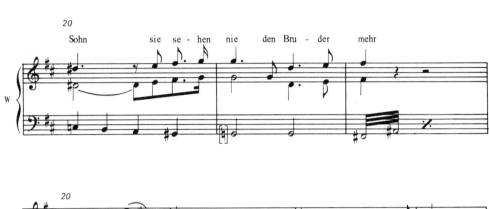

in horror and throws himself on to his father's corpse.[97] It is at this point that the present example begins: a solemn moment in which two main strands in the action are predominant—Baroncelli's bitter lament for his fellow Romans lost in the battle, and Adriano's rage at his father's death which precipitates his revolt against Rienzi.

In order to realize this contrast of mood between mourning and revenge, Wagner had an ingenious idea. As the transcription of the Wahnfried sketch in Example 23b shows, he decided to build the scene over a free application of the ground-bass form expressing the solemnity of the lament (bars 1–16, 42–8, 61–5), and interceding recitative passages expressing Adriano's rage at his father's death. But this clear-cut combination of forms did not suit Wagner's limited technique; we can see in the process of composition how these forms are dissolved into freer and more dramatically effective elements in keeping with the paradox of his calculating, and at the same time unwieldy approach to the composition of the music.

By using a modified form of *basso continuo* as the scaffold of Baroncelli's (and later Rienzi's) song of mourning, Wagner returned to a long-standing operatic tradition: the lament sung over a recurring figure in the bass. Egon Wellesz has identified the origins of this form in the early Italian madrigal and Venetian opera of the seventeenth century.[98] He points out a feature common to most laments of the period which clearly suggests the existence of an acknowledged convention: the ground-bass built around the interval of a descending fourth, i.e. a downward progression, usually chromatic, between two pitches a fourth apart as in the following example from Climen's aria in Cavalli's *Egisto*:[99]

EXAMPLE 24

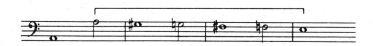

Although in slow march tempo, the recurring bass figure in the Wahnfried sketch is clearly related to this tradition. The first four bars, for example,

[97] Cf. *Vocal Score*, ii. 90 (414); *Sämt. Werke*, iii (3). 216.

[98] 'Cavalli und der Stil der venezianischen Oper von 1640–1660', *Studien zur Musikwissenschaft*, Denkmäler der Tonkunst in Österreich, i (1913), 38–42.

[99] Ibid. 39. The example is one of several quoted by Wellesz. Another, which he does not quote, is the lament in the third act of Purcell's *Dido and Aeneas*.

contain a partially chromatic descent from the tonic to the dominant
degree of the scale, and a clearly implied modulation to the dominant key
itself. The opening phrase is therefore centred around an initial melodic,
as well as over-all, descent from B to F sharp. In contrast, the second half
of the bass figure is a rising, partially chromatic phrase, which, also
characteristic of the older tradition, embraces the interval of an octave
while returning to the tonic key. The two halves of the figure and their
essential interval structure are shown in the following example:

EXAMPLE 25

A striking feature of Wagner's bass is the unexpected delay of the final
cadence: once again, he thwarts the anticipation of both a regular four-
bar phrase and a perfect cadence in B minor by suddenly reverting to an
E sharp after the downward octave leap on F sharp. In addition, he uses
the ground-bass formula to create a feeling of forward motion by leading
the ear into a repetitive pattern which is then disrupted.[100] Thus at bar 16
of the Wahnfried sketch in Example 23b (p. 105 above), the bass-line is not
taken to its conclusion, but is continued in sequence[101] until it reaches an
F sharp pedal-point supporting Adriano's announcement of the motif
'Weh dem, der ein verwandtes Blut . . .'.[102] After a passage of free recitative (mostly accompanied), the bass figure returns at Rienzi's words
'Ihr Jungfrauen weint . . .' (bars 41–2) only to dissolve before the final
cadence is reached, and, significantly, over a chromatically descending
fourth from D to A in the bass (bars 49–51). This second 'interruption'
leads again to a free recitative ('Fluchtwürdiger . . .'), this time shorter

---

[100] Wagner possibly intended the bass figure to sound alone before the addition of a counter-
melody (as he did with its variant in the Burrell draft), but did not bother to write it out in the
Wahnfried sketch which begins in mid air. This would have reinforced the ground-bass pattern and
hence the effect of its eventual disturbance.

[101] The sequence is built on a series of descending phrases in the bass, the last two of which
embrace the interval of a fourth. See bars 18–21 of the Wahnfried sketch in Example 23b.

[102] An exact reference to Rienzi's announcement of the same motif in Act I. Cf. bars 23–7 of the
Wahnfried sketch and p. 33 above.

and more concentrated. At Adriano's words 'Geschieden sind wir . . .' (bars 61–4), the first phrase of the recurring bass figure appears fleetingly, only to give way to another dramatic passage in freer style.

In the Wahnfried sketch, then, Wagner clearly wanted to confront a fixed form with more flexible passages of free recitative, possibly in the hope that the antithesis would heighten the intensity of the scene. The total impression of the sketch, however, is not one of dramatic tension, but rather one of disunity and lack of direction. There are two reasons for this: first, Wagner's inability to create convincing transitions between the static and freer forms (e.g. bars 16–21, 35–41), and, second, his stiff handling of the 'ground-bass', a form which, even in his free application of it, requires a highly flexible technique to give its essentially inflexible nature the greatest variety of expression. In order to correct these deficiencies, Wagner decided to expand the time-scale of the entire passage— again returning to the verse draft to provide himself with more text[103]— and to do away with the idea of a recurring bass figure as relief for Adriano's outbursts of emotion. The result, as shown by the Burrell composition draft in Example 23b above, is a passage of far greater length—199 as opposed to 80 bars—and one in which the traditional flavour of the fragmented *basso ostinato* is reduced to a shadow.

The Burrell draft, which corresponds in most details with the finished score, shows that the bass figure of the initial sketch has been simplified; it is announced alone, as a real ground-bass would be, and has even been reduced, so to speak, to its historical common denominator: the descending perfect fourth—an interval also predominant in its continuation:

EXAMPLE 26

[103] The additional lines are printed in *italics* in the extract from the verse draft in Example 23a. The quantity of extra text was so great that Wagner had to write it on a separate piece of paper which he then glued over the original text. On the microfilm of the Burrell Collection it is not possible to see the complete text of the original since it is partially obscured by the extra sheet Presumably it was as Wagner wrote it down in the Wahnfried sketch (bars 36 ff.). The additional text is an elaboration of the original no longer intended as an isolated solo for Rienzi, but as an ensemble for the entire company on stage.

As the first sixteen bars of the Burrell draft in Example 23b show (pp. 103–5 above), the bass is not repeated in its original form, but as a variant which leads to the dominant key (F sharp major) and an extended pedal-point on F sharp. After this passage, it is not heard again. It is significant, though, that the stylistic essence of the traditional lament, i.e. the chromatic bass, the descending fourth and lyrical intensity of the voice part, continues to colour the style of Wagner's music, even though the ground-bass form itself is relinquished. The F sharp pedal-point, for example, is adorned with a chord progression both melodically and rhythmically similar to the older ground-bass formulae in its chromatic descent by step and alternation of long and short durations.[104] Further, the ensemble 'Ewiger Tod . . .', which is not in the Wahnfried sketch, is built from a descending bass encompassing the interval of a fourth at Cecco's words 'Furchtbar entschied . . .':

EXAMPLE 27

Burr. draft
bars 50·1

Furcht - bar   ent - schied

The phrase is subsequently inverted (complete with vocal ornament[105]) to form the first two bars of Rienzi's lament 'Jungfrauen weinet . . .'[106]— the lyrical centre-point of the scene and one of Wagner's best inspirations in the whole opera. In order to accommodate the Wahnfried sketch and the Burrell draft, it is not transcribed complete in Example 23b above; it is therefore shown here in full—a regular, Italianate melody of symmetrical structure:[107]

---

[104] See bars 16–24 of the Burrell draft in Example 23b. The progression is one of the first in Wagner's *oeuvre* to show an affinity with the harmonic language of J. S. Bach. It is similar, for example, to the descending sequence over an F sharp pedal-point at bars 14–15 of the Prelude and Fugue in B minor for organ (BWV 544). Indeed, Wagner may have heard or studied the work during his lessons with the cantor of the Thomaskirche in Leipzig, Theodor Weinlig—according to *Mein Leben*, the only training of any value he ever received. See *Schriften*, xiii. 75.

[105] The ornament is an interesting example of Wagner's vocal characterization. It appears twice in Act I, for example, both times in association with Rienzi. See Examples 14 (bar 7) and 15 on pp. 56–8 above.

[106] In the Burrell draft, Wagner uses a different form of the second person plural ('weinet' instead of 'weint') to fit the emphasis of the new melody.

[107] Cf. *Vocal Score*, ii. 93–4 (418–19); *Sämt. Werke*, iii (3). 227. The second phrase of the melody closely resembles the opening of Adriano's 'In seiner Blüthe . . .' in the scene and aria earlier in Act III—another Italianate melody of similar structure. (See Example 10, p. 47 above.)

EXAMPLE 28

Jung - frau - en wei - net, ihr, Wei - ber kla - get,

nicht wehrt der Thrä - nen hei - li - gem Strom!

Doch, eu - ren Her - zen trö - stend auch sa - get:

die ihr ver - lo - ren fie - len für Rom

As indicated in the example, the descending and ascending range of the perfect fourth also pervades the rest of the melody. If this seems a pedantic observation—especially since the fourth is frequent in all tonal music—other examples make it plain that Wagner, whether intuitively or by design, intended the interval to dominate the passage. We have already noted the descending fourth written into the prose draft next to Adriano's curse 'Fluchwürdiger . . .'[108]—an interval transformed into a rapidly descending scale covering a diminished fifth in both the Wahnfried sketch (bar 55) and the Burrell composition draft (bar 167). In addition, the last and fleeting occurrence of the 'ground-bass' in the Wahnfried sketch at Adriano's words 'Geschieden sind wir fortan . . .'[109] is transformed in the Burrell draft into a simple declamation of the text over a heavily accented scale which descends through the interval of a fourth (bars 180–1, 184–5). Finally, at Rienzi's words 'Ha, diese Schmerzen . . .' which, in the finished work, come after a stage fanfare at the transition to the final movement of Act III, the vocal line contains a distinct reminiscence of the beginning of the 'ground-bass' in the Wahnfried sketch:[110]

[108] Cf. Example 1, p. 16 above and Ap. ii. 181.

[109] See bars 61–4 of the Wahnfried sketch in Example 23b (p. 111 above). The sketch shows a clever combination of opposites at this point. While Adriano speaks of 'separation' from Rienzi, he does so over a fragment of the ground-bass which, until this moment, has formed a clear antithesis to his recitatives. Significantly, when Adriano mentions the vengeance he now has 'in common' with Rienzi ('nur Rache haben wir gemein . . .'), the ground-bass immediately disintegrates.

[110] Cf. *Vocal Score*, ii. 115 (441–2); *Sämt. Werke*, iii (3). 248. Wagner did not reach this stage in the Wahnfried sketch. Since the Burrell draft has been transcribed in Example 23b to the point in the text where the Wahnfried sketch breaks off, the passage is not to be found in the transcription.

EXAMPLE 29

Ha,   die - se   Schmer - zen   tief   und   groß !

Although Wagner returns to a traditional 'ensemble' in the Burrell draft, the combination of musical events *vis-à-vis* the Wahnfried sketch has a significantly new complexion: Adriano's recitatives no longer serve as diversions from the recurring 'ground-bass' form, but attain an independence and autonomy of their own. Whereas the Wahnfried sketch shows an alternation of 'free' and 'fixed' forms, the Burrell draft contains more subtle transitions between the 'lament' (or 'ensemble') and Adriano's outbursts in freer form, with the result that the boundary between them becomes far less distinct.[111] Apart from the fact that Adriano's recitatives are far more incisive in the Burrell draft, i.e. with a more sharply defined effect due to the inclusion of longer note values in the voice part,[112] it is the addition of the instrumental bars after Adriano's first outburst 'Fluch über dich . . .'[113] and the ensemble based on the extra text in the verse draft which serves to emphasize the intensity of the adjacent recitative passages by offering a longer period of repose—a traditional moment based on 'purely musical' principles. As in the case of 'Rienzi, dir sei Preis', however, the relief offered by this 'purely musical' movement consists less of consequent musical thought[114] than of ideas sewn together to create another powerful *Steigerungseffekt*. The passage in the ensemble where the music begins to 'develop' towards its climax, for example, is based on the sequential repetition of a phrase to be found in the Wahnfried sketch—a moment which clearly looks forward to *Tristan*:[115]

[111] e.g. the F sharp pedal-point leading to Adriano's 'Weh dem, der ein verwandtes Blut . . .' in the Burrell draft is a far more gradual and subtle preparation than the perfunctory two bars in the Wahnfried sketch (Example 23b, p. 106 above).

[112] e.g. Adriano's words 'der du von mir stießest . . .' in Example 23b, p. 110 above, bars 56–59 (Wahnfried sketch) and bars 172–7 (Burrell draft).

[113] Not transcribed in Example 23b. Cf. *Vocal Score*, ii. 92 (416); *Sämt. Werke*, iii (3). 222–3.

[114] As the clumsy sequence at bars 49–56 of the Burrell draft proves (Example 23b, p. 108 above).

[115] Cf. *Vocal Score*, ii. 107–8 (432–3); *Sämt. Werke*, iii (3). 233–4. For the origin of the phrase in the Wahnfried sketch, see Example 23b, p. 105 above, bars 16–17. Although the erotic element is not important in the traditional lament form (including its remnants in *Rienzi*), the form could be regarded as a stylistic ancestor of the intense chromaticism in *Tristan* and its association with death and suffering. There is no external evidence to suggest that Wagner was consciously aware of the tradition. It is possible, however, that Wagner had some knowledge of the form from the 'Crucifixus' of Bach's B minor Mass. Although the 'Credo' was not published until 1845, Wagner's teacher Weinlig, who was an expert on 18-century music, may have possessed a copy of it, or at

EXAMPLE 30

The climax comes a few bars later when the entire on-stage assembly (except Adriano) sings a massive cadence in B major to the words 'für Rom!'—an affirmation of Rienzi's call for the integration of the warring Roman factions in Act I.[116] The final chord of the cadence is supported by full orchestra which carries through the impetus of the climax until it breaks into Adriano's subsequent recitative:[117]

EXAMPLE 31

[116] *Nobles:* 'Für Colonna!—Für Orsini!' *Rienzi:* 'Für Rom!' Cf. *Vocal Score*, i. 60 (57); *Sämt. Werke*, iii (1). 115. Adorno interprets Rienzi's cry for 'integration' as a prophetic antecedent of totalitarianism. See *Gesammelte Schriften*, xiii. 12.

[117] Cf. *Vocal Score*, ii. 111–12 (436–7); *Sämt. Werke*, iii (3). 236–7.

---

least heard a performance of it. (According to Smend, parts of the 'Credo', including the 'Crucifixus', were performed by Spontini in Berlin, and by Schelble in Frankfurt during 1828. There were no MS. sources in Leipzig to which Weinlig could have had access. See F. Smend, *Kritischer Bericht, J. S. Bach: Sämtliche Werke*, Kassel/Basel, 1956, II/i. 15–21, 40–1.)

By means of this transition, the gestural force of the 'più vivo' section is brought into focus with the climax of the preceding ensemble: Adriano's tirade is no longer part of a hierarchy between 'set piece', arioso and recitative, but a musical element on equal footing with other parts of the total fabric. Instead of writing a simple recitative to fill in the gap between the last two movements of the finale, as he had done in Act II,[118] for example, Wagner merges the climax of the ensemble into the ensuing recitative in such a way that both sections form a unified complex which, until the exaggerated banalities of the final movement,[119] has a rhetorical power equal to some of the best moments in his later works.

Once again, as with 'Rienzi, dir sei Preis' in the finale of Act II, the calculated climaxes of the scene are seriously jeopardized by extensive cuts in most performing editions.[120] Small wonder, then, that the originality of the scene has never been pointed out, for it is an originality which relies less on intrinsic musical excellence than on large-scale dramatic effect— an effect not immediately obvious from the printed page, and so well timed that any cut, however small, inevitably weakens the quality of the whole. In this respect, the emergence of the scene in the Wahnfried sketch gives a valuable insight into Wagner's growing awareness of his strengths and weaknesses as a composer. While the original plan involves an interplay of two definite musical styles, Wagner, who probably sensed his inability to articulate this effective idea, resorts to a larger time-span and a less organized style, or combination of styles in the Burrell draft in order to build a longer, but essentially simpler line of dramatic tension better suited to his lyrical talent and melodramatic sense of theatrical effect. Although we could reproach him for not working to improve the musical invention of the original idea, there is also something positive in the fact that his instinctive and somewhat haphazard approach in the Burrell

[118] Cf. *Vocal Score*, i. 323 (306); *Sämt. Werke*, iii (2). 297.

[119] The final movement of Act III is even longer than 'Rienzi, dir sei Preis' in Act II (238 as opposed to 180 bars). As in the trio of Act I (see pp. 78–9 above), Wagner, having shown resourcefulness in the adaption of convention to his dramatic needs, no longer has the stimulus of a changing dramatic situation in the final ensemble. The result is again a paucity of ideas for which he compensates with imitative themes and exaggeration of effect. Cf. *Vocal Score*, ii. 116–56 (442–82); *Sämt. Werke*, iii (3). 249–67.

[120] The only complete versions of the Act III finale are in the Burrell composition draft and *Vocal Score* (Klink and Singer). Even the full score in *Sämt. Werke* has to exclude some passages for lack of authentic sources. All other copies and editions introduce large cuts, especially in the B minor section discussed above. The Cosima Wagner/Kniese version, as if to make up for its inclusion of Rienzi's 'Jungfrauen weinet ...' missing in other editions, introduces even more extensive and eccentric cuts in the rest of the ensemble.

draft (an altogether different solution to the one in the Wahnfried sketch) leads him to unexpected combinations of stylistic elements which, had he been a more 'conscientious' composer, he might never have discovered. The remnants of the 'lament' form and the gestures of *recitativo accompagnato* which recur in freer combination in the Burrell draft are among the first signs of a development which, by an arduous process of trial and error, was to become a central feature of his later music: the separation of traditional musical style from its formal context, and its re-application apart from accepted structural norms according to extra-musical criteria such as the meaning of a text or the efficacy of a dramatic situation.[121]

6. Verse draft, composition sketches and drafts: Acts IV–V, overture

Unfortunately, there are few extant examples of Wagner's working methods in the last two acts of *Rienzi* which illuminate his changing attitude towards composition in the second half of the work. The evidence presented so far, however, suggests that the additional entries in Acts IV–V of the verse draft might well have been the result of changes made during the composition of the music. Evidence that this was probably the case is an autograph libretto in French now in the Wahnfried Archives Bayreuth. According to *Mein Leben*, a rough prose translation was made with the help of a French teacher in Riga just before Wagner's departure for Paris. It is likely, therefore, that the autograph in verse was made shortly after his arrival in Paris, either late in 1839 or in the first months of 1840.[122] This is confirmed by the fact that Acts III–V are translated according to the unaltered form of the text—a sure sign that the additions in the original verse draft were made at a later date, probably during the composition of the second half of *Rienzi*, which began in February 1840. Theoretically, then, it should be possible to compare these additional entries with the finished score in order to ascertain, as far as we can, the probable reasons for their existence.

There are two additions to the verse draft in Acts IV–V substantial enough to give a reliable indication of Wagner's working methods in

[121] For proof of Wagner's later awareness of this process, see his essay 'Über die Anwendung der Musik auf das Drama' (1879), *Schriften*, x. 229 ff. (176 ff.).

[122] See Ap. i. 160 (sources 5 and 6).

the absence of further evidence.[123] The second of these larger additions—
the extended Latin text of the priests' chorus at the end of Act IV[124]—need
not concern us further. It may be regarded simply as a prolongation of an
effective dramatic idea which, musically speaking, shows little innovation
beyond the fact that its later repetition serves as an original and powerful
close to the act. The first addition, however, deserves closer scrutiny.
As shown by the italicized text in Example 32a below, it occurs at Adriano's
entrance in Act IV and begins with the words 'Colonna, ach, darf ich ihn
nennen? . . . .'.

When compared with the finished score, this addition can be seen to
correspond with a passage of 28 bars containing perhaps the clearest
premonition of Wagner's mature style in the opera. The fact that the
passage begins and ends with an almost identical interrupted cadence
(Example 32b) is a strong indication that the intervening bars, which
correspond exactly to the added text, were inserted after the surrounding
music had already been composed:[125]

EXAMPLE 32a

Verse draft
Ap. i. 160 (source 3, p. 11)

ADRIANO

Colonna's Sohn!

Colonna, -- ach, darf ich ihn nennen?
Der aus dem Grab mir fluchend dräut?
Laß dich versöhnen, blut'ger Schatten,
Wend' ab von mir den düstren Blick!
Nicht eher soll mein Arm ermatten,
Bis er gerächet dein Geschick!
Ihr Männer, ja, ich bin Colonna's Sohn!
Hört mich! Unwürdig seiner Macht. . .

---

[123] Other additions in Acts IV–V are either alternatives replacing deleted lines or short fragments
consisting of one line or less. Cf. *Sämt. Werke*, xxiii. 193–206.

[124] Cf. *Vocal Score*, ii. 200–4, 209 (525–30, 534); *Sämt. Werke*, iii (4). 66–74, 81–2.

[125] Cf. *Vocal Score*, ii. 168–70 (494–5); *Sämt. Werke*, iii (4). 23–7. Examples 32b and 33 (below)
are transcribed from the Burrell composition draft. The dotted rhythm which dominates the
succeeding bars is introduced immediately after the double bar, and not two bars later as in all
other scores. For further comments on the discrepancies between the composition draft and subsequent sources, see Chapter IV below.

EXAMPLE 32b

Burrell composition draft
Ap. i. 161 (source 8, p. 134)

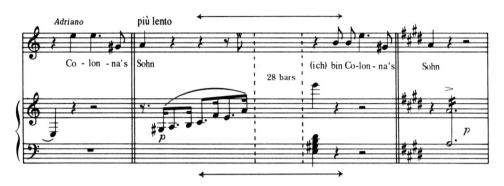

On the evidence of these parallel cadences, it is reasonable to suppose that Wagner originally intended to lead from Adriano's words 'Colonna's Sohn!' to the new key-signature and string tremolo, and then, after an announcement of the 'vengeance' motif in the bass, to the words 'Höret mich!'[126]—a transition which follows the original form of the verse draft. It also seems reasonable to assume that, instead of this, he then decided to insert an interlude for Adriano (perhaps in a sketch no longer extant) and wrote the extra words he needed for it in the margin of the verse draft.

As with Adriano's words 'Schon eilt' ich ohne dein Geheiß . . .' in the finale of Act III,[127] the expansion of the verse draft adds nothing to the action. The episode can be described as a lyrical meditation by Adriano on the fate of his father, his obligation to avenge this fate, and a certain resignation towards the possible consequences of his actions. Thus the additional text does not serve to bring the action forward, but rather to deepen the characterization of Adriano. In view of Wagner's statement that he intended the libretto of *Rienzi* to be little more than an 'efficient play'[128] for the operatic stage, this addition to the initial draft of the text suggests a different approach at odds with the closely packed, and often perfunctory nature of the original conception. Indeed, when we turn to the music associated with the additional text, we find a relaxed and subtle texture very different from the hectic exaggeration predominant in the

---

[126] 'Hört mich!' in the verse draft. Wagner uses the alternative form of the second person plural in the composition draft to accommodate a second version of the vocal line.

[127] See Example 22a, p. 93 above.

[128] *Schriften*, i. 3 (3) 'ein tüchtiges Theaterstück . . .'

rest of the work. Not only this, Wagner also takes the opportunity to
establish a clear musical association with another part of the work. Immediately before the setting of the extra text in the composition draft,
he introduces a pointed rhythmic figure which he then weaves through
the whole passage:

EXAMPLE 33

Using bar numbers corresponding to the 28 bars containing the extra
text, the same figure occurs at bars 9 (after 'blut' ger Schatten'), 13 ('düstren
Blick') and 24 (before 'Ihr Männer, ja').[129] Judging by its first appearance
in the composition draft, it is clearly associated with Adriano's naming
of his father Colonna. Although the comparison seems far-fetched at
first sight, it is also linked to the duet and trio in Act II[130] where Adriano
opposed his father's plan to assassinate Rienzi, the opening of which
presents a similar figure on bassoons and bass strings:[131]

EXAMPLE 34

[129] Cf. *Vocal Score*, ii. 168–9 (494–5); *Sämt. Werke*, iii (4). 24–6.

[130] Like the opening scene of Act IV to which it is parallel, the scene is marked in both the
Klink and Singer vocal scores as a 'Terzett und Chor'. In the prose, verse and composition drafts,
however, Wagner originally provided both scenes with the heading' 'Duett u. Terzett. Chor'.

[131] Cf. *Vocal Score*, i. 178 (162); *Sämt. Werke*, iii (2). 36–7.

The similarity of this figure to its counterpart in the 28 bars of the duet
and trio in Act IV suggests an intuitive, if not deliberate attempt to create
a musical connection between the two scenes. This is borne out by the
fact that both rhythmic figures are repeated in their respective contexts
to an extent where they clearly become identified with the action.[132]
Further, it is obvious from the analysis of the prose draft that both scenes
were intended as opposite poles in the quasi-symmetrical groundplan
of the work as a whole.[133] Thus the antithesis between Adriano's resis-
tance to Rienzi's murder in Act II, and, after a change of heart in Act
III, his support of a similar plan in Act IV, is greatly enhanced by a
musical cross-reference which subtly defines his bitter, not to say tragic
dilemma. Indeed, it may even be true to say that Wagner added the extra
text in Act IV in order to give himself an opportunity of relating the two
scenes more closely not only with outer symmetry of action, but also in
terms of their inner musical fabric.

Besides the associations evoked by the reference to Act II, the music
accompanying the extra text also shows a number of other features which
foreshadow Wagner's mature style. The falling thirds at the words
'Laß' dich versöhnen . . .', for example, are an unmistakable sign of his
melodic individuality, and a clear premonition of the 'Ring' motif, to
name only one instance (see Example 35 below). Also, the form of the
passage presents a scheme frequently found in the later music. Instead of
a varied repeat typical of the italianate melodic form dominating much
of the work, especially Acts I–III,[134] the phrase in Example 35 is repeated
exactly and with identical orchestration (to the words 'wend' ab von
mir den düstren Blick'). The repetition is followed by a third expansive

[132] See e.g. the development of the figure at Orsini's words 'Verräther, frecher Knabe . . .' in
the duet and trio of Act II. Cf. *Vocal Score*, i. 183ff. (167 ff.); *Sämt. Werke*, iii (2). 48 ff.
[133] See p. 30 above.
[134] See p. 47 (esp. note 37) above. Also Example 28, p. 117 above.

EXAMPLE 35

phrase which forms a sharp contrast to the compact, static quality of the first two:

EXAMPLE 36

The three phrases together constitute a model AAB, or 'Bar' form which, according to Lorenz,[135] permeates both the small and large aspects of the mature works. In this case, the feeling of motionlessness created by the first two phrases (corresponding to the stage direction 'vor sich starrend'), and the subsequent rise and fall of the last climactic section, are similar to the effect which Wagner often creates with the same pattern in his later music.[136] The effect is also dramatically justified. The enclosed, introspective

---

[135] *Das Geheimnis der Form bei Richard Wagner*, Berlin, 1924–33. Lorenz's analysis of small-scale structure is often convincing; but his view of the larger aspects of Wagner's music as a potentiated form of its smaller elements often takes on ludicrous proportions. His assumptions and methods have been rightly criticized by Carl Dahlhaus, 'Formprinzipien in Wagners "Ring des Nibelungen"', *Beiträge zur Geschichte der Oper*, ed. H. Becker, 1969, pp. 95–129; and Rudolph Stephan, 'Gibt es ein Geheimnis der Form bei Richard Wagner?', *Das Drama als musikalisches Kunstwerk*, ed. C. Dahlhaus, 1970, pp. 9–16. (Both volumes appear as 15 and 23 respectively in the series: *Studien zur Musikgeschichte des 19. Jahrhunderts*, Regensburg.)

[136] A good example is the beginning of the 'Todesverkündigungsszene' in *Walküre* (II/iv). The first twelve bars are a regular AAB form (4+4+4). The only difference with the example in *Rienzi* is that the first half of the form (AA) is not an identical repetition, but a rising sequence of identical phrases—a characteristic to be found in most examples of the (small-scale) form in the later works.

stillness of the Bar-form—the feeling of 'nothing has happened', as Adorno maliciously remarks[137]—matches the numb emotion of Adriano's words exactly. Indeed, the 'self-negating' gesture which Adorno claims to see in Wagner's later application of the Bar-form[138] can also be felt in the present instance. Not only does the final phrase of the form fail to develop (it remains in A minor), the passage as a whole turns in on itself, so to speak, by leading back to its opening cadence at the words 'Colonna's Sohn' (Example 32b). But while Adorno puts a negative emphasis on this effect, it is, in this instance at least, a moment of great originality which enriches the action precisely by its static, meditative quality, not to mention the motivic cross-reference to Act II. If the supposition is correct, therefore, that the extra text on which the passage is based originated during the musical composition of the second half of the work, the entry in the verse draft is a clear indication of Wagner's growing sensitivity towards a type of dramatic situation in which he could give full reign to his instinct for expansive melodic forms and the direct emotional intensity which was to become one of the most powerful ingredients of his mature style. It was a real awareness of this which first came to him in his early Paris years and eventually led to the more intense, and altogether simpler realization of *Holländer*.

Of the remaining examples of Wagner's working methods in *Rienzi*, those connected with the composition of the overture (which was written last[139]) are of particular interest as far as his stylistic development is concerned. The first extant sketch fragment of the overture is a fleeting outline of the opening written on a single stave into an empty space at the end of a fair copy of Claudio's cavatina from *Liebesverbot* arranged with French text for piano and voice. The main interest of the fragment is that it appears in close conjunction with another fleeting sketch containing part of the overture to *Holländer*. In fact, as the following example shows, the two fragments appear so close together (with the *Holländer* sketch coming first) that they appear to have been written down in the same moment of inspiration:

---

[137] *Gesammelte Schriften*, xiii. 37.

[138] Ibid. 'Die Entwicklungslosigkeit der Geste und die Unwiederholbarkeit des Ausdrucks [both of which Adorno sees embodied in the Bar-form] will er [Wagner] versöhnen, indem die Geste sich selbst widerruft.'

[139] Cf. the dates in the composition draft, Ap. i. 161 (source 8).

EXAMPLE 37

Composition sketches (fragments)
Ap. i. 163 (source 14)

Unfortunately it is impossible to determine the date of the *Holländer* and *Rienzi* fragments with certainty. We know from *Mein Leben* that Wagner had arranged three pieces from *Liebesverbot* for audition at the Théâtre de la Renaissance by Easter 1840.[140] Since Wagner succeeded in having his second opera accepted by the theatre after appealing to

[140] *Schriften*, xiii. 238–9, 246.

Meyerbeer in a letter dated 18 January 1840,[141] the arrangements must have been made sometime during the first three months of that year. This means that the fragments of the two overtures were written some time between January and 20 September 1840, when Wagner began the outline composition sketch of the *Rienzi* overture.[142] The exact date of the fragments during this period is not important; it is only necessary to make clear that they were written down in a period later than that of the Conservatoire rehearsal of Beethoven's Ninth Symphony in November or December of 1839, the experience of which, according to Wagner, was a 'turning point' in his development.[143] As already stated,[144] the experience prompted him to write an overture on Goethe's *Faust*. But on closer consideration of the two fragments in question, it seems possible that the initial conception of the overtures to *Rienzi* and *Holländer* were also coloured by this reawakened interest in Beethoven.

The very proximity of the fragments suggests that the two overtures were somehow related in Wagner's mind, although this is not immediately clear from the sketch. The first fragment consists of sixteen incomplete bars corresponding roughly to the passage beginning 'a tempo' at bar 97 of the *Holländer* overture.[145] The second is an even rougher outline of the beginning of the *Rienzi* overture. It is written without key signature (although it is clearly intended to be in D major) and contains only the first bar of the main melody[146] followed by a gap and a number of transitional bars corresponding roughly to the passage following bar 34 in the finished work. The most interesting feature of the fragments, however, is not what they contain, but precisely what they do not. The fact that Wagner does not notate the beginning of the *Holländer* overture leading up to the D minor figure shown in the fragment, or the entire melody in the *Rienzi* sketch, suggests that these two moments were already clear in his mind, i.e. that the fragments constitute an attempt to find two different contexts for two ideas which had already been formed. If any connection

---

[141] *Sämt. Briefe*, i. 378–9.

[142] See Ap. i. 161 (source 9b).

[143] *Schriften*, xiii. 236. 'Doch gewann ich bei einer dieser Proben unerwartet einen so bedeutenden Eindruck, daß ich ihm eine wichtige Entscheidung für eine jetzt neu sich begründende Wendung meiner künstlerischen Entwickelung beimessen muß. Dies geschah durch meine Anhörung der neunten Symphonie Beethovens . . .'

[144] See p. 39 above.

[145] The D minor figure also occurs at bar 26 ff. of the *Holländer* overture. However, this is only a fleeting premonition of its later, and more definite form.

[146] Cf. bar 12 of Example 37 (ii).

is to be found between the two fragments, therefore, it is to be found in those ideas for which they were intended as extensions.

Keeping in mind the approximate period when the fragments were presumably sketched, it is not difficult to find out where this connection lies. The keys of the two fragments (D minor, D major) immediately suggest a reference to the first and last movements of the Ninth Symphony.[147] In the final works, this reference is made more specific— so much so, in fact, that the beginnings of both overtures were almost certainly intended as an act of homage to the Beethoven work. The resemblance of the *Holländer* overture to the first movement of the Ninth Symphony needs little elaboration:

EXAMPLE 38

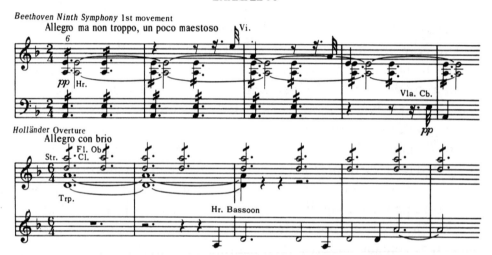

The connection between the D major melody in the *Rienzi* overture and the final movement of the Ninth, however, is not so immediately obvious. It is not until we turn to both the outline sketch and detailed draft of the overture that we find a surprising difference in the opening not to be found in the finished work,[148] and one which unmistakably suggests an indebtedness to Beethoven. Instead of introducing the main melody on violins after a short introduction for solo trumpet, wind instruments and

[147] Wagner only heard the first three movements in Paris. However, he was acquainted with the choral movement as well, partly from a performance he had heard of the whole symphony in Leipzig, and also from an intensive study of the work in his youth. Indeed, Wagner was the first to make a piano arrangement of the work (1830), the MS. of which is now in the Wahnfried Archives, Bayreuth. See also *Sämt. Briefe*, i. 117–21.

[148] In the finished work there is a cut of 17 bars equivalent to bars 4–20 in Example 39. The cut is discussed more fully on pp. 151–2 below.

III. The Burrell Composition Draft, page 1, Overture

EXAMPLE 39

Burrell composition draft, overture from bar 12
Ap. i. 161 (source 8, p. 1 – see Plate III)

Beethoven *Ninth Symphony*, last movement from bar 88

bass strings (as at bar 18 of the final work), it is clear from both the outline sketch and the detailed draft, as well as from the initial fragment,[149] that Wagner originally intended to introduce the entire melody on 'cellos and basses alone, just as Beethoven introduces his 'Freude' melody on octave-unison bass strings in the last movement of the Ninth. Indeed, the comparison of the composition draft with the Beethoven work in Example 39 not only shows that the four bars leading into the *Rienzi* melody follow the course of the final instrumental recitative before the

[149] Except for the A natural (instead of A sharp) at bar 9 of the *Rienzi* fragment in Example 37 above, the transition to the main melody corresponds to the later outline sketch and detailed draft and not to the final work. The transition proves that Wagner intended the unison melody on bass strings from the beginning. The melody is transcribed in Example 39 from the composition draft; the passage in the outline composition sketch is, except for some changes in dynamics, largely the same.

main melody in the Beethoven movement, but also that the two melodies are identical in structure and similar in contour. Each is constructed in regular four-bar phrases, beginning with a repetition of the opening phrase. Although the Italianate contour of Wagner's melody contrasts strongly with the step-by-step compactness of its counterpart in Beethoven, the upward and downward movement of both melodies tends to correspond, with the exception of the third phrase, which, in Wagner, remains stationary on an F sharp, unlike the continual movement of the Beethoven melody at this point (bars 13–14). Also, the continuation of the *Rienzi* overture (as it stands in the finished score) resembles Beethoven in the sense that the main melody is repeated with more elaborate orchestration each time. But most interesting of all is the fact that Wagner clearly wanted to combine 'the sound of a single trumpet'[150]—the symbol of Rienzi's revolution which comes at the very beginning of the overture—with a passage on bass strings modelled on the last movement of Beethoven's Ninth, i.e. the very piece of music which later became an important ideological precursor of Wagner's 'revolutionary' *Gesamtkunstwerk*.[151] Bearing in mind that Rienzi's political ideal of the 'people's community' foreshadows the type of community which Wagner imagined for the reception of his *Gesamtkunstwerk*, the combination of musical ideas at the beginning of the *Rienzi* overture may be regarded as the first glimmer of an ideological association which became the backbone of Wagner's later social and artistic philosophy.

The relation between the beginnings of the *Holländer* and *Rienzi* overtures and Beethoven's Ninth Symphony does not necessarily mean, of course, that Wagner was profoundly influenced by Beethoven. Although the character of each beginning resembles the corresponding moments in the first and last movements of the Ninth, it cannot be said that Wagner penetrates any deeper into Beethoven's musical personality. The thematic integration of the opening fifths later in the first movement of the Ninth, and the variation form of the last movement are nowhere to be found in Wagner. The opening of the *Holländer* overture, for example, develops into an intensified imitation of the overture to Marschner's *Der Vampyr*; and the *Rienzi* overture, after a promising opening of seventy-three bars, rapidly degenerates into a

[150] See p. 32 above.
[151] See e.g. the essay 'Das Kunstwerk der Zukunft' (1849), *Schriften*, iii. 53 ff. (42 ff.), esp. 115 (96).

melodic potpourri of the type to be found in the works of Rossini, Auber, and Boieldieu. Wagner does not attempt to take Beethoven's music as a technical foundation; rather, he attempts to acknowledge the spirit of Beethoven with resemblances of key and melodic shape, while at the same time keeping to the letter of early nineteenth-century opera with procedures modelled on those of composers of lesser stature.

This cleavage between Wagner's clear-sighted admiration for Beethoven's greatness on the one hand, his imperviousness towards the latter's technical achievements on the other, is symptomatic of a disparity between his own ambition and real ability. If the experience of hearing the Ninth Symphony in Paris had any positive effect, it was to make Wagner more aware of this deficiency, and to prompt him (as his teacher Weinlig had done in earlier years)[152] to set about a self-improvement. Not surprisingly, then, there are more frequent attempts to revise initial ideas in the sketches and drafts for the second half of *Rienzi*, and also signs of a more contrapuntal way of thinking which was clearly intended to enhance the limited homophonic style Wagner had adopted for the work.

A good example of the latter is contained in a sketch fragment now in the possession of Wolfgang Sulzer in Marburg. The fragment shows that Wagner originally intended to combine the A major opening of the Rienzi/Irene duet in Act V with the main melody of Rienzi's prayer (V/i)—the same melody which dominates the beginning of the overture:[153]

EXAMPLE 40

Composition sketch (fragment)
Ap. i. 163 (source 13)

---

[152] Cf. *Schriften*, xiii. 75–7.

[153] Jack Stein has pointed out the discrepancy between the melody of the prayer and its text in Act V (*Wagner and the Synthesis of the Arts*, pp. 23–4)—a disparity suggesting that the melody was not composed with regard to the text, but as a purely instrumental invention. It is possible, therefore, that the Burrell fragment with the beginning of the melody (Example 37) originated before Act V was begun (5 September 1840).

As the transcription of the fragment demonstrates, the combination proved to be an awkward one, largely because the harmonic rhythms of the two melodic shapes were at odds with one another. Wisely, Wagner decided not to pursue the idea and omitted it from the later sketches and the final work. Nevertheless, the idea of linking the two melodies was a good one; coming immediately after the prayer at the beginning of the act, it would effectively have symbolized Irene's expression of solidarity with Rienzi during the duet, and her identification with his lonely idealism. Once again, Wagner was not hampered by his dramatic instinct, but by his inability to find an equivalent musical style.

The difficulty, demonstrated by the Sulzer fragment, of mixing a contrapuntal approach with a decidedly homophonic style is well illustrated by another example from the outline sketch and detailed draft of the overture. As shown by Example 41 below, Wagner originally intended to enhance his four-square treatment of the 'Santo Spirito Cavalieri' motif at the centre of the overture[154] with a canonic elaboration of no less than thirty-six bars. In addition, the outline sketch now in the Wahnfried Archives contains an extra half-sheet slipped into the beginning of the folder which is covered with fragmentary sketches showing numerous attempts to combine themes (most of them later abandoned) and a number of preliminary sketches for the canonic

[154] Cf. *Vocal Score*, i. 10–11 (8–9); *Sämt. Werke*, iii (1). 33–9.

passage in question—a slender, but nevertheless clear indication of Wagner's more assiduous approach to composition.

EXAMPLE 41

Burrell composition draft
Ap. i. 161 (source 8, p. 4)

The canon itself is more accurately described as a series of canonic imitations with free accompaniment. After a homophonic sequence of the 'Santo Spirito' motif in its original and inverted forms,[155] Wagner begins a canonic treatment with simple imitation at the octave which is then inverted (bars 4–13). The second phase of the passage begins with a canonic imitation at the sixth which is then repeated a tone lower (bars 13–21). After a free four-bar phrase, this process is reversed with a third stage—an inverted canon at the octave beginning on D and then repeated a tone higher on E (bars 25–32). In order to crown his ingenuity, Wagner introduces, as a fourth stage, a four-part canonic imitation beginning on B, C sharp, D, and G sharp respectively (bars 33–9), which leads into a further simple homophonic treatment of the 'Santo Spirito' motif as it stands in the finished score.

It is not at all clear from either the outline sketch or the Burrell composition draft whether Wagner incorporated the canonic passage into the finished score. Only the final seven bars are heavily deleted in the Burrell draft, whereas the remainder is intact except for the middle stave. It is possible that Wagner included some of the passage in the finished score and decided to delete it only later. In any event, nothing of this strange series of canons is to be found in the finished version as we now have it, and for reasons not difficult to see. Apart from the fact that the sudden complication of musical events would, if included, slow down the impetus of the overture, the passage is forced, harmonically wayward, and only serves to emphasize the banality of the theme it tries to strengthen. Above all, the canonic imitations were clearly intended as the equivalent of a development section in the rough sonata form of the overture's second part,[156] and, as such, reveal Wagner's greatest technical weakness at this point in his development: his inability to vary his material in a real sense, without resorting to sequence or simple repetition. It must be said, however, that even if he included the passage in the original MS. of the full score, his critical judgement was honest enough to reject the passage in the subsequent versions which have survived—a sign, perhaps, that he was more than subconsciously aware of his deficiencies and the need to overcome them if he was to rise above the world of second-rate early nineteenth-century opera in which he was rooted.

[155] Only the final 3 bars of this treatment are shown in Example 41.

[156] The second part may be divided up as follows: bars 74–129—1st melodic group; 130–95—2nd melodic group; 195–262—development; 262–345—protracted recapitulation of melodic groups; 346–408—coda.

7. Summary

What, then, do the sketches and drafts tell us about the stylistic character of *Rienzi* which cannot be gleaned from the work itself? And do they present enough evidence to support Hanslick's opinion that Wagner's 'new path', i.e. his later musico-dramatic style already noticeable, as we have seen, in the second half of *Rienzi*, was simply a way out of his mediocre musical inventiveness?[157]

To take the second question first, it is true that the revisions and extensions analysed in the foregoing discussion are relatively few for a work as long as *Rienzi*, but they nevertheless provide enough material for a fair estimation of Hanslick's argument. Indeed, the idiosyncrasies of Wagner's working methods are so clear that we can arrive at a more differentiated conclusion which both confirms Hanslick's position and defines its limitations. Before proceeding to consider the evidence of our analysis, however, it is necessary to elaborate a little on Hanslick's point of view, and to place it in a broader perspective.

The immediate objection to Hanslick's critique (written, it must be remembered, in 1871) is that Wagner's 'new path' was not new at all, but a practical reflection of an already long-standing discussion among German intellectuals about the validity of the number opera as a contemporary art form. Judging from Wagner's printed essays which began to appear while he was at work on the second half of *Rienzi*, he was aware of these discussions even at this early stage.[158] E. T. A. Hoffman, for example, is only one writer of the period who offers an accurate pre-echo of Wagner's ideas on operatic reform, and who also sensed, like Wagner, that the 'set' forms of traditional opera were out-dated and opposed to the highly subjective needs of the contemporary artist.[159] But with the word 'mittelmäßiges',[160] Hanslick pinpoints a characteristic not only of *Rienzi*, but also of Wagner's early works in general, which has a disturbing pervasiveness not to be found in the early works of any other

---

[157] See p. 10 above.

[158] See e.g. the novella 'Eine Pilgerfahrt zu Beethoven' (1840), *Schriften*, i. 115 ff. (90 ff.).

[159] See e.g. E. T. A. Hoffmann, 'Nachträgliche Bemerkungen über Spontini's Oper "Olympia"', *Gesammelte Werke*, ed. Ellinger, 15 vols., Berlin/Leipzig, 1927, xiv. 106–46, esp. 109, 115, 117 ff., 129 ff. First published in *Zeitung für Theater und Musik zur Unterhaltung gebildeter, unbefangener Leser. Eine Begleiterinn des Freimüthigen*, ed. August Kuhn, Berlin, 1821, nos. 23–38, 9 June–22 September.

[160] See p. 10 above '. . . Wagner hätte in dieser Richtung nur mittelmäßiges geleistet . . .'

front-ranking composer with the exception of Gluck. Indeed, Hanslick's
point that Wagner's 'new style' was a way out of his musical limitations
is strikingly reminiscent of Tovey's remark that Gluck's ability to overcome the weaknesses of his 'technique' was largely due to a librettist who
knew how to exploit Gluck's points to their best advantage.[161] Broadly
speaking, the same is true of *Holländer*: after hearing the rehearsal of the
Ninth Symphony at the Paris Conservatoire in 1839 and realizing, as
Wagner tactfully puts it, that his 'taste' had been 'running wild',[162] he
set out to provide himself with a libretto in which the action was reduced
to its barest essentials, thus enabling him to expand simple musical ideas
in broad lines of emotional tension without the distraction of a complicated plot.[163] One reason why *Rienzi* proved to be of such impossible
length, and therefore subject to extensive cuts, was that his growing need
to let music expand against a simple background[164] went against the
grain of the work's ornate action, which, despite its Utopian time-scale,
actually required a more flexible and concentrated approach.

It would be unjust, of course, to berate Wagner for simply recognizing
his limitations; but for Hanslick, a more fundamental question was at
stake than this. His point about *Rienzi* is that it not only proves Wagner's
inability to write a good 'opera', but also his inability to write good music.
Rienzi is not a bad opera, he says, because Wagner used the 'obsolete'
forms of Spontini, Donizetti, and Meyerbeer, but because he was incapable
of injecting life into these forms with original musical ideas.[165] Hanslick
is therefore implying, as Nietzsche said explicitly in his essay 'Der Fall
Wagner',[166] that Wagner was not an instinctive musician, but a 'poetic-
theatrical'[167] talent who was compelled to find a 'new path' because he
knew that his lack of technique, or more precisely, his inability to create

---

[161] D. F. Tovey, 'Christopher Willibald Gluck', *Essays and Lectures on Music*, ed. H. Foss,
London, 1949, pp. 74–5.

[162] *Schriften*, xiii. 237. 'Die ganze Periode der Verwilderung meines Geschmackes . . . versank
jetzt vor mir wie in einen tiefen Abgrund der Scham und Reue.'

[163] It is significant that, after Wagner had sold his first sketch of *Holländer* to the Académie
Royale, the authors commissioned to rework his idea for the French stage found it necessary to
complicate the plot in order to make a proper 'opera' libretto for another composer. See G. Leprince,
'The Flying Dutchman in the setting by Philippe Dietch', *Musical Quarterly*, L (1964), 311.

[164] The plan for *Holländer* was already finished in May, 1840, i.e. while Wagner was working
on the second half of *Rienzi* (see p. 39 above).

[165] *Die moderne Oper*, p. 276.

[166] *Gesammelte Werke*, xvii. 25.

[167] See p. 10 above '. . . Wagner's eigenartiges, mehr poetisch-theatralisches als musikalisches
Talent . . .'

an autonomous musical style would carry him no further in the direction *Rienzi* was taking him.

In terms of this argument, the most significant feature of Wagner's working methods in *Rienzi* is his preoccupation with the text, especially in the second half of the work. Alone, the fact that the revisions in the musical documents correspond, in the majority of cases, with alterations in the verse draft suggests that he was already on the verge of challenging the notion of music as an autonomous mode of expression which Hanslick represents in his later critique of the work. Two of these revisions—in the trio of Act I[168] and the finale of Act III[169]—tend to confirm Hanslick's point of view. Both examples show that Wagner began with a free application of 'purely musical' forms (a canon and a ground-bass), and, after unsuccessful attempts to realize them, was forced to find different solutions: in the first instance by the substitution of a musical gesture underlining Adriano's glance towards Irene,[170] and in the second by an extension of text and looser constellation of stylistic elements—two moments which clearly point to Wagner's later music. In addition, the canonic passage in the outline sketch and detailed draft of the overture[171] is a further indication of Wagner's inability to handle a purely musical situation of any complexity without the stimulus of extra-musical associations.

Above all, it is the 'set pieces' of *Rienzi*, most notably the last movements of finales and the ensembles, which add most fire to Hanslick's argument. There is no need to look further than the finished score to see that these 'purely musical' moments show Wagner, when deprived of dramatic movement and a workable text, at his weakest and most imitative.[172] But an examination of his working methods is useful here also, for it shows in one instance—the outline sketch for 'Rienzi, dir sei Preis'[173]—how he compensates for his trivial musical inspiration by deliberately extending the repetitive form of the movement to a point where the mass disposition of the music (as opposed to its inner substance) becomes the carrier of its effect on the audience. The sketch shows that the calculated mass effects in *Rienzi*—its *Massenhaftigkeit*, to use Hanslick's

---

[168] Example 19b, pp. 74–7 above.
[169] Example 23b, pp. 103–12 above.
[170] Cf. *Vocal Score*, i. 75 (73); *Sämt. Werke*, iii (1). 144.
[171] Example 41, pp. 136–7 above.
[172] E.g. 'Noch schlägt in seiner Brust'—the final ensemble of the trio in Act I. See pp. 78–9 above.
[173] Example 21, pp. 82–8 above.

term[174]—also served as a substitution for good musical ideas. Indeed, this is doubtless one reason why these large-scale effects are the most unpleasant feature of the work.

It would be a mistake, though, to see *Rienzi*, as Hanslick does, simply as the prelude to an opportunistic 'change of style',[175] serving to conceal Wagner's musical weaknesses. It is true that the sketches and drafts provide some evidence of Wagner escaping from the difficulties of using 'purely musical' forms; but they also show that some of the alternative solutions are definitely superior in quality to the original versions. Although the sketches and drafts tend to confirm Hanslick's argument, therefore, they also demonstrate that his critique was based on a misunderstanding of Wagner's creative personality and a limited, not to say reactionary, conception of what music could and could not express.

Hanslick's remark that Wagner is unable to 'delight' with the 'richness and beauty of musical ideas'[176] reveals, at one stroke, his most fragile assumption: that music is an autonomous mode of expression of necessarily positive or affirmative import. It is probably true to say that *Rienzi* marks Wagner's first step beyond this notion, not only with its aggressive fanfares and 'musical clash of weapons',[177] but also with clear signs shown by the sketches and drafts of an attempt to form a closer relationship between text and music. In this respect, it is interesting to note that with one exception—Rienzi's introductory recitative in Act I[178]—the changes in the verse draft corresponding to the revisions in the musical documents are all closely associated with the role of Adriano, or with situations in which Adriano plays a prominent part. The additions of text and music to Adriano's scene and aria in Act III,[179] the additional lines 'Schon eilt' ich . . .' and 'Colonna, ach . . .' in Acts III and IV,[180] and 'Ach, blutig ist die Strafe' in Act IV where recitatives for Adriano are especially prominent,[181] all suggest a lively interest in this role, and

---

[174] *Die moderne Oper*, p. 279.

[175] See p. 10 above. 'Für das Verständniß von Wagner's späterer auffallender Stylwendung ist dieser Rienzi unschätzbar.'

[176] See p. 10 above. '. . . in den alten Formen durch Reichtum und Schönheit musikalischer Ideen zu entzücken, erlaubten seine Mittel nicht . . .'

[177] *Schriften*, iv. 320 (259). '. . . musikalische(s) Waffengeräusch'.

[178] Example 13a, p. 53 above.

[179] Example 8, pp. 45–6 above.

[180] Examples 22a and 32a, pp. 93, 122 above.

[181] Example 23a, pp. 102–3 above.

one which prompted Wagner to take considerable pains with the composition of the music.

The relevance of this observation to Hanslick's critique is evident when we consider that Wagner's conception of Adriano was greatly influenced by the unusual dramatic talents of Schröder-Devrient—the singer who was the first creator of the role and the artist who did more than any other to bring home to Wagner the fact that the ideal world of music and the real world of spoken language are not mutually exclusive, but can serve to complement each other's limitations. Wagner himself describes in his later writings how Schröder-Devrient's performance in *Fidelio*—according to *Mein Leben*, the earliest and most decisive experience of his career[182]—brought him to a realization of this:

Welche Wirkung ein im übermäßigen Affekt mit Annäherung an den reinen Sprach-Akzent ausgestoßenes entscheidendes Wort hervorzubringen vermag, hatte [Schröder-Devrient] bereits im "Fidelio" zur höchsten Hingerissenheit des Publikums oft bewährt, wenn sie bei der Stelle: "Noch einen Schritt und du bist tot!" das *tot* fast mehr sprach als sang. Diese ungeheure Wirkung, die gerade auch ich empfunden, beruhte auf dem wunderbaren Schreck, der sich meiner bemächtigte, aus der idealen Sphäre, in welche die Musik selbst die grauenhaftesten Situationen erhebt, plötzlich auf den nackten Boden der schrecklichsten Realität, wie durch einen Beilschlag des Henkers, mich geschleudert zu sehen. Hierin gab sich die unmittelbare Erkenntnis der äußersten Spitze des Erhabenen kund . . .[183]

What is remarkable about this quotation is that Wagner is prepared to see music not only in terms of what it can express, but also in terms of what it cannot. Unlike Hanslick, he was not prepared to accept that music is a language based on 'natural' laws independent of social reality, and demanding only a positive response to the 'beauty' of abstract forms.[184] Indeed, the profoundly disturbing character of some of his later music is doubtless a result of the insight that the worlds of music and spoken word do not form an antithesis, but two complementary modes of expression which, in combination, are capable of heightening negative as well as positive feelings—the gulf between the 'most terrible reality' and the

---

[182] *Schriften*, xiii. 50.

[183] Ibid. xiv. 92. A similar account appears in the essay 'Über die Bestimmung der Oper' (1871), ibid. ix. 183–4 (152–3).

[184] See e.g. E. Hanslick, *Vom Musikalisch-Schönen*, 1st edn., Leipzig, 1854, p. 35. 'In dieser negativen, inneren Vernünftigkeit, welche dem Tonsystem durch Naturgesetze inwohnt, wurzelt dessen weitere Fähigkeit zur Aufnahme positiven Schönheitsgehaltes.'

'summit of the sublime' which Wagner himself experienced when listening to Schröder-Devrient.

The above quotation from *Mein Leben* was written more than twenty-five years after the completion of *Rienzi* and represents, of course, an observation coloured by Wagner's later theories. Nevertheless, the revisions in the verse draft of *Rienzi* associated with the role of Adriano suggest that Wagner was already prepared at this early date to draw on an interaction of words and music which could lead to the discovery of new forms and a musical style capable of reaching beyond the 'ideal' sphere of absolute music later emphasized by Hanslick.

Wagner has often been criticized for casting Adriano as a mezzo-soprano.[185] Under normal circumstances, and in view of the masculine qualities the role demands, this criticism is justified. But it must be remembered that Schröder-Devrient, without whom the unusual conception of the role would be unthinkable, was for Wagner not simply a good singing actress, but an artist who represented a revolutionary art form—an affront to the 'small-mindedness'[186] of *petit-bourgeois* German society and, in her 'ecstatic'[187] rendering of Fidelio, a symbol of sexual and political freedom. Indeed, the probable reason why all major additions to the verse draft appear in the second half of *Rienzi* composed during 1840 is that by this time Wagner had begun to despair of a Paris performance of the work, turning his eyes instead towards Germany where Schröder-Devrient was more likely to take on the role. A reunion with Laube at the beginning of 1840 in Paris may have persuaded Wagner to take this course. According to *Mein Leben*, Laube was sceptical about the chances of a Paris success for Wagner, and promised to help find support for him in Germany.[188] It was Laube, himself an ardent admirer of Schröder-Devrient,[189] who played a major part in obtaining her services as the first Adriano.[190]

---

[185] See e.g. Hugo Dinger, 'Zu Richard Wagners Rienzi', *Richard Wagner Jahrbuch*, ed. Ludwig Frankenstein, 5 vols., Berlin, 1908, iii. 119; also Adorno's review of a *Rienzi* performance in Frankfurt in *Die Musik*, xxvi/6 (1934), 448–9. Adorno goes so far as to describe the dramatic conception of Adriano as 'completely and totally incomprehensible'.

[186] *Schriften*, iv. 341 (277). 'Ich habe nie einen großherzigeren Menschen im Kampfe mit kleinlicheren Vorstellungen gesehen ...'

[187] Ibid. xiii. 50.

[188] Ibid. xiii. 244–5.

[189] See Laube's article on Schröder-Devrient in *Zeitung für die elegante Welt*, xxxiii (1833), 17–9, 21–4.

[190] See *Sämt. Briefe*, i. 455.

The identification of Schröder-Devrient with a new operatic style already had its theoretical precedent at the time *Rienzi* was composed in the writings of Theodor Mundt. In an essay published in 1831,[191] Mundt criticizes the anti-dramatic tendencies of the Rossini school and their concentration on static forms. Most interesting of all, he points to the technical means which could preserve the dramatic vitality of opera and develop its potential. Mundt's main emphasis is on the use of recitative and its combination with vocal melody. He points to a dynamic integration of word, tone, and dramatic gesture, and names Schröder-Devrient as the artist best capable of achieving this. Her ability to 'fuse poetic and musical effects into a unity',[192] Mundt writes, is the reason for her excellence in all parts which demand not simply dramatic song and recitative, but a synthesis of the two—a *Gesangspiel* in which she colours music with a 'feeling of speech'[193] and interrupts the notes of the vocal melody with 'genuine dramatic moments of emotion'.[194]

There is no indication in Wagner's writings that he knew Mundt's essay when he composed *Rienzi*. But their similar observations on Schröder-Devrient, and the correspondence of their ideas on the creation of a new dramatic style with a more judicious balance between poetry, music, and gesture suggest that Mundt was an influence on Wagner's aesthetics, perhaps as early as *Rienzi*.[195] Certainly, the sketches and drafts of *Rienzi* show that Wagner took particular trouble over the presentation of Adriano, and with modifications of text and music which point to the new dramatic style outlined by Mundt. The additions to Adriano's scene and aria in Act III,[196] and the additional lines 'Colonna, ach . . .' in Act IV[197] provide the best illustrations of this since they show in the finished score a closely-knit synthesis of recitative, aria, and arioso which comes closest to the *Gesangspiel* Mundt places at the centre

[191] 'Über Oper, Drama und Melodrama in ihrem Verhältniß zu einander und zum Theater', *Blätter für literarische Unterhaltung*, 1831, nos. 152–5.

[192] Ibid., no. 155, p. 678. '. . . sie strebt [danach], die poetischen und musikalischen Effecte in ihrem Spiel zu einer Einheit zu verschmelzen.'

[193] Ibid. '. . . die *redende* Empfindung'. (Emphasis in the original.)

[194] Ibid. '. . . echt dramatische Momente des Affects . . .'

[195] Wagner was possibly acquainted with Mundt's theories through the writings of Laube. In his article on Schröder-Devrient, Laube speaks of her ability to 'save' opera with her acting talent, and, in a striking phrase which clearly echoes Mundt, he says: 'sie [i.e. Schröder-Devrient] hat singen reden gelernt'. See *Zeitung für die elegante Welt*, xxxiii (1833), 23.

[196] Example 8, pp. 45–6 above.

[197] Example 32a, p. 122 above.

of the new operative form—a form which, prophetically, he calls a 'Musikdrama'.[198]

If the sketches and drafts of *Rienzi* reveal anything of significance not immediately apparent from the work itself, therefore, it is that Wagner's 'new path' did not simply originate as a way out of his musical limitations, but rather as an unusual mixture of *laissez-faire*, audacious intuition, and a real effort to provide his artistic ideal, Schröder-Devrient, with a dramatic style worthy of her unique acting and singing abilities.[199] The famous forging-scene in *Siegfried* provides a parallel, perhaps a deliberately autobiographical one. In one of Wagner's technically most sophisticated works, it is Siegfried's naive recklessness, and not Mime's 'expertise' which succeeds in creating the sword used to win Brünnhilde. Like Siegfried, the young Wagner's disregard for the rules of 'good craftsmanship' was perhaps his greatest asset: it enabled him, without inhibition, to forge the beginnings of a new style counter to the subjective limitations of traditional forms, and ostensibly at odds with the society which had produced them. If *Rienzi* is not exactly the shining sword in Wagner's *oeuvre*, a study of his methods reveals at least a glimmer of the process which, in his later works, was to enlarge the expressive boundaries of music to an unprecedented degree.

[198] Mundt, op. cit., no. 155, p. 677. '∴ . . aber Das leuchtet ein, daß die Oper, ungeachtet ihrer lyrisch-phantastischen Behandlungsweise, doch immer ein Musik*drama* bleiben muß, wenn sie überhaupt eine Kunstform sein und bleiben soll.'

[199] See e.g., Wagner's later remarks on Schröder-Devrient in his essay 'Über Schauspieler und Sänger' (1872): 'Außerdem verstand sie es, einen Komponisten dazu anzuleiten, wie er zu komponieren habe, wenn es der Mühe wert sein solle, von einem solchen Weibe "gesungen" zu werden . . .' *Schriften*, ix. 264 (221).

IV

The Composition Draft
and the Problem of Performance

1. Sources

GENERALLY speaking, the sketches for a work of art, if they show any-thing at all, serve to give us valuable insights into the mind of the artist. They can show us how he absorbed influences and formed his ideas in a way which often illuminates interesting new perspectives in the finished work of art as we know it. In the case of *Rienzi*, however, the sketches and drafts are important in another sense, for they sharpen not only our awareness of the finished work, but also our knowledge of its content as Wagner originally conceived it. In fact, they provide the only reliable reference for a performing edition of the work, which, in the absence of the original MS. score,[1] comes closest to an authentic restitution of Wagner's intentions. To make this clear, we shall begin with an account of the existing sources bearing on this problem.

A central difficulty in the study of *Rienzi* is the fact that no printed score has ever been made from the original without introducing cuts made by Wagner[2] and others before and after the first performance in Dresden (20 October 1842). Of the copies made in Dresden from the original score, with Wagner's cuts included, only two have survived. The first was obtained by the *Städtische Musikbücherei*, Hamburg from the Hamburg *Theater- und Leihbibliothek*, Emil Richter; the second was presented by Wagner to Theodor Krüttner in Einsiedeln on 16 February 1846, and is now preserved in the Wagner Museum in Eisenach —it contains some autograph corrections by Wagner, but is unfortun-ately incomplete (Act I, the end of Act III and the beginning of Act IV are missing).[3]

---

[1] See p. 2 above and *Sämt. Werke*, iii (5), for which this chapter (1970) was a preliminary study.

[2] For Wagner's account of cuts in *Rienzi*, see *Sämt. Briefe*, i. 558–9. Also *Schriften*, xiv. 9–10, 21–3.

[3] Two facsimile sides of the original MS. score are contained in Robert Bory, *Richard Wagner: sein Leben und sein Werk in Bildern*, Leipzig, 1938, p. 70 (from Act V/ii) and in Erich W. Engel, *Richard Wagners Leben und Werke im Bilde*, 2 vols., Vienna, 1913, i. 73 (from Act I/ii). The facsimile

The first printed score appeared in Dresden in 1845 as a written copy lithographed by the *Hoflithographie- und Steindruckerei* Fürstenau and Co. (25 copies) and contains the cuts which Wagner made for Dresden in late 1842 or 1843.[4] Two further performing editions which have been traced in Vienna and Karlsruhe are copies of this lithographed score with additional alterations made for the performances in those cities.

As mentioned in the introduction to this study,[5] a further complication arises from the fact that the orchestral and vocal scores published by Fürstner (1898/9) are based on a considerably shortened and, one is inclined to say, mutilated version by Cosima Wagner and Julius Kniese. Despite this, the full score of this version is a valuable source because it includes the full orchestration of a number of passages not in the sources already mentioned. The longest and most important of these is the 'Rape of Lucretia' pantomime which Wagner introduced into the ballet of Act II, but which he had to omit in Dresden owing to the lack of three good actors to take the principal roles—a condition on which he insisted if the piece was to be performed at all.[6] The pantomime has been excluded in all copies and prints of the full score with the exception of the C. Wagner / Kniese version which, despite numerous cuts and insertions, preserves most of its original orchestration.[7] Even this, however, is something of a mixed blessing since the excisions preclude the possibility of restoring a complete authentic version of the piece.[8]

[4] The sequence of sides in this score corresponds exactly to the Einsenach score. The latter may have been the first attempt to produce a fair copy to be lithographed which was then considered unsatisfactory by Wagner. This would account for the incomplete nature of the score and the corrections introduced by Wagner, probably for the benefit of the copyist.

[5] See pp. 2–3 above.

[6] For Wagner's discussion of this problem, see *Sämt. Briefe*, i. 528, 532, 552–3, 556, 558.

[7] There exists another orchestration of the pantomime by M. Ruzek. It was made for a performance of *Rienzi* in Karlsruhe on 13 January 1889 under Felix Mottl. The original score was sent only later to Karlsruhe by Cosima Wagner in order to let Mottl have the original orchestration copied. A copy of the whole score was eventually made, but so far it has not been traced. See Martin Geck, 'Rienzi-Philologie', *Das Drama Richard Wagners als musikalisches Kunstwerk*, ed. C. Dahlhaus, Regensburg, 1970, pp. 187–9.

[8] For this reason, the full score of the pantomime is excluded in *Sämt. Werke*.

---

correspond exactly to the same sides in the copies made from the original MS. This may be chance, but it does show that the copyists in Dresden used the original score wherever possible to keep the same ordering of sides. Between the beginning of Act V and the facsimile side in Bory, for example, no cuts were introduced by Wagner, and the copyist was able simply to follow the page sequence of the original score. The other facsimile is more difficult to account for since Wagner introduced a substantial cut preceding it in the same scene. However, it is possible that the cut corresponds exactly to the ends of two sides in the original score.

In a sense, the key source is a vocal score made by Gustav Klink which was published by C. F. Meser in Dresden in 1844. Wagner himself described this score as 'complete' in a letter to his sister Cäcilie dated 28 July 1844.[9] Formally speaking, it is the most complete source, and so far, it has been assumed that it was made directly from the original MS. score before any cuts were implemented by Wagner. However, a close comparison of the Burrell composition draft[10] with the Klink vocal score has revealed a number of differences between the two—too many to rule out the possibility that Klink could have made his arrangement after Wagner had already introduced cuts into the original MS. score.[11] For this reason, it is necessary to return to the composition draft to form a clear idea of how Wagner originally conceived *Rienzi*.

2. Comparison of sources: two examples

In order to demonstrate the importance of the composition draft in estimating the original extent of the music in *Rienzi*, we shall take two intensive examples—the introduction to the overture, and 'Rienzi, dir sei Preis' from the finale of Act II.[12] The comparative length of the latter movement, from its origin in the composition sketch (fragment)[13] through the composition draft and the most important sources which have survived, is shown by the following table (see p. 150 below).[14] It can be seen from this table how Wagner gradually expanded the movement in the sketch and composition draft, and how it was gradually, and substantially reduced in the sources subsequent to the original MS. score. The overwhelming mass effect which Wagner intended with the movement is therefore weakened in the early performing scores, and, in the C. Wagner/Kniese version, practically destroyed.

In December 1841, Wagner received a letter from Wilhelm Fischer, the chorus-master of the Court Theatre in Dresden, voicing doubts about the extreme length of *Rienzi* and, judging from Wagner's reply,[15]

---

[9] *Sämt. Briefe*, ii. 390.

[10] Ap. i. 161 (source 8).

[11] The main formal and textual differences between the two sources are shown in Ap. iii. 188–9.

[12] Cf. Ap. iii. 188 (items 1, 11–13).

[13] British Library MS. Egerton 2746, f. 3. See Example 21, pp. 82–8 above.

[14] Although the most recent edition in *Sämt. Werke* does not count as a 'surviving source', it has been included here for comparison. For lack of authentic sources, the edition at this point corresponds to the Hamburg and Eisenach copies.

[15] *Sämt. Briefe*, i. 548.

Source	Allegro vivace $\downarrow = 88$	Presto $\downarrow = 160$	Tempo I (orchestral conclusion)
composition	version 1: 79	63	0
sketch (fragment)	version 2: 84	71	0
composition draft	112	73	18
autograph score	?	?	?
vocal score (Klink)	96	73	12
copies: Hamburg⎫ Eisenach ⎭	80	49	12
full score (first edition)	80	49	12
Fürstner score (C. Wagner/Kniese)	64	22	12
Sämt. Werke, iii (2)	80	49	12

asking for suggestions about cuts. In his reply, Wagner states that although the producer in Dresden, Ferdinand Heine, has calculated the length of the opera as five hours, he himself has only calculated four hours.[16] Wagner also enclosed a sheet containing suggestions about casting and cuts. But from this letter, and also from Wagner's account in *Mein Leben* of a meeting with Fischer in Dresden to decide upon how to shorten the opera,[17] it is impossible to determine exactly how many of Wagner's suggestions were decided on for the first performance. What is certain is that a number of them were taken up in the Hamburg copy, later in the Eisenach copy, and eventually in the print of 1845. In his letter to Fischer Wagner makes only one suggestion for the final movement of Act II:

Schlußsatz des Finales. Hier ist mir wiederum, trotz der Ausdehnung dieses Stückes, unmöglich einen schicklichen Punkt zum Streichen aufzufinden:

---

[16] See Ap. iii. 189–90.

[17] *Schriften*, xiv. 9–10. 'Leichten Herzens warf ich ihm [Fischer] als Beute die große Pantomime und das meiste Ballett des zweiten Aktes hin, wobei ich anzunehmen glaubte, daß wir eine ganze halbe Stunde ersparten. So wurde denn in Gottes Namen das ganze Ungeheuer den Kopisten zum Ausschreiben übergeben: das Übrige sollte sich alles finden.'

höchstens im PRESTO, wo nach dem 40sten Takt 24 Takte gestrichen werden können, was jedoch nicht viel ausmachen wird, nur die Schlußkraft hinwegnimmt.[18]

In slightly altered form,[19] this cut was included in the three sources mentioned above. However, Wagner made no mention of cuts in the 'Allegro vivace' and certainly the history of this section, particularly between the Burrell draft and the Klink vocal score where there is a discrepancy of sixteen bars, is considerably less clear. The actual length in the original score of both the 'Allegro vivace' and the 'Tempo I' (see table) may be surmised as follows: either Wagner decided while he was writing the full score from the composition draft to cut one or both sections as they stand in the latter; or he included one or both sections into the full score without changes and decided to make cuts at a later stage. The likelihood that the original score itself already contains cuts made by Wagner is shown by his suggestion for shortening the overture included in the letter to Fischer mentioned above:

In der Einleitung der OUVERTURE kann ich ebenfalls das SOLO der Violoncelle u. Contrabässe kürzen; jedoch wünschte ich dieß nicht eher zu thun, als bis ich mich in einer Orchester-Probe überzeugt habe, daß die von mir angegebenen Nüancen im Vortrage nicht hinreichend sind, dieser Stelle das Ermüdende zu nehmen, was bei einem ganz glatten Spiele ohne Zweifel nicht ausbleiben kann.[20]

Wagner is clearly referring here to a longer passage for unaccompanied 'cellos and basses than the eight bars which exist in all the available scores —a short passage not likely to prove tiring even for an amateur orchestra. Indeed, as we have seen, both the outline sketch and detailed composition draft of the overture reveal that Wagner originally intended the 'solo', as he calls it, to be as long as twenty-four bars.[21] Since Wagner was writing his letter to Fischer over a year after the original MS. score of *Rienzi* had been completed,[22] it is safe to assume that he had included this passage in the score and then decided to omit it either by rewriting

---

[18] *Sämt. Briefe*, i. 559.

[19] Cutting after the 36th and not the 40th bar of the 'Presto'. The number of bars (24) remains the same.

[20] *Sämt. Briefe*, i. 559.

[21] For a transcription of these bars as they stand in the outline sketch and detailed draft of the overture, see Example 39, pp. 131–2 above. The 'nuances' which Wagner mentions in his letter are already present in detail in both documents.

[22] According to *Mein Leben*, the opera was completed in Paris on 19 November 1840. See *Schriften*, xiii. 254.

the first page of the overture again, or simply by crossing it out. It is
therefore not unreasonable to suppose that he may have revised other
passages in the original score itself before any copies were made from it.
It is possible that when Klink made his vocal score from the original MS.
score, he simply left out passages which had already been cut by Wagner.
Unless the original MS. score is found, the full extent of the *Rienzi*
music as Wagner originally conceived it can only remain surmise. In
any event, as the above examples from the overture and the last chorus in
Act II have shown, the authenticity of the Klink score cannot be assumed
without the careful consideration of further evidence, particularly that
shown by the composition draft.

The cut of 16 bars in the 'Allegro vivace' of 'Rienzi, dir sei Preis' which,
when compared with the Klink score, was introduced into the Hamburg
and Eisenach performing versions and the printed scores of 1845, was
probably made by Wagner after the first performance in Dresden.[23] This
means that the orchestration of these bars has been lost, since they appear
only in the original MS. score. Of the 24 bars excluded from the 'Presto'
section, however, 18 of these are included with the original orchestration
only in the version by C. Wagner/Kniese. The orchestration of the
remaining 6 is missing.

In the 73-bar 'Presto' section as it stands in the Klink score, the massive
cut introduced by Kniese reducing the music to 22 bars[24] (18 of which are
included in the cut of 24 bars recommended by Wagner) is an indication
of the degree to which Wagner's original intentions were ignored in this
version. As our analysis of the original sketch has shown,[25] Wagner's
first instinct was to increase the dimensions of 'Rienzi, dir sei Preis' from
142 to 155 and, later in the composition draft, eventually to 203 bars (see
table)—a tendency in accordance with the gigantic proportions of the
finale which the movement concludes. Wagner's reluctance in his letter
to Fischer to suggest a cut at all in this movement would suggest that he
felt his first instinct to be the right one, and certainly, although the
movement in its original form is on an excessive and impractical scale,
this is sufficient to justify a restoration of it in its entirety as it stands in

[23] The cut is marked in Singer's vocal score, pp. 306–7.

[24] Proof that it was Kniese who instituted the cuts in the Fürstner edition is contained in a first
volume of the Klink score—originally in the Wahnfried archives in Bayreuth and now in the
Munich Staatsbibliothek. The score contains numerous emendations in Kniese's hand corresponding
to those in the final edition, including this cut in 'Rienzi, dir sei Preis'.

[25] See pp. 79–91 above.

the composition draft—firstly, with Wagner's orchestration as it can be salvaged, and secondly, with the remaining fragments in an appendix provided with suggestions for orchestration.[26]

An even stronger case can be made for the introduction to the overture. It is clear from Wagner's letter to Fischer that his suggestion for a cut in the passage for unaccompanied 'cellos and basses was based on practical rather than musical reasoning. His fears that even the Dresden theatre orchestra—at that time one of the best orchestras in Europe—could not cope with the 'solo' were probably justified, especially since this exposed passage was unique in the operatic repertoire of the time.[27] But in view of the improved technique of modern orchestras, there is no reason why this passage should not be restored in its entirety. Its orchestration and dynamics are clear enough from the composition draft, and, musically speaking, it adds a completely new dimension to the overture. When the introduction is played complete, the build-up of tension which Wagner intended with the intensified repetition of the melody is greatly increased. Furthermore, the fact that the melody is played three times instead of two, and beginning with the distant effect of unaccompanied 'cellos and basses playing softly, is an indication that Wagner originally wanted to create an effect of literal perspective in the music, i.e. a physical dimension similar to that of the approaching chorus of pilgrims in Act I/ii of *Tannhäuser*. Indeed, the opening of the *Rienzi* overture in its original form was most likely the model for the beginning of the *Tannhäuser* overture where Wagner seeks to recreate the effect of the approaching pilgrims' chorus in purely orchestral terms. Without the octave-unison passage for 'cellos and basses in the introduction to the *Rienzi* overture, however, this effect is greatly weakened since the single repetition of the melody in all current performing scores does not allow sufficient time for the idea to make itself felt.

---

[26] A similar case can be made for the cuts in the finale of Act III, i.e. for those bars contained in the composition draft, but excluded from the Klink score. See Ap. iii. 188–9 (items 14, 18–19).

[27] The 'recitative' for 'cellos and basses from Beethoven's Ninth Symphony, which is the model of the passage, was almost unheard of in Dresden. In *Mein Leben*, Wagner speaks of a performance in Dresden 'years ago' under Reissiger, i.e. a long time before Wagner's own performance in 1846. According to Wagner, the Reissiger performance had given the work a bad reputation in Dresden where, he says, it was practically unknown. For his own performance of the work, he insisted on 12 special rehearsals for the 'cellos and basses alone, even though they were excellent players. Clearly, in order not to jeopardize his chances with *Rienzi*, Wagner preferred to cut the overture rather than suggest, as an unknown composer, an inordinate number of rehearsals for the bass strings. See *Schriften*, xiv. 150, 154.

The reasons for the discrepancies between the composition draft and the Klink vocal score are probably twofold: first, while making the full score from the composition draft, Wagner doubtless made some creative decisions involving the cutting of some passages and the modification of others;[28] second, having made the full score, he may have decided to make further modifications for fear of meeting with a refusal of the work in Dresden on account of its excessive length. In the two examples above from the overture and 'Rienzi, dir sei Preis', it is clear that the cuts were a question of expediency and not simply second musical thoughts—a factor sufficient to justify the restoration of these cuts in a performance of the work. However, other alterations were certainly a result of better judgement. The omission of twenty-nine bars in the main body of the overture, for example, is clearly an improvement since the attempted development of themes it contains prolongs rather than enriches the structure of the whole.[29] On musical grounds alone, it would be difficult to justify the inclusion of these bars as they stand in the composition draft.

Each of the discrepancies between the composition draft and the Klink vocal score, therefore, has to be judged on its own merits. For this reason, it is necessary for those who want to perform *Rienzi* to be able to consult the composition draft and judge for themselves. The evidence presented above is sufficient in itself to justify publication of the draft (perhaps in the form of a new and much-needed vocal score) so that it may be used as an important source of reference for a performance of the work.

[28] From the middle of Act II, there are regular markings in the draft (every 6 or 8 bars) which Wagner used to calculate the space he needed in the full score. With the exception of the extra bars in the conspiracy scene of Act II, Ap. iii. 188 (items 7–8), the extra bars in the composition draft are accompanied by regular markings without breaks, suggesting that these bars were present in the original autograph.

[29] See Example 41, pp. 136–7 above. Reuss reports that a later, and larger cut of 48 bars in the overture, Ap. iii. 188 (item 3), was replaced in the original score by 10 bars written on a separate sheet. Although the passage is also questionable on musical grounds, Wagner, on the evidence of Reuss' description, obviously included it in the autograph, and only later saw fit to delete it. Cf. *Bayreuther Blätter*, xii (1889), 162.

V

Conclusion

IF any general conclusion is to be drawn from this study of Wagner's sketches and drafts for *Rienzi*, it is that a thorough overhaul of the work on both a practical and critical level is long overdue. Not only are the documents an important source of reference in establishing an authentic text of the work, they also provide a starting point for a critical evaluation which supersedes both the tendentious interpretations of the Bayreuth school and the derisive attitude of Hanslick and others, including some of Wagner's admirers.

In the course of this discussion we have traced the genesis of *Rienzi* from its first draft in prose to the creation of libretto and music. Alone the fact that these stages were undertaken by a single creative mind suggests that *Rienzi* is a good deal more than the extrovert imitation of 'grand opera' it is often taken to be. Without exaggeration, it is fair to say that it is the first opera in the history of the genre—the more conventional conceptions of *Die Feen* and *Das Liebesverbot* notwithstanding—in which, single-handed, a composer sought to bring text and music into a fruitful relationship with one another, and with a certain independence from the formality of operatic convention. It is already clear in the prose draft, for example, that Wagner's decision to adapt his source material himself enabled him to create a large-scale structure not at all like the typical 'number' sequence of contemporary works, but, using traditional forms, a clear symmetry in accord with the development of the action through Rienzi's rise to power, his reversal of fortune, and his subsequent downfall. Besides this unusually close identification between dramatic content and form, our analysis of the draft has also shown that its mixture of rationality and high emotion reflects the didactic and Utopian character of its political *Tendenz* in a way both more accurate and more disturbing than any of Wagner's sources. Unlike the many other adaptations of the subject in the nineteenth century, *Rienzi* still remains, for all its faults, a vital and complex presentation of the subject, largely because its dramatic conception captures a psychological truth about the nature of its hero which other versions do not. It is easy to say, of course, that Wagner's mechanistic use of symmetry and display to conjure up extravagant emotion points to a 'Fascist' element in the work not unrelated to the propaganda methods of twentieth-century totalitarianism. Indeed, Hitler's possession of the original MS. score and his indisputable attraction towards *Rienzi* would seem to support this view, if only indirectly. But the conception of *Rienzi* is a good deal more complex than this. Apart from the fact that the term 'Fascist' cannot be applied to *Rienzi* since it was a non-existent political force at the time the work was composed, Wagner's adaptation of the subject contains a decidedly critical element— notably in the presentation of Baroncelli and Adriano—which implies an awareness of the hypocrisy and potential violence beneath Rienzi's idealistic façade whose presence would be difficult to explain if one were prepared to regard the work simply as an evil premonition of Nazi Germany. It is precisely this element which is only tentatively touched on, or missing altogether, in other adaptations of the subject in the nineteenth century, including Wagner's sources. One might almost say that, momentarily, Wagner's critical consciousness reaches beyond the well-meaning idealism of *Das junge Deutschland* and the so-called 'Utopian' socialism which nourished *Rienzi* into a world of violence and terror undreamt of by his contemporaries.

But although the dramatic conception of *Rienzi* is closely bound in form and content to the essence of its subject, it is a mistake to call the work a 'Musikdrama'. While the prose and verse drafts tend towards a unity between dramatic form and content, it is the music of the work which, for the most part, remains rooted in the tinsel world of early nineteenth-century opera, a long way from the convergence of music and drama attained in Wagner's later works. Even Bekker's more differentiated evaluation of *Rienzi* as both 'grand opera' and 'drama' is without real foundation. The antithesis of genre which Bekker sees between the two halves of the work would assume, if his thesis were correct, a corresponding difference in the relation between the action and its musical articulation. Our analysis of the sketches and drafts has shown, however, that while a different emphasis in method does exist between the two halves of the work, particularly in the striking number of additions to the text in Acts III–V, this in no way alters the fundamental conception of the opera, but rather serves to work against the 'drama' with a lyrical expansion alien to the development of the action. The paradox in the second half of *Rienzi* is that the new stylistic elements, which are 'dramatic' in the sense of Wagner's latest style, have, in the context of the work's original conception, an anti-dramatic effect. While it is true to speak of a newly emerging style in *Rienzi*, therefore, it is not one organic to the conception of the work, but one which is imposed upon it. The sketches and drafts clearly show, as Hanslick surmised, that Wagner was not at ease in the medium of 'grand opera'—a genre which lies at the root of *Rienzi*, despite its unconventional use of operatic forms. They also show that his attempts to find a way out of this uncongenial situation did not lead to the creation of a 'Musikdrama', but to a more flexible relation between text and music which remained tangential to the work, particularly with respect to the role of Adriano, who, for this reason, seriously threatens the dramatic balance of the opera in its second half. Above all, the study of Wagner's working methods in the context of their biographical background shows that a quickening awareness of the scope of his musical talent—an awareness stimulated by his confrontation in Paris with the best musical minds of the day—led to a discrepancy between genre and style in the latter part of *Rienzi* which he then sought to correct by casting his next work, *Holländer*, in a simpler dramatic form.

It is one of the ironies of C. Wagner's and Julius Kniese's version of *Rienzi* that, in their efforts to convert the opera into a fully-fledged 'Musikdrama', they concentrated on the elimination of 'inessential' elements in the music which did not, in their opinion, further the course of the action. As a result, they cut out, or seriously distorted some of the best music in the work which, because of Wagner's difficulty in reconciling his musical instincts with the apparatus of 'grand opera', stands outside the main course of its dramatic development. The unquestioning acceptance of this version, which has been widely performed since its publication, is doubtless one reason why *Rienzi* has become something of a black sheep among Wagner's works. Performances based on a critical knowledge of its original form are badly needed. Only then will it be possible to appreciate at first hand the flaws and contradictions, as well as the positive elements in *Rienzi* which make it a key work in the development of Wagner's later style, and a not insignificant landmark in the history of opera.

Appendix i

Manuscript sources

TERMINOLOGY

THE most widely known terminology for Wagner's sketches is that by Otto Strobel—a German scholar whose work in the Wahnfried Archives Bayreuth during the interwar years is an important, though sometimes insecure foundation for any study of Wagner's composing methods. For reasons explained elsewhere,[1] his terms, particularly those for the musical documents, have been modified to accommodate important qualitative and quantitative distinctions not accounted for by his over-systematic view of Wagner's working methods.

As the title of the present study suggests, it is necessary to draw a clear, if somewhat artificial qualitative distinction between the terms 'sketch' and 'draft'. The word 'sketch' is used to define an improvisatory outline written in pencil and occasionally in ink. The word 'draft' indicates a more detailed document in ink showing Wagner at a more advanced stage in the process of composition. In view of the special character of Wagner's procedure, these terms are applied with a view to his working methods as a whole and refer, except when qualified with the word 'fragment', to documents which are continuous from beginning to end for a given work. Amongst the non-musical MSS., Wagner's initial outline of *Rienzi* is called a 'prose sketch'. The later and more detailed documents in prose and verse (apart from autograph libretti or fair copies) are described as 'prose draft' and 'verse draft' respectively. In the case of the musical MSS., Wagner did not make a continuous and complete initial outline of *Rienzi* before proceeding to more detailed work on the music as he did for each of his later works after *Lohengrin*. His first attempts at the composition of the music are contained in a number of isolated documents which, in order to maintain a quantitative perspective in relation to the continuous MSS. of the later works, are described in each case as a 'composition sketch (fragment)'. Since these documents are relatively few in number, it is likely that others in the same category are no longer extant. The only surviving musical document for *Rienzi* which is continuous from beginning to end is a detailed working-out in ink in the form of a vocal score. In a letter to Wilhelm Fischer (1842), Wagner described the document as a 'composition draft' (*Compositions-Entwurf*)[2] and it is this term which has been adopted here. Those documents provided with the term 'composition draft (fragment)' are also detailed workings-out in ink which, in most cases, are discarded sections of the main composition draft.

[1] See John Deathridge, 'The Nomenclature of Wagner's Sketches', *Proceedings of the Royal Musical Association*, ci (1974–5).

[2] *Sämt. Briefe*, i. 593.

The following list concentrates on authentic documents relevant to the composition and first performance of *Rienzi*. It excludes album-leaves, printed sources, copies not in Wagner's hand, and documents relating to subsequent revisions and arrangements.[3]

1	Autograph score	Presumed lost. 798 written sides bound in 4 volumes. Dates given in E. Reuss, 'Rienzi', *Bayreuther Blätter*, xii (1889), 161; Otto Strobel, 'König Ludwigs Wagner Manuscripte', *Bayreuther Festspielführer*, 1936, p. 108.

Act I (end): Riga, 6 February 1839
Act II (end): Boulogne, 12 September 1839
Act III (begin): Paris, 6 June 1840
Act III (end): Paris, 11 August 1840
Act IV (begin): Paris, 14 August 1840

Further dates are missing. According to *Mein Leben*, the autograph score was completed on 19 November 1840 (*Schriften*, xiii. 254). Facsimile from Act I/ii in Erich W. Engel, *Richard Wagners Leben und Werke im Bilde*, 2 vols., Vienna, 1913, i. 73; and from Act V/ii in Robert Bory, *Richard Wagner: sein Leben und sein Werk in Bildern*, Leipzig, 1938, p. 70.

2a Prose sketch — Curtis Institute Philadelphia—Burrell Collection 88. Small double sheet of thin cardboard (octavo)—probably originally part of a note-book. The prose sketch is written in faded pencil amidst some addresses in Paris and Travemünde. The date 'Travemünde 6 August '37' occurs beneath the sketch amongst the addresses, but with little apparent connection to the sketch itself. On the other side of the sheet are some brief musical sketches (including a theme of the later *Faust* overture) and a draft of a letter to Sir John Smart (*sic*) in London about the overture *Rule Britannia*. According to *Mein Leben* (*Schriften*, xiii. 192–3), Wagner sent his overture to Smart at about the same time he made his first 'plan' for *Rienzi* after reading Bulwer-Lytton's novel in Blasewitz in the summer of 1837. It seems likely, then, that this document is the 'plan' in question. A transcription is to be found in Ap. ii. 165.

2b Prose draft — Curtis Institute Philadelphia—Burrell Collection 127/i. 8 written sides 38 × 24 cm (2 double sheets). No date. In his 'Autobiographische Skizze' (1842), Wagner states that he did not make a draft of *Rienzi* until he was in Riga,

---

[3] For information on copies, printed sources and arrangements, see *Sämt. Werke*, and the forthcoming publication *Wagner Werk-Verzeichnis* (WWV), eds. Deathridge, Geck, Voss.

where he arrived in the latter part of 1837. See *Schriften*, i. 16–17 (12–13). Since Wagner generally used the word 'draft' (*Entwurf*) to mean a detailed working-out, this does not contradict his statement in *Mein Leben* that he made a 'plan' of the opera earlier in the same year in Blasewitz (see commentary to source 2a). If we assume that this 'plan' was the prose sketch (and not the prose draft as originally thought), he probably wrote the prose draft in Riga at some time between the autumn of 1837 and the summer of 1838. Transcriptions in Ap. ii. 165–87, and *Sämt. Werke*, xxiii. 137–50. Facsimile of side 1, ibid. xxiii. 305.

3 Verse draft   Curtis Institute Philadelphia—Burrell Collection 127/ii. 14 written sides 38 × 24 cm (3 double sheets and 1 single sheet). Concluding date: Riga, 24 July/6 August 1838. (Since Russian time in Riga was 12 days behind European time, the correct dates must be either 25 July/6 August, or 24 July/5 August.) Full transcription in *Sämt. Werke*, xxiii. 153–206. Facsimile of side 1, ibid. xxiii. 306; facsimile of side 9, Plate I in present volume.

4 Autograph libretto Presumed lost. No known date. In view of the alterations made in the verse draft during the composition of the music, Wagner probably made a fair copy of the draft between 19 November 1840 (completion of the autograph score) and 4 December 1840 when he sent both autograph libretto and score to Dresden. See *Sämt. Briefe*, i. 426.

5 French prose translation of verse draft   Curtis Institute Philadelphia—Burrell Collection 127/iv. 43 written sides with corrections in another hand 38 × 24 cm (11 double sheets and 1 single sheet). No date. According to *Mein Leben*, probably Spring/Summer 1839 (*Schriften*, xiii. 213). Facsimile of side 19 in *Sämt. Werke*, xxiii. 307.

6 Autograph libretto in French   Wahnfried Archives Bayreuth (AI c2). 52 written sides (quarto). No date. Certainly before February 1840 since the subsequent revisions in the German verse draft made during the composition of Acts III–V between February and October of the same year are not included—a certain sign that Wagner had given up hope of a Paris performance by early 1840. Full transcription in *Sämt. Werke*, xxiii. 208–50.

7	Modified autograph libretto in German	Curtis Institute Philadelphia—Burrell Collection 127/iii. 45 written sides (quarto). No date. Acts III–V written in another hand. Revised according to the requirements of the Dresden censor. Probably the text sent to Lüttichau on 23 March 1841. See *Sämt. Briefe*, i. 458–60.

8 Composition draft Curtis Institute Philadelphia—Burrell Collection 127/v. 162 written sides 35.4 × 26.8 cm (double and single sheets bound with cardboard cover). Dated as follows:

Overture (end): Paris, 23 October 1840
Act I (begin): Riga, 26 July/7 August 1838
(end): Riga, 6 December 1838
Act II (begin): Riga, 6 February 1839
(end): Riga, 9 April 1839
Act III (begin): Paris, 15 February 1840
(end): Paris, 7 July 1840
Act IV (begin): Paris 10 July 1840
(end): Paris 29 August 1840
Act V (begin): Paris, 5 September 1840
(end): Paris, 19 September 1840

Facsimile of side 1, Plate III in present volume; side 59 in *Sämt. Werke*, xxiii. 308.

9a–e
9a Composition sketches (fragments)

Wahnfried Archives Bayreuth (AI c3)
3 single sheets (quarto). No date.
(i) recto: outlines Act III/finale including orchestral list for on-stage music
verso: outlines final movement Act III/finale; march begin Act IV/finale; duet Rienzi/Irene Act V
(ii) recto: outlines Act III/finale including first sketch of 'Schütz, heilige Junfrau'
verso: heavily covered with pen strokes, last 3 lines first sketches for Adriano's aria Act III
(iii) recto: outlines Act III/finale—another attempt at 'Schütz, heilige Jungfrau' and jottings for 'Victory' chorus
verso: outline fragments for 'Szene und Arie' Act III and other jottings (unidentified)

9b Composition sketch (fragment)

$3\frac{1}{2}$ sheets (quarto) 6 numbered sides. Date (begin): Paris, 20 September 1840. Continuous outline of overture. Inserted smaller page showing attempts at contrapuntal combination of themes. Facsimile of side 1 in Richard Petzoldt, *Richard Wagner: sein Leben in Bildern*, Leipzig, 1963, Plate 35.

9c Composition draft (fragment)	5 sheets (quarto)—9 numbered sides ordered as follows: 1–3 continuous draft on 3 staves with some breaks and additions—Act III/finale from Adriano's words 'Zurück, halt ein, Tribun' to 'Nun denn, nimm Schicksal deinen Lauf!' including 2nd verse of War Hymn on p. 3. On the reverse (unnumbered) side of 2 are some sketches for the song *Maria Stuart* written in Paris in 1840.

Composition sketches (fragments)	4 'Schütz, heilige Jungfrau' incomplete outline 5 outline opening Act III 6 outline chorus 'Heil dir, du stolzes Siegesheer' through Act III/finale 7 Act III/finale—'Ach, blutig ist die Strafe' first version 2 staves. 8 Act III/finale—Ensemble 'Ewiger Tod'; second version 'Ach, blutig ist die Strafe' 1 stave only. 9 Act III/finale (end)—outline in distorted form

9d Composition sketches (fragments)	Single sheet (quarto). No date. recto: outline Act IV (end)—69 bars as opposed to 75 in finished score verso: outlines Act V—particularly A major duet Rienzi/Irene

9e Composition draft (fragment)	4 written sides (quarto). Date (begin): Riga, 26 July/7 August 1838. Identical date in main composition draft (source 8) for Act I (begin). Probably the first attempt at the composition draft which was discarded. The opening music of Act I up to Rienzi's entrance is present in vocal score with only a few variations from the final version. The last page includes outline sketches for 2 *Singspiele*: possibly the projected *Die glückliche Bärenfamilie* which Wagner mentions in *Mein Leben* (*Schriften*, xiii. 183f., 196) and another, the title of which—*Ein Wiener in Paris*—is noted on the same page.

10 Composition drafts (fragments)	New York Public Library (JOG 73–152/3) 6 written sides (quarto) comprising 1 double and 1 single sheet. Confirmation of authenticity at the bottom of side 2: 'Ein Stück aus dem Brouillon des 2 Actes [der] gr. Oper Rienzi gedichtet und componiert von *Richard Wagner* aus Leipzig (zum ersten Mal am 20 Oct. 1842 in Dresden aufgeführt). Zum Andenken erhalten bei Wagners Abreise von Paris am 7 April 1842 E. B. Kietz.'

1–4 Act I/finale beginning 'Rienzi hoch'—identical with
final version except for minor alterations in vocal line
5–6 Act I/finale Lateran chorus 'Erwacht, ihr Schläfer'
6 last half-side: Act II/finale rough outline of ensemble
'O laßt der Gnade Himmelslicht' 2 staves only.

Composition
sketch
(fragment)

11 Composition
sketches
(fragments)

Bibliothèque Nationale Paris (MS 2226) Single sheet
(quarto). No date. Confirmation of authenticity by E. B.
Kietz, Paris 1842.
recto: Act I/ii outline (single stave) of the ensemble
'Noch schlägt in seiner Brust'—bottom stave theme
for 'Rienzi, dir sei Preis' Act II/finale
verso: 4 fragments (single staves)
(a) not identified
(b) Act I/finale G major theme 'Wir schwören dir,
so groß und frei . . .'
(c) Act I/iii fanfares for central section of Adriano/
Irene duet
(d) transition into Act I/finale.

12 Composition
sketch
(fragment)

British Library (Egerton MS. 2746 f. 3) single sheet
(quarto). No date.
recto: Act II/finale outline (2 staves) of chorus 'Rienzi, dir
sei Preis' with alternative extension
verso: continuation of 'Rienzi, dir sei Preis' (extended
version) also 7 fragments not identified
Facsimile of recto, Plate II in present volume.

13 Composition
sketch
(fragment)

Private collection Wolfgang Sulzer, Marburg. Half-sheet.
No date. Act V/i–ii—attempt at contrapuntal combination
of themes: Rienzi's prayer (opening melody) with A
major melody of Rienzi/Irene duet.

14 Composition
sketches
(fragments)

Curtis Institute Philadelphia—Burrell Collection 47. No
date. Short outlines for *Holländer* and *Rienzi* overtures.
Sketched on free half-page at end of Claudio's Cavatina
from *Das Liebesverbot*—an arrangement for piano and
voice in French probably intended for audition before
Scribe and Eduard Monnaie during April 1840 (*Schriften*,
xiii. 246).

15 Composition   Wagner Gedenkstätte Bayreuth (Hs 120/S). Single sheet.
   sketches   (quarto). No date.
   (fragments)   recto: Act II/i outline of chorus 'Ich sah die Städte' and
                         further outline sketches for Act II/ii
                     verso: sketch for 'Rienzi, dir sei Preis' Act II/finale—also
                         sketches for Paris arrangements including 'Zank-
                         duett aus Fra Diavolo in G dur' and 'Donauweib-
                         schen'. Further sketches at bottom for ambassadors'
                         scene in *Rienzi* Act II/finale and a few fragments
                         for the Pantomime and Ballet in the same Act.

16 Composition   Whereabouts unknown. Formerly in the possession of
   sketch   Gustav Herrmann, Leipzig (see *Wagner Gedächtnis-
   (fragment)   Ausstellung*, Leipzig, 1913, no. 122). Offered in Auction
                     Catalogue 45, *Liepmannssohn*, Berlin, 28/29 November
                     1919. Also in Auction Catalogue, *Sotheby*, 24 January 1955.
                     recto: Act III/finale Battle Hymn
                     verso: end of song 'Der Tannenbaum' 1838, Riga

17 Composition   Princeton University Library, Single sheet (quarto). No
   sketches   date.
   (fragments)   recto: 'Lied der Mannschaft des Holländers' vocal score:
                         incomplete fair copy. Underneath: rough sketches
                         for *Rienzi* Act III/finale
                     verso: rough sketches for *Rienzi* Act IV/i.
                     The document is proof that at least part of *Holländer* was
                     composed before *Rienzi* was completed, since the MS. of
                     the fair copy (for the *Holländer* chorus) was discarded and
                     then used for the outline *Rienzi* sketches. I am grateful to
                     Paul Machlin for drawing my attention to this document.

18 Autograph   Whereabouts unknown. From the estate of Julius Rietz,
   score   Dresden. Offered in Auction Catalogue, *Sotheby*, 19
   (fragment)   December 1960 with facsimile of first side. 35 written
                     sides. No date. Act III/ii full score of Adriano's aria
                     transposed into A minor/F major—possibly used for first
                     performance. See also, Wakeling Dry, 'A Master's
                     Methods', *The Musical Courier*, xlv (1902), New York,
                     No. 25 pp. 10–11.

Appendix ii

The prose documents

A single stroke in the text indicates the end of a line. Double strokes indicate the
end of a page. Wagner's spelling and grammatical mistakes (marked *sic*), as well as
his use of short-hand for some words (e.g. m̄ for mm) have been left intact in order
to convey something of the haste with which the documents were written. Old
spellings (e.g. ß for ss between short vowels) have been retained without comment.
Italics indicate underlinings in the main text of the original. Wagner's additions
in the margin are in smaller italics. Editorial additions are in square brackets.

(a) *The Prose Sketch*
(Blasewitz or Tavemünde, Summer 1837)

Akt 1. Colonna u. Orsini im Kampf um Irene/ in den Straßen. Adriano Retter
Irene's. Liebe. Volks-/tumult. Rienzi beschwichtigt ihn. Orsini u. Colonna/
fordern sich zum Kampf am Morgen [?] außerhalb/ der Thore. Der Lateran.
Proclamation der Freiheit./ Rienzi Tribun./

Akt 2. Friedensfest. Verschwörung der Nobili./ Todesurtheil. Freigesprochen.
Unzufriedenheit./

Akt 3. Flucht der Nobili. Anrücken an Rom./ Schlacht. Adriano trennt sich von
Rienzi/ [und] Irene./

Akt 4. Kirchenbann./

Akt 5. Brand des Kapitol [*sic*]. Untergang Rienzi's./

(b) *The Prose Draft*
(Riga, Autumn 1837/Summer 1838)

Entwurf zu einer großen heroisch-tragischen Oper in 5 Akten:

Rienzi, der letzte der Tribunen.
Personen.

Steffano Colonna, Haupt der Familie Colonna, ein Greis von achtzig Jahren,—
Baß.
Marino di Ponto, Haupt der Familie Orsini,—*Baryton*.
Adriano di Castello, aus der Familie Colonna,—*tiefer Sopran*.
Cardinal, päpstlicher *Legat*,—*Baß*.
Rienzi, päpstlicher Notar,—*Tenor*.
Irene, seine Schwester.
Baroncelli, ein Bürger,—*Tenor*.
Cecco di Vecchio, ein Schmidt,—*Baß*.
Der Friedensbote.—Sopran.

Römische Nobili. Anhänger der Colonna's u. Orsini's. Bürger u. Bürgerinnen Rom's.
Päbstliche Beamten. | Priester u. Mönche aller Orden. Wachsoldaten der römischen
Nobili. |
Ort der Handlung: Rom im 14ten Jahrhundert.

Erster Akt.

1 *Introduktion.* + Eine Straße Rom's, an deren tiefen Ende die Lateran-
Kirche. Im Vorder-/grunde das Haus des Rienzi. Es ist
Nacht. *Marino di Ponto*, Nobili u. mehre [sic]/ seiner
Anhänger. Er hat an *Rienzi's* Haus eine Leiter legen laßen,—
5 zwei seiner/ Anhänger haben sie erstiegen, u. brechen durch
das Fenster ein. Alle sind in der/ lustigsten Laune eines
frechen Abentheuer's. Man hört den Hilferuf *Irene's*,/ die
jetzt durch das Fenster auf die Straße herabgeschleppt
wird. *Marino* empfängt/ sie mit roher Zärtlichkeit. Er hat
10 sie einmal auf der Straße gesehn, ihre Wohnung/ erforscht,
um sie zu rauben,—sie möge sich nur bequemen, es werde
ihr Schade/ nicht sein. Sie wollen mit ihr fort, da erscheinen
Steffano Coloña u. mehre [sic] seiner/ Anhänger.—Die
Colonna's! Die *Orsini*!—Nicht aus Gerechtigkeit sondern
15 aus Feind-/schaft nimmt *Colonna* Partei gegen Orsini,—u.
sucht ihm Irene zu entreißen/ für irgend einen seiner
Freunde. Es kommt zum Kampf.—*Adriano di Castello*/
tritt auf mit Gefolge. Er mischt sich in den Streit u. erkennt
Irene, die er schon/ früher einmal gesehen hatte; augen-
20 blicklich drängt er sich mit aller Kraft zu ihr, be-/freit sie
u. meldet sich zu ihrem Beschützer.—Gelächter.—Man
läßt sich von/ neuem zum Kampfe an. Der Lärm hat von
verschiedenen Seiten her Volk u. Bürger/ herbeigezogen.
Als sich letztere stark genug fühlen, werfen sie sich mit
25 dem/ Rufe: Nieder mit den *Colonna's*! Nieder mit den
Orsini's! Nieder mit den Räubern!—/zwischen die Kämp-
fer. Als der Tumult auf das Höchste gestiegen ist,—tritt/ der
Cardinal mit päpstlichen Gewaffneten auf, sucht den Streit
zu schlichten, u. er-/mahnt zur Ruhe im Namen des
30 heiligen Vater's. Er wird von den Nobili nicht/ beachtet
und mit Spott zurück gewiesen. Sie machen sich über
ihn her, er ist im/ Begriff, gemishandelt zu werden;—da
tritt *Rienzi* auf, begleitet von *Baroncelli*/ u. *Cecco*. Mit
gewaltiger Stimme gebietet er Ruhe; bei seinem Er-
35 scheinen/ laßen sogleich das Volk u. die Bürger, denen er
zugerufen hatte: „vergeßt ihr,/ was ihr geschworen?"—
vom Streite ab, nachdem sie den *Cardinal* befreit haben./

Rienzi ruft den Nobili zu, ob dieß ihre Achtung gegen die heilige Kirche sei,/ die sie beschützen sollten, daß sie den Pabst selbst in der Person seines/ Legaten mishandelten? —*Irene* hat sich zu ihrem Bruder gedrängt, u. sinkt/ voll Scham an seine Brust;—Rienzi erblickt die Leiter u. das erbrochene Fenster/ in seinem Haus, u. versteht sogleich was vorgefallen. Er wirft einen tödtlichen/ Blick auf die Nobili—„das ist eur Handwerk, daran erkenn' ich euch! Unsere Brüder/ erschlagt ihr im zarten Knabenalter, unsere Töchter möchtet ihr entehren! Was/ bleibt zu euren Schandthaten euch noch weiter übrig, das alte hohe Rom, die/ Königin der Welt, machtet ihr zur Räuberhöhle,— schändet die Kirche,—/ der heilige Vater mußte den Stuhl Petri' verlaßen, im fernen Avignon/ ihn neu zu errichten;— kein hohes Gnadenfest kann mehr gefeiert werden,/ kein Pilger zieht mehr gen Rom zum Völkerfeste, weil ihr rings um's/ heilige Rom die Wege belagert wie die gemeinsten Räuber,—leer bleibt/ Rom u. seine Bürger sind zur niedrigsten Armuth herabgesunken, was ihnen/ noch bleibt, raubt ihr ihnen, indem ihr wie Diebe in ihre Läden einbrecht, ihr/ erschlagt die Männer, entehrt die Weiber. Blickt um euch, u. seht wo ihr/ dieß treibt,—seht jene Säulen, jene Ruinen sagen euch,—es ist das alte/ Rom, das freie, große Rom, das einst die Welt beherrschte, deßen Bürger/ Könige der Könige waren,—Banditen, sagt mir, giebt es noch Römer?"/ Ungeheurer Beifallsruf des Volkes, das sich dadurch so stark zeigt, daß/ die geharnischten Nobili, die sich schon über Rienzi her machen wollten,/ sich zurückhalten. „Dulden wir dieß! Reißt ihm die Zunge aus! Latß ihn,—/ er schwatzt dummes Zeug,—er ist ein Narr!" Steff. Colonna [*sic*]: „Komm Morgen/ zu mir, Herr Notar, ich will dir Geld geben für deine schöne Rede!"—Sie/ machen sich über ihn lustig,—*Rienzi* hält die Bürger zurück, die die/ Nobili bestrafen wollen, er erinnert sie an ihren Schwur. *Marino—/* „was haben wir mit dem Narren zu schaffen!—Ich fordere dich zum Kampf,/ Colonna!" *Colonna:* „Zu Pferde also, kommt beim Tagesanbruch vor die Thore"/ Die Nobili erheben ihr Feldgeschrei: „Für Colonna! Für Orsini!" u. trennen sich/ tumultuarisch nach verschieden [*sic*] Seiten.—*Rienzi,*—„sie ziehen durch die Thore,—/ Nun wohl,—sie sollen ihnen auch verschloßen bleiben!"— Der Cardinal ist von den/ erlittenen Beschimpfungen noch ganz betäubt;—„wann endlich, Rienzi, wirst/ du dein

1   dem Pabst gegebenes Versprechen erfüllen, u. diese
     Belialsbrut/ unschädlich machen.—Du siehst selbst das
     päbstliche Ansehen reicht nicht mehr/ hin, ich der Legat
     werde in dem Maaße gemishandelt!"—Baroncelli u.
5   Cecco/ stürmen an Rienzi, „wann endlich machst du uns
     frei—wie lange zögerst/ du, dein Wort zu halten—" das
     Volk stimmt in diesen Ton ein. Rienzi nim̄t/ den Cardinal
     beiseite,: „werde ich mich auch immer auf euch verlaßen
     können,—bedenkt,/ was ihr verlangt, bedenkt was wir
10   verlangen; ich soll ein seit Jahrhunderten// entartetes Volk
     zu freien Bürgern machen, soll den mächtigen Uebermuth
     dieser Nobili brechen;/ kann ich mich auf dieses Volk
     verlaßen,—kann ich mich auf die Kirche verlaßen,—
     werdet/ ihr mich nicht vielleicht verdammen, wenn Blut
15   in diesen Straßen fließen müßte, wenn/ vielleicht die
     Häupter der trotzigsten Räuber den [sic] Beile weichen
     müßten?—Wenn/ vielleicht Colonna's oder Orsini's
     Haupt fallen müßte?"—Cardinal [sic], „ich habe Voll-
     macht,/ zu jedem Schritt der Nothwendigkeit,—wenn
20   nur das Ansehen der Kirche wieder hergestellt/ wird?"—
     Rienzi,—„wohlan, die Zeit ist da, die Nobili ziehen aus
     der Stadt!—Geht ruhig/ in eure Häuser, u. rüstet euch,
     zu beten für die Freiheit. Wenn ihr einen Trompeter
     durch/ die Straßen ziehen, einen langgehaltenen Ton
25   blasen hört, dann ist es Zeit, versammelt/ euch vor dem
     Lateran!"—Das Volk verspricht Gehorsam, u. trennt
     sich zu verschiedenen/ Seiten. Der *Cardinal* entfernt sich
     ebenfalls mit seinen Gewappneten.
     Szene u. Terzett.   *Rienzi, Adriano* u. *Irene.*—*Rienzi*, nachdem Alles entfernt
30   ist, umfaßt mit heftiger/ Aufwallung *Irene*: „Sprich,
     Schwester was geschah dir, was haben sie dir gethan!"—
     Irene:/ „Ich bin gerettet,—sieh dieser war mein Erlöser!"—
     Rienzi: „Adriano—du—ein Colonna rettete/ ein Weib vor
     Beschimpfung?"—*Adriano* „mein Leben hätte ich für sie
35   gegeben; kennst/ du mich nicht, Rienzi, wer hielt mich je
     für einen Räuber?"—*Rienzi*, „du verweilest, Adriano,
     / ziehst du nicht mit hinaus, um dich zu schlagen!" *Adriano*
     „—weh mir, daß ich deine Rede/ hören mußte, daß ich
     erkennen muß, was du in deinem Wesen birgst, daß ich
40   ahnen/ muß, was du beginnen willst,—u. doch nicht dein
     Feind sein kann?" *Rienzi*: „Ich erkannte/ dich stets edel,
     noch bist du nicht ein Gräul im Auge des Gerechten;—
     Adriano könnte/ ich auf dich zählen?"—*Adr:* „Wozu?
     Rienzi, was hast du vor?—ich sehe, du bist gewaltig,/—

1

wozu wirst du deine Gewalt brauchen?"—*Rienzi* „Rom
groß u. frei zu machen?" *Adr:*/ „Wodurch?—Durch Blut,
—ich ahne es, Rienzi!"—*Rienzi:* „muß es sein, so fließe
Blut." *Adr:*/ „Unglücklicher, was beginnst du? Weißt du,

5

daß es die Edlen sind, die du Feinde nennst;/ u. wer soll
dich schützen, wenn du ihrer Rache verfällst;—diesen
feilen Sclaven, diesen Plebejern,/ entartet, feig u. niedrig,
willst du dich vertrauen?"—*Rienzi:* „Erst wenn ich sie/
zu freien Bürgern, zu einem Volk gemacht haben werde!"

10

Adr. „Unseeliger, das erlangst/ du durch das Blut der
Edlen?—Rienzi, wir haben nichts gemein!"—Er will sich
zum/ Abgange wenden, sein Blick fällt auf Irene,—er naht
sich ihr zärtlich: „wie kann/ ich fliehen, kann ich mein
Herz bezwingen! Irene, fühlst du, daß du mir dankbar

15

sein/ könntest? Du blickst so sanft u. mild, giebt ein
milderes Urtheil!" *Irene* erwidert/ voll Dank u. zärtlicher
Befangenheit.—*Rienzi* hat beide scharf beobachtet. Als/
sich Adriano ~~voll~~ Beklemmung u. mit schmerzlicher
Bekämpfung seiner Liebe, sich/ von Irene wendet, ruft
ihn Rienzi zurück—„Adriano, hör' mich! Ich bezwecke/
nicht die Vernichtung deines Standes,—ich will nur das
Gesetz erschaffen, u. will/ daß auch die Nobili diesem
Unterthan [*sic*] sein sollen,—kannst du mich tadeln, wenn
ich euch/ aus Räubern zu wirklich Edlen machen will,
wenn ich eure Vorzüge dazu benützen/ will, daß ihr Beschützer u. starke Säulen von Rom's Rechten u. Freyheit,
u. der heiligen/ Kirche sein sollt?" *Adrian:* „man könnte
dich tadeln,—ich selbst bin einer der ersten, der/ das Gesetz
aufrecht erhalten will;—doch irrst du nicht in den
Mitteln,—glückt/ der Versuch, u. hast du Gewalt, werden
dann es nicht meine Brüder gewesen/ sein, durch deren
Blut du zur Macht kamst?"—*Rienzi:* „Unseeliger,
mahne mich/ nicht an Blut,—wer war es, der einst
meinen armen Bruder, den holden Knaben, als [*sic*] mit
ihm am Tiber wandelte, als wir noch unbewußt des
Jammer's waren, den/ wir ertrugen,—als er Kränze für
Irenen wandt—wer war es, der ihn aus/ brutalem Mis-
verständniß erschlug,—u. für deßen Mord ich keine
Gerechtig-/ keit erhalten konnte?" *Adria:* „Weh! es war
ein Colonna!" *Rienz:* „Ein Colonna,/ was that ihnen der
arme Knabe! Blut? Ha, Adria, ich tauchte meine Hand in
sein/ Herzblut, u. schwur einen Eid! Weh dem, der ein
verwandtes Blut zu rächen/ hat!"—*Adr:* „Rienzi, du bist
fürchterlich! Was kann ich thun, um die Schmach/

*er geht u. meinem
Schutz ver-/traut er
dich Irene—sprich/
vertraust du mir? Ir:
mein Held/ du rettetest
mein Leben, mein/
Ehre, es ist dein Gut,
u. ich ver-/trau'
es dir;—Adr:
Du fliehst/ mich
nicht den ———
—/ —Colonna,
— deßen Stamm
ein Gräul deinem
Bruder?/ Ir: O
was nennst du
dein/ Geschlecht
—mein Retter,
ja/ mir graut
vor dir, gedenke
/ ich jener Stolzen
die dir nie/
verzeihen werden,
daß du ein/ plebejisches
Mädchen vor Enteh-/
rung schütztest!—
Adr:*

20

25

30

35

40

1   meines Geschlechtes zu sühnen!"—*Rienzi*: „sei unser, sei
    ein Römer!—Verlangst/ du einen Preis, ich will dir mein
    Theuerstes geben!"—~~*Adr*: „Ha, du zeigst mir/ einen neuen~~
    ~~Zustand der Welt, wird es mir nicht verweigert, um die~~
5   ~~Schwester/eines Bürgers zu freien.~~ *Adr*: „Ein Römer?—
    Laß mich ein Römer sein!" *Ensemble.*/ *Rezitat: Rienzi*,
    „meine Pflicht, ein großes Werk rufen mich jetzt weg,
    Adriano,/ du rettetest meine Schwester,—ich vertraue sie
    dir für jetzt an, sei ihr Beschützer."/ er entfernt sich./
10 Duett. *Adriano u. Irene. Adr* „Er geht, er vertraut dich mir,—willst
    du meinen Schutz."—*Irene:*/ „Du bist edel, ich vertraue
    dir!"—Ihre beiderseitigen Gefühle steigern sich bis zur
    Erkenntnis / der gegenseitigen Liebe,—Adriano wirft
    sich zu Irenen's ~~Knieen~~ Füßen, u. leistet ihr/ den feurigsten
15 Eid dar, den sie schüchtern, aber mit Hingebung erwiedert.
    Irene: „Ich/ Unseelige, was thust du, sind wir nicht ge-
    trennt durch Stand u. Geburt; fürchtest du/ nicht deine
    Verwandten?" *Adr.* ~~„Ha, ich ahne einen neuen Zustand~~
    ~~der Welt u. der Dinge/ der Welt, dein Bruder, welch ein~~
20 ~~Geist wird er nicht fürchterlich.~~ O schweig, laß uns/
    jetzt im ersten Rausch der Liebe nicht durch das Gedenken
    an all den Jam̄er stören,/ der uns, der Rom droht;—dein
    Bruder welch ein Geist, er ist groß aber fürchterlich;—
    / was wird er wagen,—er wird zu Grunde gehen,—ihn
25 wird das Volk verrathen die/ Nobili werden ihn züchtigen,
    —welches wird dein Loos sein? Wer wird dich schützen?—/
    Irene,—dein Unglück sei das Loosungswort für mich, alle
    Bande zu zerschlagen, mein/ Leben, mein alles für dich zu
    laßen!"—*Irene.* „Und wenn ich glücklich bin?"—*Adr.*
30 „O schweige/ ich zittre vor deinem Glück;—es kom̄e
    Nacht u. Tod, u. ich bin dein für ewig!" *Ensemble.*/ Es hat
    zu tagen begonnen.—~~Sie liegen in einer Umarmung, als~~
    ~~sie aus der Ferne~~ Unter/ großem Lärmen u. Getümmel,
    ziehen die *Colonna's* gewaffnet u. gerüstet durch die/
35 Nacht. Die erschreckte Irene flieht in das Haus;—*Adriano:*
    Bleib ich schütze dich.—/ Die Orsini gewaffnet u. gerüstet
    ziehen über die Straße.—*Adrian:* „Ha, sie ziehen/ hinaus
    zum Kampfe,—Unglückseelige, sie kennen nur Mord;—
    ich schaudre,—was/wird da kommen, o Unglückszeit;—
40 ~~Es—~~Willkommen aber Tod u. Verderben,—ich bin/ dein,
    laß mich dein Retter, dein Gatte sein!" *Ensemble.*—das
Finale. Frührot glänzt an die Fenster/ des Lateran. Sie liegen in
    einer Umarmung, als die [*sic*] von Ferne den langgehal-
    tenen Ton/ einer Trompete hören.—Sie fahren auf.

„Was hat das zu bedeuten?"—Man hört den selben/ Ton
etwas näher. „Wie sonderbar u. schauerlich!" Man hört
den Ton noch näher.—/ Ein Herold kommt auf der
Straße an, u. bläßt [sic] einen langgehalt: Ton. Die Straße
wird/ auf einmal belebt, aus allen Häusern brechen die
Bürger u. das Volk hervor. Alles/ ist in wilder u. freudiger
Bewegung, „Der Tag ist da, Heil sei der Stunde!" Aus dem/
Lateran beginnt die Orgel. Alles wird bei ihrem Klange
augenblicklich ruhig. Die ganze/ Straße, der Platz bis
zum Lateran hin ist mit Knieenden bedeckt, der Lateran
glüht/ im Morgenroth! Aus ihm heraus ertönen fromme u.
erhebende Gesänge, in denen das/ Licht der Freiheit u.
des Friedens verkündet wird. Die Menge liegt noch
athemlos/ auf den Knien,—da öffnen die Pforten des
Lateran,—man erblickt die Kirche mit Priestern/ u.
Geistlichen aller Orden erfüllt,—auf die Treppe heraus
schreiten Rienzi u. ihm zur Seite/ der Cardinal,—Rienzi
ist in einer vollständigen Rüstung, nur das Haupt ist
entblöst.// Bei seinem Erscheinen erhebt sich die ganze
Masse u. bricht in den ungeheuersten Jubel aus./ Dann
beginnt Rienzi: „Erstehe aus deiner Asche du altes Rom,
Königin der Welt, du/ bist frei, frei sind alle Römer."
Enthusiastischer Zuruf des Volkes. „Hinfort herrsche/ das
Gesetz, das Gesetz sei Rom's Freiheit, ihm unterthan sei
Jeder, der Edle wie der/ Bürger. Das Gesetz bestraft hinfort
jede Gewaltthat, wer sie auch verübte; auf daß/ es keinen
Räuber mehr gebe unter den Römern. Die heilige Kirche,
die wir verehren/ sei unsere Herrscherin. Jedem Räuber
seien die Thore verschloßen, wie es jetzt sind,/ nur wer
sich dem Gesetze unterwirft, sei uns willkommen, ihm
öffnen sich die Thore./ Ziehet hinaus ihr Römer, ergreift
die Waffen u. vernichtet alle Räuber, die das Gebiet/ des
heiligen Rom's belagern. Frei u. ungehindert wandere
dann der Pilger durch/ die Thäler u. Berge, frei u. sicher
treibe der Hirt seine Heerde durch die Fluren./ Zum
Zeichen daß ihr Römer sein wollt, groß, frei u. shirmen
das Gesetz, schwört/ es bei Gott, dem Vater aller Heiligen
u. Menschen." Neuer Zuruf des Volkes u./ feierlicher
Schwur.—Cecco nähert sich der Treppe u. redet das Volk
an: „—Wisset/ denn, ihr Bürger, nun wir Römer geworden
sind,—wer machte uns dazu, wer belehrte/ uns einzeln
seit Jahren darüber, wer wir waren u. wer wir sein sollten?
Rienzi/ war es, er hat ein Volk geschaffen,—so höret
denn, es sei sein Volk, Rienzi sei/ unser König!" Unge-

1   heurer Zuruf des Volkes „—Es lebe Rienzi, der König/
der Römer!"—*Adriano*, im Vordergrunde für sich:
„Unglücklicher, sollte er es wagen?"/—*Rienzi*: „Nicht
also, ihr Römer, misbraucht nicht eure neue Freiheit.
5   Die Herrscherin/ ist die Kirche. Schenkt ihr mir jedoch
euer Vertrauen, so kenne ich in der Geschichte/ unserer
freien Ahnen eine Würde—nach der mich gelüstet, weil
ihr Träger allein/ dazu bestimmt sein soll, die Rechte des
Volkes zu schützen u. zu vertreten;—dieß/ that der Volks-
10   Tribun.—L̶a̶ß̶t̶ Römer, laßt mich euern [*sic*] Tribun sein!"
—*Cardinal*/ „in dieser feierlichen Würde bestätige u. segne
ich dich, im Namen u. am [*sic*] Stelle des/ Heiligen Vater's!"
—Jubel: „Es lebe Rienzi, der Tribun!"—*Rienzi*: „Nun
schwöre/ ich Euch treu zu sein, das Gesetz zu schirmen,
15   jeden zu vernichten, der es bricht,/ u. wanke ich, so stehe
mein Haupt euch blos.—Lang lebe Rom!"—*Adriano*/ ist
gerührt, u. da alle von neuem e̶i̶n̶ in einem erhabenen
Gebet den Schwur als freie/ Römer leistet [*sic*], stim̄t auch
er m̶i̶t̶ voll Enthusiasmus mit ein.—*Der Vorhang fällt.*/
20

Zweiter Akt.

Introduktion.   Die Säle des Capitol's,—deren Ende führt auf ein großes
offenes Portal, von/ wo eine Treppe auf den Platz hinab
25   führt, u. durch welches man R̶o̶m̶ die Straßen/ u. Häuser
Rom's erblickt. Alles ist auf das festlichste geschmückt.—
Noch eh der/ Vorhang aufgeht hört man from̄e Gesänge
der Pilger. Nachdem der Vorhang auf/ ist, bleibt die
Bühne noch eine Zeit leer, man hört den Gesang wie aus
30   *Schmach u. Verderben*   den Straßen/ näher, ein Zug Pilger mit dem Friedensboten
schwören wir/ *Dem*   an der Spitze, festlich u. antik in Weiß/ gekleidet erreicht
Frevler an der Römer   durch die Treppe des Portals den Eingang in den großen
Ehr.   Saal/ unter dem Gesange einer Friedens Hymne: „Jauchzet
ihr Thäler, jauchzet ihr Berge; ihr/ seid frei u. Friede
35   herrscht durch die Fluren!"—*Rienzi* tritt auf in der
phanta-/stischen u. pomphaften Gewändern des Tribunen,
—an seiner Seite *Cecco, Baroncelli,*/ u. mehre [*sic*] angesehene
Bürger, welche zu dem neu erwählten Senate gehören.
Rienzi./ „Friedensbote, hast du deine Sendung vollbracht?
40   Fandest du Frieden u. Seegen?"—/ *Friedensbote.* „Durch die
Thäler, über Fluren bin ich gegangen,—Friede ist in der
Romagna,/ es giebt keinen Räuber mehr; die Städte
öffnen ihre Thore, ungehindert wandert alles/ in festlichen
Zügen nach den Gnadenbildern, nach Rom, zum großen

1 Friedensfest, der/ Hirt treibt seine Heerde froh u. frei
   durch die Gefilde. Verlaßen sind die finstern/ Schlößer,—
   im Friedenszuge ziehen die letzten Nobili nach Rom."—
   Rienzi stürzt/ auf die Kniee: „Dir sei Preis, mein Gott,
5 das Werk ist vollbracht.—Die *Senatoren*—/ „Ehre dir,
   Rienzi, größter der Römer!"—*Rienzi.* „Geh, Friedensbote, ziehe durch/ alle Straßen Rom's, verkünde Allen,
   was du mir verkündest!" Der Friedensbote, setzt/ sich
   mit seinem Zuge in Bewegung u. verläßt das Capitol
10 unter Anstimmung der/ Friedens Hymne, bis sie in der
   Ferne verschallt.—/ *Steffano Colonna, Orsini* u. mehre
   [*sic*] Nobili,—sämmtlich in Friedens Gewändern treten/
   auf. Sie grüßen Rienzi mit stolzer Unterwürfigkeit.
   Rienzi: „Seid mir willkom̄en!/ Was fehlt noch Rom zu
15 seinem Glücke?—Die stolzesten u. mächtigsten Wider-
   sacher/ desselben, sind zurückgekehrt, u. treten an die
   Spitze seiner Gesetze u. Freiheit."/ *Colonna:* „Ich be-
   wundere dich Rienzi—ich ahnte deine Größe nie,—doch
   sei es drum, ich/ will sie anerkennen."—*Rienzi* „Ihr
20 erkennt nur die Größe des Gesetzes, des Frieden's/ an.
   Vergeßt es nie, daß dieß der Preis war, um den wir kämpften;— vergeßt es nie, daß ihr ihnen unterthan seid, wie
   der gemeinste der Plebejer; die Mauern eurer/ Paläste,
   durch die ihr die Stadt zum Kriegs-u. Räuberlager machtet,
25 sind geschleift; Weh euch, wenn ihr noch den heimlichen
   Groll nährt,—wenn ihr nicht aufrichtig u./ treu die
   Gesetze liebt,—weh euch, beim kleinsten Uebertritt derselben,—~~ich kann~~/ denn ich vor Allen schütze die Gesetze,
   ich—der Tribun.—Ihr Herrn u. Edlen,—ich/ erwarte euch
30 zum Festmal heute in diesen Sälen!"—Er geht ab.—/
Duett u. Terzett. Orsini—„Colonna, hörtest du die freche Rede, u. sind wir
   verflucht, sie zu dulden?"/*Colonna* „ich knirsche vor
   Wuth,—er der Plebejer, den ich an meiner Tafel hielt?"—
   Orsini/ „Was ist zu thun, wir sind besiegt;—dieser elende
35 Pöbel, den wir mit Füßen traten,/ wie ist er verändert,
   —die Masse bewaffnet,—Muth u. Begeisterung in Jedem!"
   —*Colonna,*/ „Den Pöbel fürcht' ich nicht, nimm ihm
   Rienzi, u. er ist wieder was er war;—doch in/ Rienzi ist
   der Geist, der aus jedem Plebejer einen Ritter macht."—
40 *Orsini* „Du meinst,/ so wäre der Stoß auf einen nur zu
   führen. Das Volk vergötterte ihn, nichts ist mit offner/
   Gewalt auszurichten." Die Nobili schließen sich enger
   um die beiden. *Colonna:*/ „was bleibt uns übrig. Todtet
   Rienzi in mitte [*sic*] seiner Creaturen, u. zitternd fallen

sie zu/unsren Füßen!"—*Orsini* „Der Streich, wann wäre
zu führen? [*sic*]—Heute ist das Fest in diesen/ Sälen,
erscheinet alle,—schließt euch um ihn,—den Stoß ich
führ' ihn selbst." *Colõna*—und/ bringe heimlich die
Lanzenknechte, die Rienzi nicht in die Stadt ließ, herein,—
sie besetzen/ schnell das Capitol,—Rienzi fällt,—u. Rom
ist wieder unser!"—*Adriano* war aufge-/treten, hatte die
Gruppe beobachtet, war unter sie getreten, hat alles gehört,
u. tritt jetzt/ hervor zwischen *Colonna* u. *Orsini.*—„Meu-
chelmörder?—was habt ihr vor?" —/ *Colonna*: „Wer bist
du?—bist du mein Sohn, oder der Verräther deines
Vater's?" *Adrian.* „Ich/ bin der Sohn eines Vater's, der
Ritterehre liebt bis in sein 80stes Jahr, dem niedrige
Schandthat/ fremd war von je, der deshalb ein Feind
Orsini's war, wie aller Verräther-Brut!"// *Orsini*: „Verräther *du*, frecher Knabe!"—*Colõna* „ist das die Sprache,
die dich der übermüthige/ Tribun lehrt? Adriano, ich
ahne deine Schmach, weh dir wenn ich sie für wahr
erkenne."—*Adriano*:/ „O Vater, seid ihr denn immer noch
blind?"—*Colonna*: „schweig, ungerathener,—du bist in
den/ Händen des Tribun's,—er benützt dich zum Verräther
an deinem eignen Vater;—Fluch ihm,/ dem niedrigsten
der Verrathe! [*sic*]—Laßt euch beschwören, befleckt nicht
so eure Namen, die/ schon genug befleckt durch Gewaltthat u. Raub!" *Orsini*: „Hört den Treulosen;—Colonna,
u./ du züchtigst ihn nicht."—*Colonna*: „So wisse; heute,
hier in diesen Sälen stirbt Rienzi von/ unsrer Hand—du
weißt's,—geh hin, Verworfner, u. verrathe uns, verrathe
mich deinen/ Vater!"—*Adriano's* Bitten, Aufforderungen,
Drohungen sind vergebens,—er stürzt/ auf die Kniee,—
Colonna stößt ihn von sich,—Alle entfernen sich, unter
dem Schwur/ des Todes von Rienzi.—/ *Adriano* ist vor
Schmerz zusammengesunken. Leichenblaß rafft er sich
auf;—„ich will ein Verräther/ sein! Rienzi, Bruder Irenen's,
ich rette dich!"—Er wankt,—„Verräther an deinem Vater,/
was willst du thun, dein graues Haupt, dem Henkerbeil
preisgeben! Hĩmel, schütze/ mich vor Wahnsinn.—~~Rien~~/

Finale.

Zum großen Portal heran nahet der Zug der Bürger-
schaften Rom's, mit dem Senat an/ der Spitze, ihnen folgen
die Nobili. „Laßt Festgesänge erschallen, Heil dem Frieden!" usw.—/ Als alle Säle gefüllt sind,—tritt *Rienzi,
mit Irene, Baroncelli* u. *Cecco,* auf. „Heil Rienzi,/ der Tribun!"—*Rienzi* „Seid mir gegrüßt ihr Römer;—ha
welch' ein Anblick euch/ froh u. festlich vereint zu sehen

1   zur Feier des Frieden's. Lang blühe Rom in Frieden/ u.
Eintracht!"—*Baroncelli.* „Die Gesandten stellen sich dir
vor"—der Gesandte/ Neapel's tritt auf: „Heil dir., Rienzi,
u. ewiges Gedeihen wünscht Rom Neapel."/—Der Ges-
5   andte des deutschen Kaiser's,—Mailand's,—der Lombar-
denstädte u. anderer/ Staaten, führen sich einzeln vor.—
Rienzi, in Entzückung: „Gott hat Wunder/ gewirkt
durch seiner Schwachen Kraft;—so wißet denn, es soll
dabei nicht/ stehen geblieben werden. Rom ist frei,—aber
10   ganz Italien vereinige sich/ zur Freiheit,—Heil dem
italienischen Bunde!"—machtvoll—„Wir laden auch/
kraft unsrer Eigenschaft als Representant des römischen
Volk's vor die Fürsten/ Deutschland, die sich zur Kaiser-
wahl meldeten, ihr Recht zu beurkunden auf/ den ~~Thron~~
15   Titel des König's von Rom,—denn Rom ist frei, u.
wähle fortan selbst/ seinen König!" Große Aufregung unter
den Gesandten Deutschland's.—Die/ Nobili,—„welche
Frechheit, wohin geräth er im Wahnsinn." *Rienzi* „so
mögen denn/ die Feste beginnen!"—*Adriano*, drängt sich
20   an ihn;—„Rienzi, sei auf deiner/ Hut,—weh mir, daß ich
dich warnen muß!" *Rienzi* „droht mir Verrath!—*Adr.*
„nichts/ weiter, schütze dich!"—*Rienzi:* „Verrath? Von
wem hab' ich den zu fürchten!"/*Adr.* „nur meine Ahnung!"
—*Rienzi* „Von wem anders als von den stolzen Patriciern./
25   Sei ruhig, Adr., ich weiß,—dieß mein friedliches Gewand
deckt ein eisernes Hemde."—/ Die Feste haben begonnen.
—Großes Ballet, welches in einer gemischt antiken/u.
mittelalterlichen Allegorie die Befreiung Rom's von den
Tarquiniern darstellt,—/ ihm folgt ein antiker Waffentanz
30   im alt römischen Costüm; ~~der Friedens-Engel/erscheint,~~
Ritter in mittelalterlicher Tracht greifen sie an;—die
Ritter werden besiegt,/ der Friede erscheint, u. versöhnt
das alte Rom mit dem Neuen,—festliche Tänze/ im
gemischten Costüm.—*Rienzi* hat Baroncelli mit einem
35   Auftrag entfernt./Adriano hat die Nobili streng beobachtet;—als die Tänze zu Ende gehen,—drängt/ sich *Orsini*
an Rienzi,—*Adriano* tritt hastig zwischen sie,—*Orsini's*
Dolchstoß/ verletzt Rienzi, ~~der durch ein~~ nicht,—die
Säle sind plötzlich durch Römische Trabanten/ besetzt,
40   die Nobili überwältigt. *Rienzi*—„Dieß der Lohn für
die Wiedererschaffung/Rom's!—Meuchelmord,—nicht an
mir,—an Rom's Gesetz u. Freiheit. Ich wahrte/ mich
gegen eure Liebe. Die Feste sind zu End u. das Gericht beginnt!" Alle/ trennen sich voll Entsetzen, die Senatoren

bleiben zurück. „Ihr saht Signori's/ das Verbrechen vor
euren Augen verüben!" *Cecco:* „noch mehr, die Lanzen-
reiter/ Colonna's, brachen durch die Thore, u. waren im
Begriff das Capitol zu nehmen,/ als dein Befehl es schon
durch unsre Truppen besetzt hatte."—*Rienzi:* „Ihr Edlen,
läugnet/ ihr?"—*Colonna:*—„Nein!"—*Rienzi:* „—So richtet nach dem Gesetz!"—*Senatoren:*—/ „das Gesetz bestim̄t
den Tod durch Henkerbeil!"—*Rienzi:* „bereitet sie zum
Tode."—/ Die Nobili werden in den zweiten Saal geführt,
u. ein Vorhang wird vor ihm herab/ gelaßen.—*Rienzi,*
allein,—*Adriano* u. *Irene* treten bestürtzt auf.— „Rienzi,/
was willst du thun?"—*Rienzi* „das Gesetz vollziehen
laßen!"—*Adr: Ir.* „Gnade,/ Gnade!"—*Adr:* „das wirst du
nicht, bedenke, mein Vater!—ich war's, der dich rettete,/
der jenen verrieth,—Rienzi, willst du mich zum Vater-
mörder machen?"—*Rienzi/* „Bedenke, daß du ein Römer
bist;—Colonna hat nicht *mich* ermorden wollen,—die
Freiheit/ u. Gesetze Rom's wollte er morden, u. ich schwur,
sie aufrecht zu erhalten. Dein Vater/ stirbt!"—*Adr.* „Ha,
wage es, blutdürstiger Tribun,—ich verabscheue deine
Größe!/ Der Tropfen Blutes der meinem Vater entströmt
läßt dich mir verfallen;—/ bedenke laß mich kein verwandtes Blut zu rächen haben!"—*Rienzi* „Unglücklicher,/
woran erinnerst du mich?"—*Irene* „Gnade, Gnade, mein
Bruder'—blick' auf/ zu Gott, dem Vergebenden,—willst
du seinen Vater tödten?—Adriano, Gott, dein/ Vater!"—
Adr: Ire. „Laß die Milde entscheiden,—wir knieen zu
deinen Füßen,/ um deiner selbst willen,—Gnade, Gnade!"
—*Rienzi* ist erweicht: „ich sündige an/ Rom,—wird es
sich nicht an mir rächen?"—Man hört aus dem andren
Saal,—/ den düstren Gesang der Mönche, welche die
Nobili zu ihrem Tode vorbereiten./ *Adr:* „Entsetzlich,
Entsetzlich!—diese töne,—mein Vater sein ~~graues~~ weißes/
Haupt. Rienzi, mache mich nicht mordlustig."—Noch
ferner her ertönt das Gebrüll/des Volkes nach dem Tod
der Nobili.—*Rienzi,* „Hörst du *diese* Töne, sie spechen/
meiner Milde das Todes-Urtheil!—Wohlan, erfahrt
Rienzi's Entschluß!"—Der/Vorhang wird wieder auf-
gezogen; man sieht die Nobili in Todes-Angst beten, mit/
ihnen die Mönche,—vom Portal her schallt der Ruf des
Volkes „Tod den Nobili!"/ Die Nobili werden nach dem
Vorgrund geführt, das Volk bricht durch die Wachen am/
Portal u. stürmt unter dem Schrei „Tod den Verräthern!"
herein.—*Rienzi* tritt ihnen ent-/gegen: „Die Nobili

verschwuren sich gegen mein Leben,—das Gesetz verur-
theilt sie zum/ Beil!" *Volk* „Sie sterben!" *Rienzi* „Römer,
ich begnadige sie in eurem Namen!"/ *Baroncelli u. Cecco,*
„Tribun, bist du rasend!"—*Volk* „Nie, Rienzi,—sie sterben,
sie sterben!" *Rienzi,*/ „Muß ich euch um Milde u. Gnade
für meine Mörder bitten.—Wohlan, Römer, ich flehe
euch// an,—glaubt ihr, daß ich Ansprüche auf eure Dank-
barkeit habe, so gewährt mir meine/ Bitte!"—*Baroncelli
u. Cecco*: „Hört ihn nicht, er ist rasend!" *Rienzi*: „Römer,
ich machte/ euch groß u. frei, ich schenkte euch den
Frieden;—erhaltet den Frieden, Blut bringt/ Zwietracht.
Seid gnädig Römer, ich flehe euch darum an,—ich euer
Tribun!"—/—*Volk*: „Sie wollten unsren Befreier, unsren
Tribun töden!" [*sic*]—*Rienzi* „begnadigt/ sie u. laßt sie
auf's Neue das Gesetz beschwören,—u. sie werden es nie
wieder brechen/ können!" *Colonna* „Ha, seine Großmuth
macht mich rasend!"—*Rienzi* „Aber wehe,/ dreifach
wehe ihnen, wenn sie meineidig werden!"—*Baroncelli*
„Du wirst es bereuen/ Tribun!"—*Volk*: „Du hast das
Recht, Tribun, thue wie du willst; dein Wille/ ist unsrer!"
—*Rienzi* „Dank euch, Römer,—u. in eurem Namen,
seid/ frei, ihr Verurtheilten,—bewundert die Milde Rom's,
—u. laßt es euch zum Beispiel [*sic*]/ schwört unverbrüch-
liche Treue dem Gesetz!"—Die Nobili zerknirscht: „Wir
schwören!"—/ *Rienzi* „gehet hin u. seid fortan die besten
Bürger Rom's!"—*Adriano* u./ *Irene* fallen gerührt Rienzi
zu Füßen.—Die Nobili sind in dumpfer Betäubung./ Das
Volk „Ehre Rienzi,—der große Tribun, der milde Richter!" *Baronc: u. Cecco*/ bilden einen Theil von Misver-
gnügten. *Ensemble.*

Dritter Akt.

Introduktion.

Das *Forum*,—die Sturmglocken werden hefftig [*sic*]
geläutet. Wild aufgeregte Volks-Haufen/ erfüllen die
Scene. Die Nobili sind heimlich aus Rom geflohen. Große
Bestürzung,/ man ruft nach Rienzi.—*Baroncelli* kommt:
„Römer, wir sind schändlich hintergangen,/ wer konnt
auch auf die Treue dieser Patricier zählen, der Tribun war
rasend, sie/ für ihr Verbrechen begnadigen! [*sic*] es war toll,
—nun sehen wir die Folgen,—die Geißeln des/ Friedens
sind entflohen; wer weiß, was nun kommen wird!"—
Cecco kommt: „~~Was soll das heißen~~ „Verwünschter
Streich, kaum daß wir die allgemeine Flucht/ der Nobili

erfahren, vernehme ich schon, wie sich [*sic*] auf einen[?]
Angriff auf/ die Stadt rüsten, u. fremde Söldner miethen.—
Wohin hat uns die unzeitige Milde/ des Tribun gebracht!"
Baroncelli: „Wir werden sie jetzt mit unsrem Blute, mit
unsrem/ Untergange bezahlen müssen!"—*Volk:* „Rienzi,
—wo ist Rienzi, wo ist der Tribun."/ —*Rienzi* tritt auf.
Ihr Römer, wir sind betrogen,—wehe ihnen, die mit
Gnade/ überladen Eid u. Treue brachen."—*Baroncelli,
Cecco u. Volk.* „Deine Milde, Tribun, kam/ zur Unzeit!"—
Rienzi: „ich verstehe euch, u. tadle euch nicht;—fortan sei
mein/ Herz gestählt;—das Gesetz sei eisern, wehe denen,
die es verhöhnen. Blut soll/ fließen,—u. wenn kein Tropfe
Patrizischen Blutes überbleibe.—Die Thore sind/ geschloßen, wehe ihnen, weñ sie sich nahen!"—*Baro: Cecco*
„Was wirst du thun, Tribun."/ *Rienzi* „Rom's Freiheit
vertheidigen, u. die Treulosen niederschmettern!"—
„Das/ konntest du, ohne daß es *uns* einen Tropfen Blut
kostete!" *Rienzi* „Desto volleres/ Recht haben wir nun,—
meine Gnade macht sie desto strafbarer;—vernichten wir
sie/ jetzt, so nennt uns die ganze Welt gerecht. Bewährt
jetzt eure Größe, euren Muth./ Rüstet u. waffnet euch
zum Kampfe, ich führ' euch an, Gott u. seine Heiligen/
führen euch zum Sieg; laßt uns die neuen Fahnen entfalten,
laßt ~~sie~~ uns/ sie einweihen ~~durch~~ in dem gerechtesten
Aller Kämpfe,—u. der schönste Lorbeer wird/ sie schmükken!" Er begeistert das misvergnügte u. theils entmuthigte
Volk/ von neuem;—alle rufen nach den Waffen. *Rienzi*
„Wenn ihr die große Glocke des/ Capitol's ertönen
hört, kommt gerüstet unter die Fahnen. Santo spirito,
Cavalieri!"/ *Ensemble.—Alle ab.—*
Adriano kommt. „Sie schreien zu den Waffen! Unseelger
Jammer dieser Tage! Wäre ich/ nie geboren, um ihn zu
erleben!—Wohin soll ich mich wenden? Wohin ist die
Ritterlichkeit/ meines Leben's. Dieß Schwerdt,—für wen
soll es ziehen, u. gegen wen! Meine Liebe,/ wird sie nicht
verflucht von dem der mich geboren!—O Rienzi, Unseeliger, welches/ Schicksal hast du auf mein Haupt herabbeschworen! Soll ich hinaus, soll ich für/ meinen Vater
gegen dich kämpfen,—soll ich für dich gegen den Vater
streiten!—/ Ha,—nur eines steht in meiner Macht,—ich
will hinaus zu meinem Vater eilen,/ will ihn bitten, beschwören, vom Kampfe abzulaßen,—ich will ihn erweichen
u. sollte/ ich mein Leben zum Opfer bringen;—Rienzi
ist groß u. edel, auch er wird das/ Blut der Römer schonen

*— gnadenreich/
Ha, stolze Gnade,
die er übt/*

Arie.

wollen;—Versöhnung, Versöhnung!—Herr des Hi͠mels
u./ ihr Heiligen all, steht mir bei,—gebt meinen Worten
Kraft!"—Die große Glocke/ des Kapitol's ertönt!—„Gott,
es wird zu spät!"—*ab.*/

Finale. Kriegerische Musik u. Signale auf der Bühne. Alle Römer
gewaffnet u. gerüstet/ ziehen marschmäßig auf das Forum,
—die Frauen Rom's begleiten sie,—alle Orden/ der
Mönche u. der Geistlichkeit. Als das Forum ganz erfüllt
ist, kommt *Rienzi*/ zu Pferde ganz gerüstet, an seiner
Seite Irene. *Rienzi*: „Ihr Römer, der Tag/ ist da, eure
Schmach für Jahrhunderte zu rächen, Verrath u. Meineid
zu bestrafen!/ Kämpft wie die alten Römer kämpften,—
Gott gibt uns den Sieg, u. ewig/ wird das Gesetz u. Rom's
Freiheit blühen,—denn ihr seid stark u. zittern wird/ vor
euch die Verrätherbrut!—Nun denn so sti͠mt an den
Römersang, er sei ein/ Schrecken euren Feinden: santo
spirito cavalieri!"—Alles stimmt die Römische/ Kriegs-
Hymne an, wie sie Rienzi selbst gedichtet hat,—der
Refrain ist: santo/ spirito, cavalieri!—*Adriano* tritt athemlos
auf,—„Rienzi, halt ein! Schreite/ noch nicht zum Kampfe,
höre mich!—Sende mich hinaus zu deinen Feinden,—
schlag'/ erst den Weg der Güte ein;—vertraue mir, ich
werde sie bewegen, sich mit euch zu/ versöhnen;—auch
du wirst gern das Blut der Römer schonen, Versöhnung,
Vergebung!/ Mache mich zum Vermittler!"—*Rienzi*
„Unglückseeliger, schweig; warst nicht du/ es, der mich
zu der unseligen Milde sti͠mte, um deren Willen jetzt
weit edleres/ Blut vergossen werden muß, als das jener
Verräther!"—*Adriano*: „Rienzi, bedenke/ was du thust,—
vergieb noch einmal, und sie werden nie wieder meineidig
werden."/ *Rienzi* „Schweig, unglücklicher Knabe,—es
giebt keine Treue dieser Elenden;—die Stolzen/ tragen
[*sic*] u. wollen den Kampf, er werde ihnen!" [*sic*]—*Adriano*
[*sic*] Bitten, Flehen u. Drohungen/ rühren Rienzi nicht,—
er sinkt auf das Kniee, [*sic*] u. wirft sich zur Erde vor
Rienzi,/—er bleibt unbeweglich. „Bleib hier zurück,
beschütze Irene, u. laß dem Schicksal/ seinen Lauf!"—
Adriano „Nun denn Schicksal, so ni͠m deinen Lauf!"—Die
Hymne/ wird von neuem angestimmt,—unter Kriegs-
musik setzt sich der Zug in Bewegung,/ man hört noch
lange den Schlachtgesang,—die Frauen, Irene u. Adriano
bleiben/ zurück.—Adriano im gräßlichsten Kampf mit
seinen Gefühlen. Er umfaßt ver-/zweiflungsvoll Irene,—
dann reißt er sich los.—„Leb' wohl Irene, ich muß

hinaus,// noch kann es Zeit sein!"—*Irene* hält ihn zurück. „Unglücklicher, bleib, du bist deiner Sinne nicht/ mächtig!"—*Adri*: „Laß mich,—ich muß!" — *Irene* „Treuloser, willst auch du mich verlaßen,—/ mein Bruder von Tod bedroht,—u. auch du,—wer soll sich deiner Irene erbarmen!" [*sic*]—Ich laß/ dich nicht,—du gehst in's Verderben u. ich mit dir!"—Man hört aus weiter Ferne die Schlachthymne/ u. kriegerische Töne. *Adr.* „Hörst du,—Him̃el, es wird zu spät!"—Die Frauen sind auf die/ Kniee gesunken, u. stimmen ein Gebet für den Sieg an.— *Irene* hängt sich an *Adr.*—es/ wird ihm unmöglich, sie zu verlaßen. Beide stimmen in Gebete mit ein,—*Adr*: fleht/ den Himmel um Errettung derer an, die ihm theuer sind. Das Gebet wird oft ~~mit dem~~ durch das/ ferne Schlachtge- brüll unterbrochen. Santo Spirito Cavalieri!—Endlich hört man die Römer es zwar/ in weiter Ferne wieder vollständig singen,—allmälig rückt es immer näher;— *Adr.* „Großer/ Gott, es ist entschieden!"—*Irene* u. die *Frauen*: „Hört es immer näher tönen,—das ist/ unsre Hymne,—Sieg, Sieg!"—Der Marsch rückt im̃er näher; —*Irene*: „Ha, sie nahen!/ Hoch vor ihnen mein Bruder!" —Endlich erreicht der Zug der zurückkehrenden Sieger die/ Bühne. *Rienzi*: „Heil Rom, du hast gesiegt;—aus Schrecken u. Blut gehst du neu her-/vor.—Vernichtet sind deine Feinde,—ihr Blut bedeckt das Feld, sie erstehen nicht wieder!"—/ Man bringt die Leichen *Colonna u. Orsini's. Adriano* erblickt die Leiche seines Vater's—/ u. stürzt mit einem gräßlichen Schrei über sie her.—*Rienzi* „Rom, du bist frei, es/ giebt keinen Colonna, keinen Orsini mehr!"—Allgemeiner Zuruf, gemischt von Schau- der/ u. Freude. *Baroncelli* „Ha, ihre Strafe ist blutig erkauft, —Rienzi, unser Verlust/ war ungeheuer. Weh uns, daß uns die Gerechtigkeit so furchtbar theuer zu stehen kom̃t! —/ Wie viele dieser Frauen suchen vergebens ihre Männer, Brüder u. Söhne wieder!"—/ *Adriano* richtet sich todten- bleich an Colonna's Leiche empor,—mit Bedeutung: „Wehe/ dem, der ein verwandtes Blut zu rächen hat.— Sieh her, blutiger Tribun, das ist dein Werk,/ Fluch über dich u. deine Freiheit!"—*Rienzi*: „Hört ihn nicht, er raset! Ich ehre seinen/ Schmerz! Wehe ihnen, die dieses Blutvergießen nöthig machten! Wie viele freie Römer/ ~~fielen~~ mußten fallen,—klagt ihr Weiber u. Jungfrauen, eur Schmerz ist edel u. gerecht,/ doch richtet euch auf,— seid Römerinnen,—sie fielen für Rom!"—*Adriano*:

„Fluchwürdiger/ Tribun, der du mich von dir stießest, als ich den Frieden noch erhalten konnte!—Fortan sind/ wir geschieden,—wir haben nichts mehr gemein als Rache,— die deine hast du gestillt,—zittre/vor der meinen,—du bist mir verfallen!"—*Rienzi:* „Unseeliger! Römer, verzeiht ihm!"/ *Adriano's* Blick fällt auf die hinsinkende Irene;—mit schmerzlicher Glut eilt er auf/ ihr [*sic*] zu, umfaßt sie: „Leb wohl, Irene,—uns trennt das Geschick, unsre Liebe ist/ gemordet!"—Die Glocken läuten ~~festl~~ zur Siegesfeier,—*Rienzi* reißt sich gewaltsam zu-/ sammen,—: „wie groß der Schmerz ist, Sieg u. Freiheit schweben über euch! Stimt an den/ Jubel!—Es erschallen Siegesgesänge, noch einmal schwingt sich alles mit Begeisterung/ auf. *Adriano* hält Irene noch umschlungen,—Trennung der Liebe, schmerzlich lebe wohl!/ *Ensemble.*—/

Vierter Akt.

Introduktion, Duett u. Terzett. Chor Großer Platz mit den Ruinen des Coloßeum's

Zum Himel auf schreit sein Verbrechen,/ der Frevler büß' es mit dem Tod;/ des Vater's blut'- ge Schmach zu rächen,/ treibt mich ein heiliger Gebot./

Nacht.—*Baroncelli* mit einer Anzahl/ von Bürgern. *Baronc:* „Wer war's, der euch auch hieher beschied?"—*Bürg:*— „Er war/ verhüllt, wir kennen ihn nicht."—*Baroncelli:* „u. wißt ihr schon, daß die Abgesandten/ Deutschlands Rom verlaßen haben?"—*Cecco u. Bürger* kommen dazu. *Cecco:* „Euch treff'ich/ schon,—wart auch ihr hieher beschieden?"—*Baronc:* „So ist's."—*Cecco:* „wie stets, schlim- me/ Neuigkeiten. Die Gesandten Deutschland's haben uns verlaßen." *Baronc:* „Was Wunder,/ Rienzi's Übermuth —lud er nicht die deutschen Fürsten vor, um ihnen die Wahl der [*sic*] römischen/ Königs streitig zu machen?"— *Cecco:* „wir werden diesen Übermuth schlimm büßen müßen."—*Baronc:* „der Kaiser wird uns züchtigen, umso mehr da er mit dem Pabst einver-/standen ist." *Cecco:* „weißt du was mir nicht gefällt—der Cardinal ist abgereist." / *Baroncelli:* „Was sagst du? So zieht auch der Pabst seine Hand von uns ab?—Wohl weiß ich/ daß Colonna sich an den heiligen Vater gewandt hatte,—u. ihm angeboten, den Schutz/ der heiligen Kirche in Rom durch die Macht der Nobili zu übernehmen, so daß Rienzi's/ Sendung erfüllt sei." *Cecco:* „was wird der Pabst zu dem Tod der edelsten Nobili sagen?"/ *Baronc:* „das wäre das wenigste—aber was sagt ihr Bürger, zu dem unnütz vergoßenen/ Blut eurer Söhne u. Brüder?"—*Chor.* „Fürchterlich, in jeder Familie ein Verlust?"—/ *Baronc:* „Glaubt ihr, daß es Rienzi's

1 Milde war, der sie zur Unzeit begnadigte?—/ ich sehe
schärfer, es war Verrätherei." *Chor.* „Wie kannst du das
beweisen?"—*Baronc:*/ „der Uebermüthige wollte sich
selbst mit den Nobili verbinden,—ihr wißt, Adriano
5 liebt/ Rienzi's Schwester,—um ~~dieser~~ den Preis ihrer
Begnadigung suchte er mal von den/ Nobili's ihre Ein-
willigung zu der Vermählung ~~Rie~~ Adrianos mit Irene zu
bewegen." [*sic*]/ *Cecco u. Chor:* „Ha, wehe ihm, wenn
sich dieß wahr erweist!—und darum mußte unser Blut/
10 fließen."—*Adriano* in einen Mantel verhüllt, tritt hervor:
„hier steht ein Zeuge!"/—„Wer bist du?"—„Ein Colonna!
Hört mich, Rienzi ist seiner Macht unwerth,—meinem/
Flehen gab er nach, die Ehrsucht leitete ihn; noch mehr,
Bürger, seid auf eurer Huth,—/ die Kirche zürnt, der
15 Kaiser ist ergrimmt."—*Baroncelli:* „Ha, der Ehrgeizige,
dem/ wir vertrauten, der uns mit schönen Worten speiste,
uns verrieth; unser Blut preis-/gab, er wird uns auch in's
Verderben stürzen;—Rache ihm!"—*Alle:* „Rache ihm!"
—/ *Adriano* leidenschaftlich: „Rache ihm,—und ich sei es
20 der sie vollführe!"—*Cecco:* „der/ Tag bricht an,—brechen
wir in offener Empörung los!"—*Baronc:* „der verräthe-
rische Tribun,/ sucht die gerechten Klagen durch Pomp u.
Feste zu übertäuben, indem er darüber den/ Staatssch
[—?] zudeckt. Auch für heute hat er ein Dankfest ver-
25 ordnet für den Sieg,—/ das Te Deum soll im Lateran ertönen, u. wir bluten noch an den Wunden, für die/ wir Gott
danken sollen: O Schmach!"—*Adriano:* „So macht es
denn zum Feste, und—/ bestraft den Übermüthigen!"—
Cecco, Bar, Chor: „So sei's,—vor Augen wagen wir's/
30 ihn zu bestrafen."—„Was naht dort für ein Zug?"—der
Cardinal mit Priester u. /Trabanten, begiebt sich in die
Lateran-Kirche:—*Cecco:* „was sehe ich,—der Cardinal/ ist
zurückgekehrt,—er selbst ~~wird~~ begiebt sich zur Feier nach
dem Lateran!"/ *Baronc:* „So wäre unsre Furcht falsch
35 gewesen!"—*Chor:* „die Kirche für Rienzi."—/ *Cecco:*
„wer wagt es nun noch ihn anzugreifen? Er ist allmächtig
geschützt!"—*Adriano:* / „Elende, so schnell erlischt eur
gerechter Zorn?—Sei's an den Stufen des Altar's überall/
ist er meiner Rache verfallen!"—Man hört von fern fest-
40 liche Musik.—*Cecco:* „Ha, der/ Zug naht—schließt euch
an,—erwartet, was da kom̄e.—/

Finale.   *Baroncelli, Cecco* u. die Bürger haben sich ganz auf die
eine Seite gezogen, u. verstellen die/ Treppe u. Thüre des
Lateran. Unter ihnen verhüllt *Adriano.* Der festliche Zug

nahet, *Rienzi/ Irene* an der Spitze. Als der Zug an die Kirche
gelangt, hält *Rienzi* beim Anblick der Verschworenen die
ihm ~~den Eint~~ durch ihre Stellung den Eintritt in die Kirche
streitig zu machen scheinen./ *Rienzi* sieht sie ernst an
„wie, ihr nicht beim Feste,—achtet ihr den Sieg so schlecht,
daß/ ihr in kein Te Deum stimmt?"—*Adr:* (für sich)
„weh mir, Irene ist an seiner Seite, der/ Engel schützt
ihn,—wie soll ich's hier vollbringen?"—*Rienzi*: „Oder
ist eur Muth erloschen// da ihr eure Brüder sterben sahet
in der Schlacht? Sind dafür nicht aber jene vernichtet,
die/ im friedlichen Zustande noch mehrere eure Söhne,
Väter, Brüder hinmordeten, die eure Güter raubten, die
eure Weiber, eure Töchter schändeten? O, für weit
geringere Noth, als/ diese war, kämpfte einst der Römer
um das Ehrenlos des Todes!—Und ist nicht jetzt/ Frieden
u. Ruhe, wer wird eur Glück jetzt noch beunruhigen?"—
Die Verschworenen scheinen/ wie geschlagen,—keiner
wagt zu reden,—*Rienzi*: „Ihr habt gesiegt, o laßet mich
nicht/ ahnen, daß ihr den Sieg verwünscht, dann wäret ihr
unwürdiger in der Geschichte als/ das niedrigste Sclaven-
volk;—Ihr Römer, vertraut euren [sic] Tribunen, den
Gottes Allmacht/ bis hieher trug, u. den sie nie verlaßen
wird, weil er das schönste Ziel sich steckte.—Ihr/ Bürger
schließt euch an, u. kommt zu danken für den Sieg!"—
Die Bürger theilen sich ehrfurchts-/voll,—„lang lebe der
Tribun."—*Adriano*: „ha, die feigen Sclaven,—soll meine
Rache noch/ schweigen,—soll vor Irenen Augen?"—Er
thut einen zweifelhaften Griff nach dem Dolch/ da ertönt
dumpf aus dem Innern der Kirche der Gesang der Priester,
der in düstren Tönen/ den Ausspruch eines Bannes ankün-
digt. *Rienzi* u. das ganze Volk wird von einem/ unwill-
kürlichen Schauder erfaßt.—*Rienzi*: „was soll das bedeuten? Welch' ein selt-/sames Te Deum!"—*Alle*: „uns
faßt ein Schauder, welche Töne!"—*Rienzi* rafft sich auf,/
u. besteigt die Stufen u. giebt ein Zeichen, der [sic] den Zug
in Bewegung setzt.— Der/ *Cardinal* mit Geistlichen
erscheint am Portal der Kirche. „Zurück, nur dem Heiligen/
u. Reinen ist dieser Eintritt verstattet,—Du aber bist
verflucht, im Bann,—u. mit/ dir jeder, der an deiner Seite
bleibt!"—Alles entflieht entsetzt von Rienzi's/ Seite, u.
flieht an die äußersten Einfaßungen der Bühne. *Rienzi*
steht in der Mitte der/ Bühne,—Irene ist an seiner Seite
hingesunken. Die große Kirchenthüre hat sich sogleich/
wieder geschloßen,—man sieht an ihr eine große Schrift

1   befestigt, welche die/ Bannbulle über Rienzi enthält.—
     Schauervolle Stille. Aus dem Innern der/ Kirche hört man
     noch den dumpfen Priester-Gesang. Die Bühne ist ganz
     leer/ außer Rienzi u. Irene;—am fernen Ende sieht man
5   Adriano in den Mantel/ verhüllt.—Bange, furchtbare
     Pause. ~~Irene u.~~ Rienzi steht dumpf u. wie seiner/ Sinne
     beraubt da, so daß er nicht merkt was um ihn vorgeht.—
     Adriano naht sich/ *Irenen*, beugt sich zu ihr herab u. flüstet
     ihr zu: „Irene komm, flieh diesen Ort,/ wende dich zu
10   mir,—ich bin's—dein Adriano!"—*Irene* ist erwacht:
     „—Du Adriano,/ hier was ist geschehen, was willst du."—
     Adria: „—Der Boden brennt zu deinen Füßen,/ ich bin's
     dein Freund, dein Geliebter—flieh,—eile,—" *Irene:* „Mein
     Bruder!"—/ *Adriano:* „ist verflucht,—ausgestoßen ist er
15   aus den Reihen der Glücklichen im Himel/ wie auf Erden,
     —Du darfst nicht bleiben, komm, flieh."—*Irene* „—mein/
     Bruder,—hinweg Unseeliger,—Rienzi,—o mein Bruder!"
     —sie wirft sich/ an Rienzi's Brust. *Adriano:* „Unsinnige,
     —verdirb denn!" er entflieht.—*Rienzi*/ erwacht aus
20   seiner Betäubung,—erblickt Irene, fühlt sie an seiner
     Brust—/ „Irene, du—noch gibt es einen Römer u. eine
     Römerin!"—Während der düstere/ Gesang aus dem
     Lateran wieder beginnt fällt der Vorhang.—

25   *Fünfter Akt.*

     Introduktion.   Im *Capitol.*—*Rienzi* allein. *Gebet.*—„Allmächtiger Vater
                         sieh auf mich herab, auf/ mich den du für würdig hieltest,
     In unsrem treuen ein großes, unerhörtes Werk zu vollbringen;/ du stärktest
     Bunde/ In dieser mich u. gabst mir Kraft—den niedrig denkenden zu
30   *keuschen Brust/*   erleuchten den/ niedergetretenen zu erheben,—du wandel-
     Lebt Roma noch   test den Staub in dem ich ~~dem ich~~ dieß/ Volk liegen sah
     zur Stunde/ Der   zu Glanz u. Hoheit,—o nicht zu früh laß es nur schwinden,
     Größe sich bewußt!/ das/ schöne Werk, es war zu deiner Ehre errichtet—o
                         löse die Nacht, die noch rings/ um die Seelen der Menschen
35   schwebt, schenk' uns den Abglanz deines Lichtes!/ O
                         Herr, mein Gott,—gieb mir Kraft, jegliche Prüfung zu
                         ertragen, laß nicht in/ mir zu früh dein Werk zu Grunde
                         gehn." Er versinkt in ein stummes tief/ religiöses Gebet./—
40   *Duett.*   *Irene* tritt auf. *Rienzi* erhebt sich u. erblickt sie, beide
                         finden sich mit/ glühendem Enthusiasmus des Schmerz
                         [*sic*] in die Arme. *Rienzi* „mich verläßt ~~das/~~ die Kirche, zu
                         deren Ehre u. Preis ich mein Werk begann, mich verläßt
                         das Volk/ das ich erst zu diesem Namen erhoben[*sic*], mich

verläßt jeglicher Freund den mir/ das Glück erschuf,—nur
zweies bleiben mich [sic]—der Himmel u. meine Schwester!"/ *Irene* „ich kenne recht wohl noch deine Lehren
Rienzi, in denen du mich von meiner/ Kindheit auf
erzogest;—du machtest mich zu einer Römerin,—sieh
denn ob/ ich ~~ob ich~~ deiner Lehre Ehre mache—den letzten
Römer verlaß ich nie—sei/ auch der Preis, den ich verliere,
das Glück des Leben's u. der Liebe. Rienzi, sag'/ mir, bin
ich stark u. hab' ich mich bewährt!" *Rienzi*: „Irene, meine
Heldenschwester!"/ *Irene* „Weißt du, was es heißt, einer
Liebe entsagen, o, du hast ja nie geliebt." *Rienzi*/ „ich liebte,
u. liebe glühend heiß—ich liebte meine Braut, seitdem ich
denken/ fühlen lernte, seitdem diese Säulen die Ruinen
mich auf die Vorzeit verwiesen,—als/ ich in der Geschichte
lernte, was einst Roma war.—Ich liebte meine Braut, da
ich/ sie mit Füßen getreten, grauenvoll mishandeln [sic] sah,
entstellt, entehrt, schmachvoll/ verhönt [sic]—preisgegeben
jedem Räuber,—ah, das fachte meinen Schmerz, mein
Mitleid,/ meine Liebe an, ich wollte sie erheben zur
Königin der Welt, für sie nun glüthe/ ich, ihr weihte ich
mein Leben, meine Jugend, meine Manneskraft wiße denn/
meine Braut ist Roma! *Irene* „Undankbares, treuloses
Weib,—ich verachte/ dich!"—*Rienzi* „Ermiß meinen
Schmerz,—wenn ich *dieser* Liebe entsagen soll."/ *Irene*
„Rienzi, mein großer Bruder, blick' in mein Auge, sag'
mir, ob dir Rom treu/ ist. Sieh auf den Gram dieser
Wangen, fühle was sie bekämpften,—u. sag' mir,/ ist dir
Rom untreu?" *Rienzi* „du bist mir treu,—aber zu welchem
Ende? Was/ harret mein? Ich bin im Bann, verflucht bist
auch du an meiner Seite—ich ahne/ es mein Werk ist zu
Ende,—ich sei das Opfer, doch warum du;—gedenkst du/
Adriano's,—gewiß liebt er dich noch,—sein Haß trifft
nur mich—Irene,/ sei sein, er wird dich schützen; sein
Haß wird versöhnt sein wenn ich falle.—sei/ sein Irene!"
—*Irene*: „Rienzi, was muß ich hören.—Du sprichst das
zu deiner/ Schwester!"—*Rienzi* „Es giebt kein Rom
mehr,—sei denn ein Weib." *Irene*:/ „Nicht ein Weib,—
ich will deine Schwester sein!—Ermorde mich, doch ich
verlaß dich/ nicht!"—*Rienzi*: überwältigt „So komm
denn an meine Brust, du stolze Jungfrau!"/ *Ensemble*;
Beide: „Noch lebst du Roma in unsrer Brust,—u. nur mit
ihrem letzten/ Hauch gehst du unter."// *Rienzi*: „noch
einmal will ich mich denn rüsten, noch einmal will ich es
versuchen, Rom/ aus seinem Schlaf zu wecken." (*ab.*)

1 *Szene u. Duett.*   *Irene* bleibt zurück, bald tritt in tiefer Verhüllung *Adriano* auf—er ist bis/ zum Wahnsinn aufgeregt.—*Adria:* „Noch hier Irene, in der Wohnung des Verfluchten—/ mit ihm Fluchbeladene!"—*Irene:* „Entsetzlicher, wagst du den

5   ~~Schrit de~~/ Fuß auf die Schwelle des Reinen zu setzen? Entflieh!" —*Adr:* „Wahnsinnige,/ du trotzest! Ach, du kennst nicht dein Verderben. Ich rette dich—komm!" *Irene*/ „Hier, bei dem letzten der den Römer-Namen verdient ist mein Asyl,—ihr/ seid treulose,—Schändliche,—

10   Geh—es giebt keine Liebe mehr!"—*Adr:*—„Ha,/ meine Liebe ich fühl's, sie ist Raserei! Irene, Irene,—sieh mich zu deinen Füßen—/ ich treulos,—du schwurst ewige Treue— willst du meineidigwerden,/ Tod u. Verderben sollten meine Liebe zu dir alle Schranken durchbrechen laßen,/

15   so schwur ich:—Weh—Tod u. Verderben ist [*sic*] da, deinen Bruder verfluchte die/ Kirche, wie ich ihn verfluche,— das Volk wüthet,—kennt seinen Verrath;—sieh/ diesen Palast, bald wird er nicht mehr stehn,—man wird ihn stürmen,—jeder/ der hier betroffen wird ist ein Verfluchter,

20   sein Tod ist ein Verdienst dem/ Mörder,— —sieh ich selbst bin unter ihnen,—ich selbst nähre den Brand,— dein/ Bruder fällt,—sieh Irene, Tod u. Verderben ist [*sic*] da—jetzt bist du mein,/ sieh ob ich meinen Schwur halte,—hier lieg' ich zu deinen Füßen, ich um-/faße dein

25   Kniee [*sic*], laß mich nicht meineidig werden [*sic*],—sieh' meine Liebe:/ *Irene:* „Verruchter, die Hölle brütet in dir, —sieh' denn hier stehe ich/ eine Römerin,—nur meine Leiche kannst du dein nennen!"—Man/ hört dumpfes Rasen, die wüthenden Stimmen des Volkes: *Adriano:*

30   „Hör'/ sie kom̄en,—die Flammen,—Entsetzen—Wahnsinn Irene—ich reiße dich/ fort!"—*Irene:* wehrt sich mit wüthender Kraft u. stößt Adriano von sich/ ~~Adriano nun denn se~~— *Irene:* „Vergehe, Wahnsinniger, wir haben nichts/ gemein!" Sie entflieht.—*Adriano* ist zusammenge-

35   sunken—rafft sich mit/ starrem Blicke auf:—„Nun denn du bist mein, durch die Flammen finden/ wir den Weg zu dir!" (*ab.*)/

Finale.   *Verwandlung.* Großer Platz vor dem Capitol.—Das Volk hat sich in der/ wüthenden Aufregung davor versammelt:

40   „Tod u. Verderben dem Geächteten/ der uns beherrschen wollte, er ist verfallen!" *Rienzi* erscheint auf dem/ großen Balkon, vollständig gerüstet aber in bloßen [*sic*] Haupt,— an seiner Seite/ Irene.—*Volk:* „Da ist er, er trotz [*sic*] uns,— steinigt ihn!" *Rienzi:* „Ruhe/ gebiet' ich euch, kennt ihr

noch euren Tribunen!" „Steinigt ihn!" „Entartete,/ die
ihr Stolz waret auf den Namen Römer, beweist euch
jetzt deßen würdig!"/ „Hört ihn nicht!"—„Wer machte
euch groß u. frei,—vergeßt ihr den/ Jubel mit dem ihr
mich begrüßet als ich euch frei erklärte."— „Hört ihn/
nicht, er behext uns."—*Rienzi* „Kannt [*sic*] ihr mein Ant-
litz sehen u. schämt/ euch nicht!"—„Werft Feuer in das
Capitol!"—Das Volk wirft Pechkränze/ in das Capitol.
Rienzi: „Ha, furchtbarer Hohn,—ist dieß Rom?—Elende/
unwürdig des Erbtheils, das euch hinterlaße [*sic*],—ich der
letzte Römer,/ verfluche euch,—verflucht sei diese Stadt,
vertilgt von der Erde,/ daß sie nicht den Flecken der
Nachwelt aufweise. Vermodre u. verdorre,/ Rom, denn
dein entartetes Volk will es so!"—Das Feuer hat das ganze/
Capitol erfaßt. *Rienzi* umschlingt Irene—,,Seht, so endet
der letzte der Tribunen."—Sie sind ganz vom Feuer
umgeben. Wilder/ Jubel des Volkes. Man hört ~~Adrian's~~
Rienzi's u. Irene's Stim̄e:/ „Santo spirito Cavalieri."—
Adriano an der Spitze vom Gewaffneten/ kom̄t athemlos,—
sieht Irene's Gestalt von den Flam̄en erfaßt/ „Irene, Irene!"
—das Capitol stürzt zusammen, mit einem gräßlichen
Schrei sinkt Adriano zu Boden.—

Ende.

Appendix iii

A comparison of the composition draft with the vocal score by Gustav Klink

THE following list is limited to major formal and textual differences only, as well as the timings for each act which Wagner wrote into the composition draft after the completion of the full score (see *Schriften*, xiii. 255). Numerous discrepancies between the Klink score and surviving versions of the full score are dealt with in *Sämt. Werke*, iii (5).

		Composition Draft	Vocal Score (2 vols.)
1	Overture	p. 1 bars 15–31	17 bars missing between i.3 bars 14/15
2	Overture	p. 4 bars 11–39	29 bars missing replaced by i.11 bars 9–10
3	Overture	p. 5 bars 1–48	48 bars missing replaced by i.11 bars 30–9
4	I/trio	p. 24 bars 22–5 *Text:* 'Weh' dem, der ein verwandtes Blut zu rächen hat.'	i.80 bars 13–16 *Text:* 'Weh' dem, der mir verwandtes Blut vergossen hat!'
5	I/trio	p. 26 bars 46–9	4 bars missing replaced by i.93 bar 7
6	I/duet	p. 30 bars 10–17	8 bar repeat missing i.107 bar 18—i.108 bar 6
7	II/trio chorus	p. 47 bar 32— p. 48 bar 15	30 bars missing between i.188 bars 9/10
8	II/trio, chorus	p. 50 bar 8— p. 51 bar 1	19 bars missing replaced by by i.195 bars 3–4
9	II/trio, chorus	p. 51 bars 10–23	14 bar repeat missing i.197 bar 1—i.199 bar 1
10	II/finale	p. 56 bars 7–62 Ambassadors' entry *with* text	i.214 bar 18—i.216 bar 10 Ambassadors' entry *without* text
11	II/finale	p. 85 bars 25–32	8 bars missing between i.326 bars 5/6
12	II/finale	p. 88 bars 7–14	8 bars missing between i.337 bars 2/3
13	II/finale	p. 92 bars 25–30	6 bars missing between i.351 bars 12/13
14	III/finale	p. 104 bars 60–75	16 bars missing between ii.40 bars 21/22

15	III/finale	p. 113 bar 28—p. 114 bar 14 Battle Hymn *without* text	ii.77 bar 1—ii.81 bar 5 Battle Hymn *with* text
16	III/finale	p. 115 bars 11–18	8 bar repeat missing ii. 85 bar 6—ii.86 bar 4
17	III/finale	p. 116 bar 48—p. 117 bar 1 *Text:* 'Weh dem, der ein verwandtes Blut zu rächen hat	ii.91 bars 11–14 *Text:* 'Weh dem, der mir verwandtes Blut vergossen hat
18	III/finale	p. 130 bars 7–28	22 bars missing between ii.154 bars 1/2
19	III/finale	p. 131 bars 15–26	12 bars replaced by ii.156 bars 7–21
20	V/prayer	p. 148 bars 33–40	8 bars missing between ii.213 bars 15/16

Timings in Composition Draft

Overture	(end)	p. 6	12 minutes
I	(end)	p. 38	1 hour (with Overture)
II	(beginning of pantomime)	p. 58	20 minutes
II	(end of ballet)	p. 73	$\frac{1}{2}$ hour: 2 minutes
II	(end)	p. 92	20 minutes
			42 minutes (i.e. timing of II without ballet music)
			2 hours 14 minutes (i.e. total time of Overture, I–II)
III	(end)	p. 131	*50 minutes*
IV	(end)	p. 146	*25 minutes*
V	(end)	p. 162	*30 minutes*

Added together, the timings printed in italics give a total time of

3 hours 59 minutes

In a letter to Fischer (1841), Wagner claims that the length of *Rienzi* is 'only' four hours—a calculation clearly based on the timings in the composition draft (see *Sämt. Briefe*, i. 549). According to *Mein Leben*, however, the first performance lasted six hours (with intervals) from six in the evening to midnight (*Schriften*, xiv. 21). Considering that Wagner had already cut the pantomime and 'most of the ballet' in Act II for the first performance—a cut which he assumed would 'save half an hour' (*Schriften*, xiv. 9)—a complete performance of *Rienzi* as it stands in the composition draft would probably last, with intervals, between six and a half and seven hours.

With the over optimistic calculations in the composition draft, Wagner naturally wanted to allay the fears of the Dresden authorities that his opera could well last over an hour longer than either Meyerbeer's *Les Hugenots* or Rossini's *Guillaume Tell* which, at the time, were the longest operas in the repertory. But the timings are not always inaccurate; they simply ignore the difference between playing at the piano with a metronome (where the tendency is to play too fast), and a performance with a vast ensemble requiring slower tempi and a more measured sequence of events.

Bibliography

ABRAHAM, GERALD, 'A lost Wagner aria', *Musical Times*, cx (1969), 927–9.

ADLER, GUIDO, *Richard Wagner: Vorlesungen*, Leipzig, 1904.

ADORNO, T. W., Review of *Rienzi* performance in Frankfurt, *Die Musik*, xxvi/6 (1934), 448–9.

—— *Versuch über Wagner*, Munich, 1964.

BEKKER, PAUL, *Wagner. Das Leben im Werke*, Berlin/Leipzig, 1924.

BORY, ROBERT, *Richard Wagner: sein Leben und sein Werk in Bildern*, Leipzig, 1938.

BÜCKEN, ERNST, *Der heroische Stil in der Oper*, Leipzig, 1924.

BULWER-LYTTON, E., *Rienzi—the Last of the Roman Tribunes*, 2nd edn., London, 1848.

—— *Rienzi, der letzte der Tribunen*, tr. G. N. Bärmann, 4 vols., Zwickau, 1836.

BURDACH, KONRAD, *Briefwechsel des Cola di Rienzo*, 5 vols., Berlin, 1913–29.

BUTLER, E. M., *The Saint-Simonian Religion in Germany*, Cambridge, 1926.

CHAMBERLAIN, H. S., *Richard Wagner*, Munich, 1901.

—— *Das Drama Richard Wagners*, 3rd edn., Leipzig, 1908.

DAUBE, OTTO, *Ich schreibe keine Symphonien mehr*, Cologne, 1960.

DEATHRIDGE, JOHN. 'The Nomenclature of Wagner's Sketches', *Proceedings of the Royal Musical Association*, ci (1974–5).

DINGER, HUGO, 'Zu Richard Wagners Rienzi', *Richard Wagner Jahrbuch*, ed. Ludwig Frankenstein, 5 vols., Berlin, 1908, iii. 88–132.

DRY, WAKELING, 'A Master's Methods', *The Musical Courier*, xlv (1902), New York, No. 25, pp. 10–11.

EICHBERG, O., 'Zum 50jährigen Jubiläum des "Rienzi"', *Bayreuther Taschenbuch*, viii (1892), 51–85.

ENGEL, ERICH W., *Richard Wagners Leben und Werke im Bilde*, 2 vols., Vienna, 1913.

ENGEL, HANS, 'Wagner and Spontini', *Archiv für Musikwissenschaft*, xii (1955), 167–77.

ERCKMANN, FRITZ, 'Der historische Rienzi', *Musikalisches Wochenblatt*, 1910 (Heft 45/6), 641–3, 656–8.

FRIEDRICH, HANS, *Die religionsphilosophischen, soziologischen und politischen Elemente in den Prosadichtungen des jungen Deutschlands*, Leipzig, 1907–8.

GECK, MARTIN, 'Rienzi in Bayreuth', *Neue Zeitschrift für Musik*, 1968, 331–3.

—— 'Rienzi-Philologie', *Das Drama Richard Wagners als musikalisches Kunstwerk*, ed. C. Dahlhaus, Regensburg, 1970, pp. 183–97.

GERATHEWOHL, FRITZ, *St. Simonistische Ideen in der deutschen Literatur*, Munich, 1920.

GIBBON, EDWARD, *The History and Decline of the Roman Empire*, 12 vols., London, 1790.

GLASENAPP, CARL F., 'Aus dem deutschen Dichterwalde', *Bayreuther Blätter*, iii (1880), 31–45.

—— *Das Leben Richard Wagners*, 5th edn., 6 vols., Leipzig, 1916–23.

GOLTHER, W., 'Rienzi—ein musikalisches Drama', *Die Musik*, i (1902), 1833–9.

GREGOROVIUS, FERDINAND, *Geschichte der Stadt Rom im Mittelalter*, vol. vi, Stuttgart, 1867.

HANSLICK, E., *Die moderne Oper*, Berlin, 1875.

HOFFMANN, E. T. A., 'Nachträgliche Bemerkungen über Spontini's Oper "Olympia"', *Gesammelte Werke*, ed. Ellinger, 15 vols., Berlin/Leipzig, 1927, xvi. 106–46.

HORKHEIMER, MAX, 'Egoismus und Freiheitsbewegung' (1936), *Traditionelle und kritische Theorie*, Frankfurt, 1970.

IGGERS, GEORG G., *The Cult of Authority. The Political Philosophy of the Saint-Simonians*, The Hague, 1958.

KIRCHMEYER, HELMUT, *Das zeitgenössische Wagner-Bild*, Regensburg, 1967–72.

KOCH, MAX, *Richard Wagner*, 3 vols., Berlin, 1907.

KÖHLER, W., 'Wagners "Rienzi" in alter und neuer Gestalt', *Musikalisches Wochenblatt*, xxii (1901), 648–9.

KOHUT, ADOLF, 'Zur Erstaufführung des Rienzi', *Neuer Theater Almanack*, 4, Dresden, 1893, pp. 8–19.

—— *Der Meister von Bayreuth*, Berlin, 1905, esp. pp. 117–33.

KOLNEDER, WALTER, 'Die Partitur der Rienzi-Ouverture', *Zeitschrift für Musik*, cxi (1950), 589–92.

KUBIZEK, A., *Adolf Hitler mein Jugendfreund*, Göttingen, 1953, esp. pp. 133–42.

LAUBE, HEINRICH, *Gesammelte Schriften*, 50 vols., Leipzig, 1908/9.

LAUX, K., *Die Dresdener Staatskapelle*, Leipzig, 1964, pp. 48–52.

LEPRINCE, GUSTAV, 'The Flying Dutchman in the setting by Philippe Dietch, *Musical Quarterly*, L (1964), 307–20.

LYTTON, *The Life of Edward Bulwer by his Grandson*, 2 vols, London, 1913.

MANN, THOMAS, 'Leiden und Größe Richard Wagners', *Gesammelte Werke*, 12 vols. Frankfurt, 1960, ix. 363–426.

MEHLER, EUGEN, '"Rienzi" und die Dresdener Theaterzensur', *Die Musik*, xii (1913), 195–201.

MITFORD, MARY, *Rienzi*, London, 1828.

MUNDT, THEODOR, 'Über Oper, Drama und Melodrama in ihrem Verhältniß zu einander und zum Theater', *Blätter für literarische Unterhaltung*, 1831, nos. 152–5.

NATHAN, HANS, *Das Rezitativ der Frühopern Richard Wagners*, Diss., Berlin, 1934.

NEUMANN, FRANZ, *Behemoth*, New York, 1963, esp. pp. 465–7.

NEWMAN, ERNEST, *Wagner as Man and Artist*, 2nd edn., London, 1923.

—— *The Life of Richard Wagner*, 4 vols., New York, 1933.

NIETZSCHE, F., *Gesammelte Werke*, 23 vols., Munich, 1922.

PAPENCORDT, FELIX, *Cola di Rienzo und seine Zeit*, Hamburg, 1841.

PETSCH, R., 'Das tragische Problem im "Rienzi"', *Zeitschrift für Philosophie und philosophische Kritik*, cxxviii (1906), 44–55.

PETZOLDT, RICHARD, *Richard Wagner: sein Leben in Bildern*, Leipzig, 1963.

PFORDTEN, H. v. d., *Handlung und Dichtung der Bühnenwerke Richard Wagner's* Berlin, 1893.

Rè, Zefirino (ed.), *La Vita di Cola di Rienzo*, Fiorli, 1828.

Reichelt, J., 'Zur Uraufführung des "Rienzi"', *Allgemeine Musikzeitung*, xlii (1912), 716–9.

Reuss, E., 'Rienzi', *Bayreuther Blätter*, xii (1889), 150–62.

Sade, Abbé de, *Memoires pour la vie Patrarque*, 3 vols., Amsterdam, 1764–7.

Schmid, Otto, *Richard Wagners Opern und Musikdramen in Dresden*, Dresden, 1919, esp. pp. 7–14.

Seidl, Arthur, 'Der Doppelschlag im Rienzi', *Wagneriana*, 2 vols., i. 62–74.

—— 'Das tragische Problem im "Rienzi"', *Neue Wagneriana*, 3 vols., Regensburg, 1914, i. 174–83.

Shaw, B., *The Perfect Wagnerite*, Leipzig, 1913.

Stein, Jack, *Richard Wagner and the Synthesis of the Arts*, Detroit, 1960.

Stravinsky, Igor, 'Wagner's Prose', *Themes and Episodes*, New York, 1966, pp. 138–44.

Strobel, Otto, 'Richard Wagner als Arbeitsgenie', *Allgemeine Musikzeitung*, lvi (1929), 523ff.

—— *Skizzen und Entwürfe zur Ring-Dichtung*, Munich, 1930.

—— 'Aus Wagners Musikerwerkstatt', *Allgemeine Musikzeitung*, lviii (1931), 463ff.

—— 'König Ludwigs Wagner Manuscripte', *Bayreuther Festspielführer*, 1936, pp. 106–10.

—— *Richard Wagner, Leben und Schaffen—Eine Zeittafel*, Bayreuth, 1952.

Suhge, Werner, *Saint-Simonismus und junges Deutschland*, Berlin, 1935.

Voss, Egon, 'Wagners fragmentarisches Orchesterwerk in e-moll', *Die Musik-Forschung*. xxiii (1970), 50–4.

Wagner, Richard, *Briefwechsel zwischen Wagner und Liszt*, 2nd edn., 2 vols., Leipzig, 1900.

—— *Die Briefe Richard Wagners an Judith Gautier*, ed. Willi Schuh, Leipzig, (no date).

—— *Gesammelte Schriften und Dichtungen*, 10 vols., Leipzig, 1871.

—— *Richard Wagner an Freunde und Zeitgenossen*, ed. Erich Kloss, 2nd edn., Berlin, 1909.

—— *Sämtliche Briefe*, eds. W. Wolf/G. Strobel, 15 vols. projected, Leipzig, 1967–

—— *Sämtliche Schriften und Dichtungen*, 16 vols., Volksausgabe, Leipzig, 1911.

—— *Sämtliche Werke*, 30 vols., Mainz, 1970–.

—— *Wagner Briefe. Die Sammlung Burrell*, ed. John N. Burk, Frankfurt, 1953.

—— *Wagner Werk-Verzeichnis* (WWV), eds. John Deathridge, Martin Geck, Egon Voss, Regensburg, 1977/8.

Wahle, Werner, ' "Ferdinand Cortez" von Spontini als Vorbild zu Wagners "Rienzi"', *Allgemeine Musikzeitung*, lxvi (1939), 3–4.

Warncke, A., *Miss Mitfords und Bulwers englische Rienzibearbeitung*, Dissertation, Rostock, 1904.

Wolf, W., *Richard Wagners geistige und künstlerische Entwicklung bis zum Jahr 1848*, Dissertation, Leipzig, 1966.

Index

* .. example(s)